my revision notes

OCR A Level

MEDIA STUDIES

Michael Rodgers

HODDER
EDUCATION
AN HACHETTE UK COMPANY

The Publishers would like to thank the following for permission to reproduce copyright material.

Photo credits

p.8 © DMG Media via Solo Syndication; **p.11** © Guardian News & Media Limited ; **p.19 top** © DMG Media via Solo Syndication, **bottom** © Guardian/Twitter; **p.29 left** © Daily Express/Express Syndication, **right** © Telegraph Media Group; **p.80** © Shelter; **p.81** © Hugh Kretschmer via Wieden+Kennedy; **p.90 both** © The Big Issue; **p.105 left** © Everett Collection, Inc. / Alamy Stock Photo, **right** © Disney/Kobal/REX/Shutterstock; **p.113** © Yui Mok/PA Archive/PA Images; **p.115** Minecraft.net © 2018 Microsoft; **p.116** © Sharon McTeir/Hodder Education; **p.156** © Teakwood Lane Prods./ Cherry Pie Prods./Keshet/Fox 21/Showtime/Kobal/REX/Shutterstock; **p.168** © Netflix/Kobal/REX/Shutterstock; **p.178** © Moviestore/REX/Shutterstock; **p.192** © RVK Studios.

Acknowledgements

p.18, Katherine Viner, *'A mission for journalism in a time of crisis'*, Guardian, 16 November 2017 © Guardian News and Media Limited. Reprinted with permission; **p.18, Paul Dacre,** *'Why is the left obsessed by the Daily Mail?'*, Guardian, 12 October 2013 © Guardian News and Media Limited. Reprinted with permission; **p.38, Table of average newspaper circulation figures in August 2018,** © abc.org.uk; **p.104, Table of national and global film audiences for the 2016** *Jungle Book* **film:** © *BoxOfficeMojo.com,* Reproduced with permission; **p.110, Extract from Top 12 video games conglomerates/ publishers,** www.newzoo.com (https://newzoo.com/insights/rankings/top-25-companies-game-revenues/). Reprinted with permission; **p.127, Nick Levine,** *'Nick Grimshaw's Radio 1 breakfast show ratings fall to new low'*, NME, 18 May 2017. Reproduced with permission of Radio 1; **p.189, USA Network,** Quote about scheduling of Mr. Robot. Reproduced with permission of Entertainment Networks, NBCUniversal Cable Entertainment.

Every effort has been made to trace all copyright holders, but if any have been inadvertently overlooked, the Publishers will be pleased to make the necessary arrangements at the first opportunity.

Although every effort has been made to ensure that website addresses are correct at time of going to press, Hodder Education cannot be held responsible for the content of any website mentioned in this book. It is sometimes possible to find a relocated web page by typing in the address of the home page for a website in the URL window of your browser.

Hachette UK's policy is to use papers that are natural, renewable and recyclable products and made from wood grown in sustainable forests. The logging and manufacturing processes are expected to conform to the environmental regulations of the country of origin.

Orders: please contact Bookpoint Ltd, 130 Park Drive, Milton Park, Abingdon, Oxon OX14 4SE. Telephone: (44) 01235 827827. Fax: (44) 01235 400401. Email education@bookpoint.co.uk Lines are open from 9 a.m. to 5 p.m., Monday to Saturday, with a 24-hour message answering service. You can also order through our website: www.hoddereducation.co.uk

ISBN: 978 1 5104 2921 5

© Michael Rodgers

First published in 2018 by
Hodder Education,
An Hachette UK Company
Carmelite House
50 Victoria Embankment
London EC4Y 0DZ

www.hoddereducation.co.uk

Impression number	5	4	3	2	1
Year	2022	2021	2020	2019	2018

Cover photo: Copyright to Jacquie Boyd from Debut Art Agency

Typeset in Integra Software Services Pvt. Ltd., Pondicherry, India

Printed in Spain

A catalogue record for this title is available from the British Library.

MIX
Paper from
responsible sources
FSC
www.fsc.org
FSC™ C104740

Get the most from this book

Everyone has to decide his or her own revision strategy, but it is essential to review your work, learn it and test your understanding. These Revision Notes will help you to do that in a planned way, topic by topic. Use this book as the cornerstone of your revision and don't hesitate to write in it — personalise your notes and check your progress by ticking off each section as you revise.

Tick to track your progress

Use the revision planner on pages iv and v to plan your revision, topic by topic. Tick each box when you have:

- revised and understood a topic
- tested yourself
- practised the exam questions and gone online to check your answers and complete the quick quizzes.

You can also keep track of your revision by ticking off each topic heading in the book. You may find it helpful to add your own notes as you work through each topic.

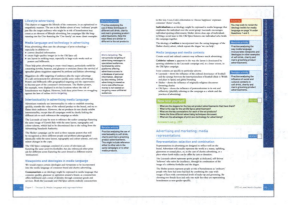

Features to help you succeed

A number of key terms are used and defined for you as you work through this guide. Make sure you learn them so that you can use the terms accurately and precisely in the exams in order to gain top marks. The full glossary can be found at **www.hoddereducation.co.uk/ myrevisionnotesdownloads**.

Exam tips are given throughout the book to help you polish your exam technique in order to maximise your chances in the exam.

Practice questions are provided for exam questions, together with some sample answers and assessment

comments. Use these to consolidate your revision and practise your exam skills. The sample answers can be found at **www.hoddereducation.co.uk/ myrevisionnotesdownloads.**

These activities will help you to understand each topic in an interactive way.

These sections are summaries of how to revise for each topic.

These short, knowledge-based questions are the first step in testing your learning. Answers are at the back of the book.

My revision planner

REVISED   TESTED   EXAM READY

Paper 2, Section B: Long form television drama

Question 3

Question 4

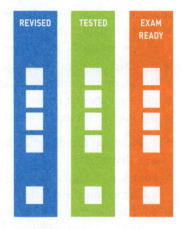

Introduction

In your A Level Media Studies course you will have learned about:
- the nine media forms
- the set products in each form
- the three in-depth studies in online newspapers, print newspapers and long form TV drama
- the theoretical framework covering media language, audiences, industries and representations
- the theories that apply to each area of the framework
- the media contexts – social, cultural, political, economic, and historical – that influence media products.

This Revision Guide will take you through this content by working through the questions in the two exams that assess:
- your knowledge and understanding of the theoretical framework and/or media contexts and their influence on the media
- your application of knowledge and understanding of the theoretical framework to:
  - **analyse** products (including in relation to their **contexts** and using media **theories**)
  - **evaluate academic theories**
  - make judgements and draw **conclusions**.

You only need to be able to use and evaluate theories in relation to your three in-depth studies:
- newspapers – the *Daily Mail* and the *Guardian*
- online, social and participatory media – the *Mail Online* and the *Guardian* websites plus their social media feeds
- television – long form television drama (one US, one European).

For each of these in-depth studies you need to apply the whole of the theoretical framework – media language, audiences, industries and representations – plus any media context.

You only cover some areas of the framework and some contexts for the other six media forms:

Media form	Set Product	Area of framework	Contexts
Film	Jungle Book (1967 and 2016)	Industries	Economic, Historical
Advertising and Marketing	Old Spice, Lucozade, Shelter	Media Language, Representations	Social, Cultural
Radio	The BBC Radio 1 Breakfast Show	Industries, Audiences	Economic, Political, Cultural
Magazines	The Big Issue	Media Language, Representations	Social, Cultural, Political
Video Games	Minecraft	Industries, Audiences	Economic, Social
Music Video	Two videos chosen from two set lists	Media Language, Representations	Social, Cultural

This Revision Guide will take you through each question looking at the content you may need to know. It includes exam practice questions, for which sample answers are available so you can see how the questions may be set out and what you would have to do to answer them.

What you have to do in the exam

The Exam Papers

You will have to complete two examination papers, each worth 35% of your final grade and lasting 2 hours each:

- **Paper 1: Media messages**
- **Paper 2: Evolving media**

You are expected to complete **all** the questions in each paper.

Paper 1 **Media messages** 90 marks 6 questions	**Section A: News** **Two** in-depth studies: • newspapers • online, social and participatory media. Some questions will relate to unseen sources on newspapers and/or online, social and participatory media	• Knowledge and understanding of the **whole framework** and/or **contexts**: 15 marks. • **Analysis** (including **contexts** and **theories**)/**theory evaluation**/judgements and **conclusions**: 30 marks.	• **Three** 10 mark questions • **One** 15 mark question **Total marks:** 45 marks
	Section B: Media Language and Representation **Three** media forms: • advertising and marketing • magazines • music videos. Some questions will relate to unseen sources on advertising and marketing, and/or magazines. You may have to compare the set advertising and marketing products you have studied with the unseen sources.	• Knowledge and understanding of **media language** and **representations** and/or **contexts**: 10 marks • **Analysis** (including **contexts**)/judgements and **conclusions**: 15 marks	• **One** 10 mark question • **One** 15 mark question **Total marks:** 45 marks
Paper 2 **Evolving Media** 70 marks 4 questions	**Section A: Media Industries and Audiences** **Three** media forms: • radio • video games • film (industries only).	• Knowledge and understanding of **media industries** and **audiences** and/or **contexts**	• **Two** 15 mark questions **Total marks:** 30 marks
	Section B: Long Form TV Drama **Three** media forms: • advertising and marketing • magazines • music videos. Question 3 of Paper 2 is worth 30 marks and will require you to draw upon your knowledge and understanding from the whole course of study.	• Knowledge and understanding of the **whole framework** and/or **contexts**: 10 marks • **Analysis** (including **contexts** and **theories**)/**theory evaluation**/judgements and **conclusions**: 30 marks.	• **One** 30 mark question • **One** 10 mark question **Total marks:** 40 marks

- Questions about knowledge and understanding of the theoretical framework (mostly found in Paper 2 Section A, and possibly one question in each section of Paper 1) will test knowledge about the media form as a whole, with reference to the set products.
- Questions asking for analysis will be about unseen sources in the exam (found in Paper 1) or the set products you have studied (found in Paper 2 Section B).

Countdown to my exams

6–8 weeks to go

- Start by looking at the specification — make sure you know exactly what material you need to revise and the style of the examination. Use the revision planner on pages iv and v to familiarise yourself with the topics.
- Organise your notes, making sure you have covered everything on the specification. The revision planner will help you to group your notes into topics.
- Work out a realistic revision plan that will allow you time for relaxation. Set aside days and times for all the subjects that you need to study, and stick to your timetable.
- Set yourself sensible targets. Break your revision down into focused sessions of around 40 minutes, divided by breaks. These Revision Notes organise the basic facts into short, memorable sections to make revising easier.

REVISED ☐

2–6 weeks to go

- Read through the relevant sections of this book and refer to the exam tips, exam summaries, typical mistakes and key terms. Tick off the topics as you feel confident about them. Highlight those topics you find difficult and look at them again in detail.
- Test your understanding of each topic by working through the 'Now test yourself' questions in the book. Look up the answers at the back of the book.
- Make a note of any problem areas as you revise, and ask your teacher to go over these in class.
- Look at past papers. They are one of the best ways to revise and practise your exam skills. Write or prepare planned answers to the exam practice questions provided in this book. Check your answers online and try out the extra quick quizzes at **www.hoddereducation.co.uk/myrevisionnotesdownloads**
- Use the revision activities to try out different revision methods. For example, you can make notes using concept maps, spider diagrams or flash cards.
- Track your progress using the revision planner and give yourself a reward when you have achieved your target.

REVISED ☐

One week to go

- Try to fit in at least one more timed practice of an entire past paper and seek feedback from your teacher, comparing your work closely with the mark scheme.
- Check the revision planner to make sure you haven't missed out any topics. Brush up on any areas of difficulty by talking them over with a friend or getting help from your teacher.
- Attend any revision classes put on by your teacher. Remember, he or she is an expert at preparing people for examinations.

REVISED ☐

The day before the examination

- Flick through these Revision Notes for useful reminders, for example the exam tips, exam summaries, typical mistakes and key terms.
- Check the time and place of your examination.
- Make sure you have everything you need — extra pens and pencils, tissues, a watch, bottled water, sweets.
- Allow some time to relax and have an early night to ensure you are fresh and alert for the examinations.

REVISED ☐

My exams

Paper 1: Media messages

Date:..

Time:..

Location:..

Paper 2: Evolving media

Date:..

Time:..

Location:..

▶ Paper 1 – Section A: News

What you have to do

This section of the exam asks four questions on your study of news across two media forms:

- an in-depth study of online newspapers, with the *Mail Online* and the *Guardian* websites and their use of social and participatory media such as Twitter, Instagram and Facebook as the set products
- an in-depth study of print newspapers, with the *Daily Mail* and the *Guardian* as the set products.

Which areas of the theoretical framework must I study?	
Online newspapers	The whole theoretical framework: • media language • representations • industries • audiences Social, cultural, economic, political and historical contexts Academic ideas and arguments (theories)
Print newspapers	The whole theoretical framework: • media language • representations • industries • audiences Social, cultural, economic, political and historical contexts Academic ideas and arguments (theories)

The four questions in Section A will be as follows:

Q1	10 marks	This question will ask you to analyse the media language or the representations in two sources. The sources will be extracts from different genres of online or print newspapers and may include one of the set products. This short essay should take about 17 minutes to plan and write.
Q2	15 marks	This will be a complex question including a number of bullet points asking you to: • show knowledge and understanding of the theoretical framework as it applies to news • analyse the two sources provided, probably in terms of media language or representation (this might entail comparing the two) • make judgements and draw conclusions. This extended essay should take about 25 minutes to plan and write.
Q3	10 marks	This question asks you to show knowledge and understanding of the influence of media contexts on print and/or online news, including your set products. This short essay should take about 17 minutes to plan and write.
Q4	10 marks	This question asks you to evaluate an academic theory in relation to news – how useful is it in understanding news? You may be given a choice between two theories. This short essay should take about 17 minutes to plan and write.

Questions 1 and 2

What these questions involve

You will be given two sources to analyse in the exam. The two sources may be extracts from print newspapers, from newspaper websites, or from newspaper social media feeds such as Twitter, Instagram and Facebook.
- One will be an extract from a 'popular' newspaper such as the *Daily Mail*, the *Sun*, the *Daily Mirror*, the *Daily Star*, or the *Daily Express*, or possibly their Sunday editions.
- One will be an extract from the 'quality' press, such as the *Guardian*, the *Daily Telegraph*, *The Times*, the *Financial Times* or the *Independent* (online only), or possibly their Sunday editions or sister papers.

The two sources cannot be both of the two set products – the *Daily Mail* and the *Guardian*. At least one source will be a newspaper that you might not have studied in any depth, because these questions will be testing your ability to analyse any newspapers based on your knowledge and understanding of the media form as a whole.

The following information is based on the specimen assessment materials produced by OCR. These are likely to be the format of exam questions in the live exam papers, but OCR reserves the right to make changes.

Question 1 will probably ask for analysis of the two sources with the focus most likely on analysis of media language or representations. It may require you to use a specific concept or theory in your analysis.

Question 2, as well as testing your knowledge and understanding of print and/or online newspapers as media forms and analysis skills (probably of media language or representations), will also ask you to make judgements and draw conclusions.

Timing

These two questions will be 10-mark or 15-mark questions.

If, as expected, Question 1 is a 10-mark question, you should spend about 17 minutes answering this question.

If, as expected, Question 2 is a 15-mark question, you should spend about 25 minutes answering this question.

> **Revision activity**
>
> Past papers and practice papers are published on the OCR Interchange – ask your teacher to access these so you can check whether the format for Questions 1 and 2 has changed over time.

What the examiner is looking for

In the following exam practice Question 1, examiners are looking for:
- how well you apply your knowledge of the area of the theoretical framework (e.g. media language or representation) to analyse the two sources
- how convincingly, accurately and perceptively you analyse the sources, with logical connections and lines of reasoning in your answer

- how relevantly and precisely you refer to any theoretical concept specified in the question
- the detail and accuracy of your references to the sources.

Exam practice

Question 1

Analyse the representations in Sources A and B. Use Van Zoonen's concept of patriarchy in your answer.   [10]

Sources A and B can be found in the sample assessment material on the OCR website at: www.ocr.org.uk/Images/316674-unit-h409-01-media-messages-sample-assessment-material.pdf.

Sample answer available online   ONLINE

In exam practice Question 2 below, examiners are looking for:
- knowledge and understanding of the theoretical framework
- how accurately and relevantly you use Media Studies terminology
- how well you apply your knowledge of the area of the theoretical framework (such as media language or representation) to analyse the two sources
- how convincingly, accurately and perceptively you analyse the sources, with logical connections and lines of reasoning
- how accomplished and developed are your judgements and conclusions.

Exam practice

Question 2*

How far has genre influenced the media language in Sources A and B?
In your answer you must:
- outline genre conventions in British newspapers
- analyse the contrasting use of media language in the sources
- make judgements and reach conclusions about how far genre has influenced the media language used.   [15]

Sources A and B can be found in the sample assessment material on the OCR website at: www.ocr.org.uk/Images/316674-unit-h409-01-media-messages-sample-assessment-material.pdf.

Sample answer available online   ONLINE

Extended response questions   REVISED

The asterisk (★) next to exam practice Question 2 is to signpost that this is an extended response answer, meaning that you will be marked on the quality of your essay:
- how well you develop a line of reasoning
- how relevant your answer is throughout
- how well you provide evidence for the points you make.

Making judgements and reaching conclusions   REVISED

If a question asks 'how far' something is true or whether or not you agree with a statement, then this should be the focus of your conclusion, which one bullet point will ask you to provide. In exam practice Question 2 above you might argue one of the following:

- that the differences in media language **do** reflect generic conventions
- that the differences in media language **do not** reflect generic conventions
- that some media language **does** and some media language **does not** reflect generic conventions.

Examiners will be told to credit any argument that is backed up by analysis of the extract, so there is no 'right answer' to these questions with which you have to agree. In fact, examiners are told to reward nuance in the conclusion, meaning that careful and thoughtful views will be rewarded more highly than simple assertions. This means:

- it would be good practice to argue and offer some counterargument in the essay and test ideas against the evidence before coming to a conclusion based on your analysis
- your conclusion can argue that both sides of an argument are correct to some extent.

You may find it useful to end this type of essay with a paragraph starting with the phrase 'In conclusion' – reminding you to reach a conclusion and signalling to the examiner that you are drawing one.

Example

In conclusion, the differences in media language between the Sun and the Telegraph do reflect the generic conventions of the popular and quality press in terms of layout, use of photography, language use and typography, as I have demonstrated. However, the domination of both front pages by the same hard news story – the resignation of the Prime Minister – does not reflect the typical entertainment focus of the red top tabloid press, but rather the exceptional news value of this very unusual event. Even so, the way the story is more personalised in the Sun reflects its tabloid conventions, as does the more objective treatment in The Times.

This would count as a conclusion. It is nuanced as it covers both sides of an argument. It appears to rely on the analysis already made earlier in the essay.

However, if you see immediately that the analysis would point to a definite conclusion to a particular question, it is perfectly fine to start the essay with a strong assertion of this conclusion. A confident beginning to an essay often suggests to the examiner that this might be a high-quality essay.

Exam tip

Simply repeating or rephrasing the question in an opening paragraph often suggests a middling or low-quality answer. Examiners always mark each answer on its merits, but a good initial impression cannot do any harm.

Bullet-pointed questions

REVISED

Look again at the three bullet points in Question 2 on page 3. They tell you exactly what the examiners are looking for in your answer and state everything you have to do to meet the demands of the mark scheme. Bullet 1 is worth 5 of the 15 marks and bullets 2 and 3 together are worth 10 of the 15 marks available.

Recommended revision for these questions

You need to practise textual analysis of a range of different newspapers, looking especially at media language and representation.

For media **language**, you should:
- analyse and explain the combination of elements to create meaning using **semiotics**
- study a range of newspapers to become familiar with the **generic conventions** of print and online newspapers, looking at variations, change over time, **hybridity** and challenging/subverting conventions
- compare a range of print and online newspapers in order to understand the relationship between media language and technology
- analyse and explain examples of **intertextuality**
- analyse and explain the way media language incorporates viewpoints and **ideologies**
- practise applying the ideas of Barthes, Todorov, Levi-Strauss, Neale and Baudrillard in analysing newspapers
- analyse and explain media language in newspapers in terms of media contexts.

For media **representations**, you should:
- analyse and explain how selection and combination create representations of events, issues, individuals and social groups
- analyse and explain how news makes claims about **realism** and constructs versions of reality
- analyse and explain the impact of the media industry and social, cultural and historical contexts on how producers choose to represent events, issues, individuals and social groups
- analyse and explain positive and negative uses of **stereotyping**
- analyse and explain how social groups may be under-represented or misrepresented
- analyse and explain how representations, particularly those that systematically reinforce values, attitudes and beliefs about the world across many representations, invoke **discourses** and ideologies, and **position audiences**
- suggest how audience response and interpretation reflects social, cultural and historical circumstances
- apply the ideas of Hall, Gauntlett, Butler, Van Zoonen, hooks and Gilroy in analysing newspapers.

Semiotics: The study of signs. (See Barthes in the Academic Theories section at: www.hoddereducation.co.uk/myrevisionnotesdownloads.)

Generic conventions: The shared understandings of what elements fit in which genres.

Genre hybridity: The stable mixing of different genres in one product.

Intertextuality: Media products (texts) that refer to other media products.

Ideologies: Sets of beliefs, values and assumptions shared by a social group and embedded in social, cultural, political and economic institutions. Usually thought to reflect the interests of powerful groups. Consumerism, freedom, equality and individualism are often considered dominant ideologies in free market capitalist societies as they reflect the economic basis of these societies.

Realism: Realism is the set of conventions by which audiences accept a representation as 'real' or 'realistic'. There are different sets of rules for different genres and for different media forms, and there are many different forms of realism.

Stereotyping: A commonly repeated generalisation about a group, event or institution that carries judgements, either positive or negative, and assumes any example of this group, event or institution will fit the stereotype. This generalisation is inaccurate because it is an over-simplification, even if it is based in reality. It can refer to a representation that comprises a simple stereotyped characteristic rather than a complex and individualised set of characteristics.

Discourses: A system of shared knowledge embedded in social institutions, such as medicine, that exercise power over people.

Positioning audiences: How products try to put their audiences in particular positions. This might be emotional positioning (e.g. making them feel fear or sympathy), cognitive positioning (how they think about representations in the products), social positioning (e.g. as males or females) or cultural positioning (e.g. being positioned as British or American).

Exam tip

The specification lists the subject content on pages 23–27 of the document. Examiners may write their questions using the same wording as the subject content. So, it is important you read through the subject content to check you understand all the wording.

For Question 2, revise media **audiences** and media **industries** as well, as they could be covered in the first bullet point about the media form. However, these two areas will be dealt with under Question 3, as they are best understood in relation to their contexts, which Question 3 is likely to ask about.

Exam tip

You may be asked to discuss media language or representation in either Question 1 or Question 2.

Question 1 in the exam practice above is an **analysis** question, so you may be asked to **apply** your knowledge and understanding of media language or representations when analysing the unseen sources you are given in the exam.

Question 2 in the exam practice above is both a **knowledge** and **understanding** question on the whole media form (the first bullet point) and an *analysis* question based on the sources (the second and third bullet points).

Newspapers

Newspapers: media language

REVISED ☐

Semiotics – combining elements to create meaning

The media language elements in print newspapers include:

- colour
- layout (e.g. page size, the **masthead**, the **skyline**, use of columns, headlines, image, space)
- images (e.g. photography, graphics, cartoons)
- language use (e.g. **formal and informal registers**, **mode of address**)
- typography (e.g. **serif and sans-serif typefaces/fonts**, gothic typefaces/fonts).

Media language elements in online newspapers and their social media feeds include all the above, plus:

- elements of specifically webpage layout (e.g. page size and margins, headers and footers, navigation bars, tabs)
- functionality (e.g. hyperlinks, embedded audio/visual content, interactivity)
- media language elements determined by the social media site (e.g. Twitter, Facebook and Instagram house styles).

Semiotics or semiology is the study of signs. There are many different versions of semiology/semiotics, but this need not concern us here. Meaning is created by difference (how one sign is different to another) and combination (how signs are put together, such as words in a sentence).

Mode of address: How a media product addresses its audience. This might be warm and inclusive, or formal and objective, for example, as in tabloid and broadsheet newspapers.

Serif and sans-serif typefaces/fonts: Serifs are small ornaments on fonts, sans-serif fonts do not have these so look cleaner and more modern. A typeface is a family of fonts. Arial is a common sans-serif typeface. Times New Roman is a common serif typeface.

Masthead: Often used to describe the title of a printed publication (though technically it is the title above the editorial).

Skyline: A line of text or boxes (sometimes called skyboxes) above the masthead promoting a newspaper.

Formal and informal language registers: A **formal language register** is used in formal situations, e.g. in a lecture, to communicate information, and may include complex sentences and an elaborate vocabulary. An **informal language register** is used in informal situations, e.g. in a chat with a friend, to communicate the relationship between the participants and uses simple language including slang.

Barthes put forward this theory of the different levels of signs (he called them 'orders') in the 1960s:

- A **sign** consists of a signifier (a word, an image, a sound) and its meaning – the signified.
- The **denotation** of a sign is its literal meaning. For example, the word 'dog' denotes a mammal that barks.
- Denotations signify **connotations** – the associations of the denotation. For example, we need to make up the rather strange word 'dogness' to suggest the thoughts and feelings associated with dogs. Connotations are often expressed as nouns in this way.
- Denotations and connotations are organised into **myths**– the ideological meaning. These make ideology seem 'natural'. For example, an image of a Bulldog might activate a myth of Britishness.

This all sounds complicated, but in practice you simply have to analyse front pages, websites or social media feeds from newspapers by:

- explaining why each key element has been selected (imagine it replaced with the opposite)
- explaining why each key element has been combined with the other elements (especially the **anchorage** effect of written language)
- suggesting the connotations of these combinations
- suggesting the ideologies activated by this media language (see the section on media language – the way media language incorporates viewpoints and ideologies).

Example: the *Sun*'s 'Gotcha' headline

The *Sun* used this headline for the story of an attack on two Argentinian warships during the Falklands Conflict of 1982. It was changed for later editions when the large number of sailors killed became known. The headline is combined with two photographs of Argentinian warships; these are long shots, a detached observer's point of view that tries to minimise any emotional involvement the audience might feel with dead sailors.

The headline implies '*we* got *you*', positioning the audience on the side of the attackers. The slang term 'gotcha' rather than 'got you' connotes a heightened emotional involvement in the attack and triumphant identification with the British armed forces personnel. This one word activates ideologies of nationalism and militarism – the patriotic pride in the military that was aroused in some sections of the population during this controversial conflict.

Imagine the page with the opposite connotations and ideologies. For example, in a pacifist version the headline might read 'Slaughter' and anchor images of grieving relatives.

(The front page may be found at: https://editdesk.wordpress.com/2009/08/28/memorable-headlines-gotcha/).

Sign: Any unit of language that designates an object or phenomenon. It consists of a signifier (a word, an image, a sound) and its meaning – the signified.

Denotation: The literal meaning of a sign.

Connotation: The associations of the denotation. Often expressed as nouns. May vary in their meaning – be 'polysemic'. For example, the sign 'dog' connotes 'dogness' which could mean 'warmth and devotion' or 'fear and danger'.

Myth: The organisation of meanings into commonly repeated forms that express ideology (e.g. the myth of Britishness may be signified by bulldogs, Union Flags, the monarchy, Big Ben).

Anchorage: Use of language to 'anchor' the meaning of an image to suit the purposes of the producer.

Example: the *Mail Online* logo

Figure 1.1 The *Mail Online* logo

Selection and combination are evident in the two very different fonts used for the *Mail Online* logo.

The word 'Mail' uses a heavy gothic font that is the font used for the masthead in the print edition. This connotes tradition, craft, solidity, reliability and other such virtues from its association with medieval calligraphy. This is a masthead font style that the *Daily Mail* shares with another staunchly conservative newspaper, the *Daily Telegraph*.

The word 'Online' uses a contrasting font. It is elegant, sans-serif and seems to stand tall. It connotes modernity, lightness and youth, especially when compared to the heavy gothic font.

The combination of the two fonts tries to connote that the *Mail Online* combines the reliable virtues of print journalism with the fast-moving online world. This also combines two ideologies, that of conservatism (a belief in conserving existing institutions) and modernism (a belief in change and progress), which are usually held to be opposites.

> **Revision activity**
>
> Revisit your set products – the *Guardian* and the *Mail* print and online editions and use of social media – and note how this semiotic analysis can apply to the whole front pages of these set products.

Print newspaper generic conventions

The traditional genre classification for print newspapers referred to their paper size. By the 1970s most of the more downmarket popular press had adopted tabloid size paper – half the size of the traditional broadsheet size – as it was cheaper to print, had a more accessible feel, and enabled the newspaper to fill the page with photographs or **banner headlines** for impact. The more upmarket quality press chose to retain the broadsheet format as it retained an element of formality and served to demarcate the quality press from the popular press.

> **Banner headlines**: Large headlines that fit the width of the printed page.

The terms 'broadsheet' and 'tabloid' are still in common use to describe the style of a newspaper, although few newspapers (the *Daily Telegraph* and *Financial Times*, for example) are still printed in the broadsheet format. The quality press that have moved over to the tabloid size sometimes refer to their format as 'compact', as they feel the term 'tabloid' carries negative connotations of sensationalism and gutter journalism.

The generic conventions of tabloid and broadsheet newspapers are as below:

Print newspaper generic conventions table	
Tabloid	**Broadsheet**
Softer news agenda – e.g. human-interest stories, celebrities	Harder news agenda – e.g. politics, finance, international news
Less formal language register	More formal language register
Bold mastheads in sans-serif often white on red	Traditional mastheads in serif fonts, often black on white
Headlines (often banner) in bold, capitalised sans-serif fonts	Headlines in serif fonts capitalised as in a sentence
Pages dominated by headlines and images	Pages dominated by **copy**
Addresses a more downmarket (primarily working class) audience	Addresses a more upmarket (primarily middle class) audience
Offers news as entertainment	Offers news as information

This simple division does not always work in practice:
- newspapers such as the *Daily Mail* position themselves as mid-market, combining conventions of both the tabloids and broadsheets
- some traditionally 'tabloid' features – such as extensive use of photography, human-interest stories and stories about celebrities, are increasingly common in the broadsheet press, especially in supplements such as the *Guardian's G2*. This process is sometimes called 'broadloidisation'.

The following newspapers are considered the 'quality press' or 'broadsheets':
- *The Times* and *Sunday Times*
- the *Daily Telegraph* and *Sunday Telegraph*
- the *Guardian* and *Observer*
- the *Financial Times*
- the *Independent* (now online only).

The following newspapers are considered the 'popular press' or 'red top tabloids':
- the *Sun* and *Sun on Sunday*
- the *Daily Mirror* and *Sunday Mirror*
- the *Daily Star* and *Daily Star Sunday*.

One newspaper – the *i* – is an unusual hybrid in that it was launched as the compact sister of the *Independent*, though it has now changed ownership. It offers a short, cheaper version of a quality newspaper.

Two other newspaper titles are considered to be **middle-market tabloids**:
- the *Daily Mail* and *Mail on Sunday*
- the *Daily Express* and *Sunday Express*.

These lie in between the quality press and red top tabloids in that:
- they deliver more hard news than the other tabloids (though this was less true of the Express newspapers under their pre-2018 owners); the *Daily Mail*, for example, runs campaigns on serious issues such as freeing British captives in Guantanamo Bay
- their media language is a hybrid of tabloid and broadsheet conventions.

Copy/body copy: The written element of a newspaper or advertisement. Body copy is the main body of a newspaper article.

Middle-market tabloids: Generic hybrid newspapers that share conventions of both tabloid and broadsheet newspapers to target a middle-market audience.

Daily Mail hybrid conventions
Mix of hard and soft news
More formal than the popular press, more opinionated than the quality press
Traditional serif masthead
Capitalised, often banner headlines
Front page dominated by headlines and images, but usually some copy
Addresses a middle-market (lower middle class and skilled working class) audience
A mix of both news and entertainment

Newspapers can vary from their house style and generic conventions on occasions. The day after the 9/11 attacks on the twin towers in New York, for example, the *Guardian* ran a full-page picture story with the image of the burning building, disrupting the usual layout. The day after a photograph of a drowned refugee boy was released the *Daily Mail* ran a full-page picture story (3 September 2015) using the photograph with the following headline in a lower-case font that challenged the generic conventions and house style: 'Tiny victim of a human catastrophe'. The muted media language fitted the sympathetic tone of the headline.

Online newspaper generic conventions

The traditional classification of print newspapers as broadsheet and tabloid extends at least in part to their online editions, though here the process of hybridisation continues even further.

Broadsheet newspapers online all tend to follow a similar format, which echoes the connotations of objectivity and seriousness in the print newspapers:

- the home page of the website is filled with headlines, with hard news stories towards the top of the home page
- the same traditional masthead is used as in the print edition – the *Guardian* before January 2018 used a white on blue sans-serif masthead but has since reverted to the traditional black on white serif format
- most home pages in their PC editions use a four-column layout, which fills the home page with news
- most typography is serif
- although the pages consist of mostly headlines and **standfirsts** the quantity of photographs (and other images) roughly matches that of writing.

The home pages of broadsheet newspapers do contain many more hybrid features:

- there is more extensive use of colour
- opinion, lifestyle and sports pieces appear on the home page, these would be buried inside the print newspaper or in supplements
- there is some use of sans-serif fonts.

Tabloid newspapers online also mirror some conventions of their print versions and hybridise others. Conventions shared with the print editions include:

- lifestyle, 'showbiz' and human-interest stories feature prominently towards the top of the home pages
- fonts are sans-serif
- there is use of saturated colour, especially red
- photography dominates the home pages
- the language register is more informal
- the *Mirror, Star* and *Sun* all use the same red top masthead as the print newspaper.

Standfirst: A block of text that introduces a newspaper story under the headline, normally in a different style (often bold) to the body copy and headline.

Hybridised features:
- there is little use of banner headlines, rather a large number of headlines are offered, connoting 'newsiness'
- most headlines are not capitalised (except in the *Sun*)
- the home page layout is generally less photograph/image and headline dominated than the print front page
- the large number of headlines means that some hard news stories are covered on the home page that might only make the inside pages of the print newspaper.

Print and online technology and media language

These hybridised features in online tabloid newspapers might reflect the influence of online technology: large capitalised banner headlines, for example, would be the equivalent of shouting in an online environment, whereas they are appropriate for the front page of a print newspaper to be quickly scanned by possible customers in a newsagent. Online headlines, such as those in the *Mail Online*, are often much longer than those in the print newspaper; this may be due to their role in attracting clickthroughs from the home page or to act as 'clickbait' in social media, which means they have to explain more of the narrative hook in the headline.

The large number of headlines in the online editions of all newspapers reflects audience expectations of a cornucopia of choice in the online media, whereas print readers are more content to be guided by the layout of the newspaper as to the hierarchy of stories. The online media are less effective at showing photographs compared to the print media, so photographs online tend to be cropped more as close-ups and smaller scale.

The newspaper home pages follow many online conventions and offer the usual functionality of the webpage, suggesting that the media form is as powerful an influence as the genre of newspapers in the choice of media language.

Intertextuality in media language

You should be able to analyse why media products use intertextuality. The reasons are as varied as the uses of intertextuality so you need to be able to analyse its use in context rather than applying pre-learned ideas.

However, some common significances of intertextuality include:
- to create humour
- to parody (criticise) the referred text or person (e.g. political cartoons)
- to honour the referred text (e.g. reference to universally revered people or texts)
- to create a flattering mode of address for the audience – the product may be assuming that they are clever or well informed enough to understand the intertextual reference
- to attempt to transfer the value of the referred media product to the referring one (e.g. a newspaper quoting Shakespeare or references to currently high-status celebrities)
- to create a sense of shared experience with the audience (e.g. reviews of last night's television).

Within the news sections of newspapers, headlines and standfirsts are often good sources of examples of intertextuality as they have to draw attention and summarise in a pithy manner. For example, the 3 March 2018 edition of the *Guardian* (see Figure 1.2 for the front page) contains the following instances:

Figure 1.2 *Guardian* front page, 3 March 2018

- 'Oscars so right?' – an intertextual reference to the 'Oscars so White' hashtag, which combines humour in the pun with a flattering assumption that the readers would understand it
- 'Walk on the poetic side: Lou Reed's lost verse published' – an intertextual reference to Lou Reed's song 'Walk on the Wild Side', which suggests homage to the original
- 'MI5 agents licensed to commit crime in UK' – an intertextual reference to James Bond, which suggests a similar level of lack of regulation of spies to that shown in Bond films.

The opinion section yields:
- 'Will we get a sleeping beauty or our first woke princess?' – punning intertextual references to children's fairy tales and a term for anti-racist political awareness for an article about a mixed-race soon-to-be princess, which surprises with this unlikely conjunction of connotations
- 'Don't cry for Theresa May. The truth is, this is her fault' – an intextextual reference to the lines 'Don't cry for me Argentina, the truth is I never left you' from the musical *Evita*, which works by replacing the expected gentle second line with a brutal one.

Revision activity

Look at the front pages and home pages of a range of newspapers (both print and online versions can be found online). Note examples of intertextuality and suggest reasons why they have been used. Note examples of intertextuality in the pages of your set products.

Viewpoints and ideologies in media language

'Viewpoints and ideologies' crop up in both media language and representations and will be covered in more detail in the latter. For media language, you need to be able to analyse how the choice of media language is never neutral. This is true whether or not the viewpoints being expressed are obvious. Let us take one example where the viewpoint/ideology is not obvious and one in which it is obvious.

For the more obvious example, let's take the *Daily Mail* front page for 13 June 2016, which can be found at: www.huffingtonpost.co.uk/entry/daily-mail-front-page-fails-to-mention-orlando-mass-shooting-at-all_uk_575e67c8e4b014b4f253df35.

The headline reads, 'FURY OVER PLOT TO LET 1.5M TURKS INTO BRITAIN'. This choice of language incorporates viewpoints and ideologies in a few words. The headline connotes that there is a plot, that it is right and proper to be angry about these plotters, that immigration is a bad thing, that Turks are particularly bad immigrants, possibly because they may be Muslims (the language may be read by the audience in terms of racist and Islamophobic ideologies even if these are not intended), that the plotters are most probably the 'metropolitan liberal elite' who are soft on immigration, hand-in-hand with the EU, and never to be trusted. The ideologies at play here are British, or perhaps English, nationalism (the belief in the superiority of the British/English nation) and social conservatism (the belief in the role of the common people in maintaining traditional values and resisting social liberalism). It is, in fact, newspapers such as the *Guardian* that represent the ideologies of internationalism and social liberalism that the *Daily Mail* wants to resist. Alongside this headline, the choice of the word 'dazzling' on the front page to describe the Queen, alongside a 'glamour' photograph of the young queen, again reinforces what feminists and republicans would see as traditional patriarchal views of femininity and monarchism that fit with social conservatism.

As a less obvious example, on the front page of the *Guardian* (3 March 2018) is a large photograph of a woman looking pensive and sad (see Figure 1.2). She is shot in medium close-up so her facial expression is clearly visible. She is a conventionally attractive woman who is wearing make-up, so the presence of this photograph does not disturb the patriarchal ideology that women are to be looked at, but the photograph has been shot and cropped to minimise sexual objectification. The lighting is not that used for 'glamour' photography: she is side-lit in a natural light, there are no eye-lights to bring her eyes to life. Her image has been cropped so we only see face and scarf. Why this media language? The meaning is anchored by the use of captions such as 'Hellish limbo: Widow fights for answers'. The woman has been shot in such a way as to suggest 'widowness'. A quote, 'I dread the moment when my daughter asks, "Where's Dad?"' anchors this meaning and links this to 'motherliness'. The media language used for this tragic story does not threaten what feminists call the ideology of the family, because this is the lived experience of many of the producers and audience.

Barthes called this the 'naturalising' of ideology – the way it is encoded into media language so it seems 'normal' and 'natural'. If Barthes is right, then it should be really quite difficult to analyse ideology. If an ideology is one we take for granted, one we all don't question, then it is going to be hard to spot.

It is easier to analyse the way media language incorporates viewpoints and ideologies when there are two products with different viewpoints about the same event. This means that the sources chosen for the exam paper are likely to demonstrate clearly different viewpoints on the same event, perhaps where there is obvious disagreement in ideologies, in order to make their influence clearer.

For example, look at the two sources – the front pages of the *Sun* and *The Times* for exam practice Questions 1 and 2 at: **www.ocr.org.uk/ Images/316674-unit-h409-01-media-messages-sample-assessment-material. pdf**. The two cover stories are both about the resignation of the Prime Minister after the Brexit vote in 2016. The two newspapers had different views on Brexit and these different viewpoints are embedded in the media language:

- The *Sun* has chosen a close-up of David Cameron's emotional face with a headline that anchors the story as about how the Prime Minister feels: 'Why should I do the hard s★★t?' This media language creates focus on the personal pain felt by the loser in the Brexit debate.
- *The Times* uses a two-shot of the Prime Minister and his wife coming out of number 10 Downing Street that connotes a historic as well as a personal event. This is anchored by the choice of headline: 'Brexit earthquake'. This metaphor connotes an unexpected disaster that nobody can control, a reading emphasised by a standfirst stating 'Vote to leave threatens break-up of UK'.

Now which viewpoint did each newspaper take on the Brexit debate? The media language should give you a clue. The *Sun* was passionately pro-Brexit, while *The Times* advised its readers to vote to remain in the EU.

However, though on different sides in the debate, both these front pages share a wider ideological commitment to democratic politics. Both see the resignation of a Prime Minister as an exceptionally newsworthy event. Both have chosen images of the Prime Minister looking emotional as symbolic of the high drama of political leadership.

Here is an example of an ideology toolkit that you might use to analyse media language. Note that some of these ideologies also count as media contexts, especially multiculturalism, feminism, consumerism and democracy.

Ideology 'toolkit'	
Ideology	**How it might influence the media language used**
Sexism/**patriarchy**	Emphasises sexual objectification, or a stress on women's appearance. Reinforces sexist stereotypes
Feminism	Supports women's rights and gender equality
Racism	Connotes racial stereotypes or Whiteness as normal and race as a problem
Multiculturalism	Promotes inclusivity and multicultural viewpoints
Ethnocentrism	Connotes distrust or hatred of foreigners (e.g. headlines connoting immigration as a problem, antipathy to EU officials because they are foreign)
Internationalism	Connotes care for and responsibilities towards other countries and peoples
Consumerism	Markets consumerist views to its audience (e.g. lifestyle advice, skylines/skyboxes, connotations of glamour or entertainment, extensive use of colour)
Individualism	Emphasises the individual (e.g. close-up photographs of people, headlines about prominent individuals) over the group or the society
Democracy	Emphasises the importance of politicians and political issues (e.g. prominent photographs of politicians looking like leaders – or not looking like leaders, if the article is critical of the politician)

Patriarchy: The system and ideology of male power described by feminism. Literally it means 'rule of the father'. Patriarchal ideology includes the male gaze, stereotypes of male power (including violence) and activity, and female submissiveness and passivity, the ideology of romance and the family, and the separation of a masculine public realm from a feminine domestic realm.

Ethnocentrism: Belief that your own culture is natural and normal, and that other cultures are inferior and strange.

Consumerism: The ideology that we should judge ourselves and others on our material possessions, that our lifestyles (e.g. our clothes, houses, cars, media use) should define our individual identities. The opposite is ideas of duty or religious renunciation.

Individualism: The ideology that assumes people are essentially individuals. Taking exams is an example of competitive individualism. The opposite is collectivism – that people are essentially collective, i.e. members of a group.

You are not expected to know newspapers' viewpoints in detail, but the following table outlines the political position – as far as this is possible – of each national newspaper, as this may affect their media language use in some stories.

As you cannot know which newspapers, print or online, you will be asked to analyse in the exam and it would be too great a task to learn the viewpoints and ideologies of all British newspapers, assemble a 'toolkit' of ideologies that might apply to the front pages, websites or social media feeds of newspapers.

Revision activity

See if you can add other ideologies you come across in your analyses to this list.

Newspaper	Political position
The Times	Right of centre, most often supports the Conservative Party but supported the Labour Party under Tony Blair
Daily Telegraph	Right wing – staunchly supports the Conservative Party
Guardian	Left of centre – usually supports the Labour Party but has supported the Liberal Democrats
Financial Times	Pro-business – usually supports the Conservative Party
Independent	Centrist – the name suggests a desire not to be politically affiliated, but the paper has endorsed the Liberal Democrats
i	Centrist – not politically affiliated
Daily Mail	Right wing – staunchly supports the Conservative Party
Daily Express	Right wing, usually supports the Conservative Party but has also once this century endorsed the Labour Party (under Tony Blair) and, more recently, UKIP
Sun	Right of centre, most often supports the Conservative Party but supported the Labour Party under Tony Blair
Daily Mirror	Left of centre – staunchly supports the Labour Party
Daily Star	No clear political affiliation

Media language theories

See the Academic Theories section at www.hoddereducation.co.uk/myrevisionnotesdownloads for a list of what you have to know about these writers.

Using **Barthes** in analysis will usually be a case of analysing connotations and the ways these embed ideologies, as discussed on page 7.

Todorov's theory of narrative can be applied to newspaper stories insofar as any 'bad' news story acts as a **narrative disruption** of an implied equilibrium. For example, in the story from the *Guardian* above – 'Hellish limbo: Widow fights for answers' – the disruption can be seen as the killing of her husband, implying an initial equilibrium of stable family life. The new equilibrium which the disruption is driving towards is that the woman will achieve some sort of resolution when she gets some answers.

Levi-Strauss's idea of **binary oppositions** can be readily used in analysis. For example, the cases from the *Guardian* and the *Daily Mail* headlines discussed above:

In the *Guardian* example the set of binary oppositions are as follows, with the valued term first:

family : individual

whole : separated

In the *Daily Mail* example they are:

Brexiteers : Remainers

authentic : plotters

truthful : lying

the people : elites

Narrative disruption: The event(s) that disrupt an initial equilibrium and drive a narrative towards a resolution. For example, a murder can disrupt the peace of a community and cause investigation and solution.

Binary opposition: This consists of two concepts that mean the opposite of each other, e.g. hot:cold. Levi-Strauss analysed communication in terms of these oppositions.

Using **Neale** in analysis will be in relation to genre or genre conventions, especially Neale's insistence on the dynamic nature of genre as a **shared code** that changes over time with every addition to the **generic corpus** rather than being fixed, and that is often hybridised.

Neale's argument that genre may be communicated outside the texts themselves in an intertextual relay does not apply so much to newspapers as it did to film in his original discussion.

Using **Baudrillard** in analysis is extremely difficult, so he may be less likely to appear in an analysis question. His idea of **implosion** could be applied to a news story or image about a person constructing an identity ignoring traditional social differences – celebrities who transcend their backgrounds, for example. His idea of **hyperreality** (signs that refer to other signs and not a reality) can be applied to absolutely anything, but would particularly apply where audiences will know nothing of events except for media representations of them and also to events about other media events (e.g. news stories about promotional activities such as film premieres).

Implosion: The collapse of traditional social distinctions in postmodern society. (See Baudrillard in the Academic Theories section at: www. hoddereducation.co.uk/ myrevisionnotesdownloads.)

Hyperreality: A sense of reality constructed by media products that refer to other media products in a never-ending chain. (See Baudrillard in the Academic Theories section at: www. hoddereducation.co.uk/ myrevisionnotesdownloads.)

Shared code: The idea the genres are defined by codes and conventions that come into existence in the interrelationship between media products, their producers and their audiences. A producer looks at existing products that have been successful with audiences and produces new products using the same conventions to meet the audiences' expectations, but with subtle variations to maintain interest.

Generic corpus: The body of media products in a genre. Each subtly adds to, and thus changes, the genre.

Media language and media contexts

Some media contexts may influence the use of media language in newspapers, though this impact is more oblique than the effect on representations.

Consumerism – can count as a social, cultural, economic and even political context, as it affects all these areas of society. It influences media language particularly through the dominance of marketing in contemporary media. Comparing today's print newspapers with their 1950s counterparts shows that audiences are now used to colour, extensive use of photography and self-promotion in a way that would have appeared gaudy in the black-and-white world of 1950s newspapers. The cornucopia of content in online editions and the targeting of audiences through bite-sized social media feeds further suggests that consumer needs are paramount in the current media age as compared to the austere authority of traditional newspapers.

Celebrity culture – a social, cultural and even political context – infuses the media language of many newspapers with large images of celebrities dominating the layout of front pages, home pages and social media feeds.

Multiculturalism – a social and cultural context – affects the use of language in newspapers, where editors aim to use inclusive language and avoid racist terms.

Revision activity

Return to the media language revision activities on pages 11, 12 and 15 and see if you can insert an appropriate reference to Barthes, Todorov, Levi-Strauss, Neale or Baudrillard. Note where the theories don't help you very much – this is relevant to Question 4.

The impact of **feminism** – a social, cultural and political context – may be reflected in language use – avoiding sexist terms and stereotyping – and photographic practices. The persistence of patriarchy may express itself in sexist language and sexually objectifying photographic practices.

Postmodernism – a social and cultural context – may have led to increasing intertextuality in newspapers.

Paper 1 – Section A: News

Revision activity

Revisit your analysis of the set products – the *Guardian* and the *Mail* print and online editions and use of social media – and note how media contexts have affected the media language.

Newspapers: media representations

REVISED

The subject content for representation covered here, though separated into different sections, is all highly interrelated: misrepresentation of social groups, for example, is closely linked to other sections such as those on stereotyping, the impact of contexts, and ideologies. So, in order to weave together these sections, we will use the set products – the *Guardian* and the *Daily Mail* – as exemplars as we explore how each section applies specifically to news, then illustrate how they might be applied to the front pages of two newspapers that you could be asked to analyse in the exam.

Representation: selection and combination

We have seen how the meanings created by media language depend on how the various elements are selected and combined and that the repetition of these meanings reflects ideologies. Representation works in the same way. Our view of the world is mediated by newspapers that select which events, issues, individuals and social groups to represent and which to ignore.

One simple way to illustrate selection is to draw a map of the world based on how many stories about each continent (or countries) are reported in British newspapers. Britain, especially London, is huge. North America, especially the USA, is large. Europe is medium sized. Australasia, Africa and Asia are tiny. South America is usually non-existent.

These biases in representation are caused by the application of **news values**, which include bias towards powerful people, celebrities and entertainment, events or issues already in the news and seen as relevant to the audience, 'big' news, 'bad news', 'good' news, and the unexpected, as in the old journalistic saying 'dog bites man is not news, man bites dog is'. Different newspapers will also have their own agendas (such as the 2017 *Daily Express*'s obsession with weather, the royal family and health stories). Online versions of newspapers will be more likely to have a bias towards what plays well on Facebook, such as entertaining stories that are 'shareable' or stories with strong visual or audio-visual images.

Newspapers combine representations to create a view of the world. In newspapers with a strong ethos, such as the *Guardian* and the *Daily Mail*, a fairly consistent world-view will be represented. In the case of these two newspapers, this will often but not always be diametrically opposed.

Exam tip

Both presence and absence are important in representation analysis, but analysing what is present in a representation is much easier than analysing what is absent. Listing which groups are not included in a representation does not count as effective analysis. Comparing two sources might show, however, that a representation is absent in one source and present in another – you should explain why this is, trying to link to the viewpoints and ideologies of the different sources.

News values: The values that govern which events are selected as news and which events are rejected.

The *Guardian* world-view

The *Guardian* supports liberal, progressive values.

Katherine Viner, the *Guardian* editor, wrote in 2017:

> Our moral conviction, as ... codified by Scott, rests on a faith that people long to understand the world they're in, and to create a better one. We believe in the value of the public sphere; that there is such a thing as the public interest, and the common good; that we are all of equal worth; that the world should be free and fair.

She added:

> the Guardian will embrace as wide a range of progressive perspectives as possible. We will support policies and ideas, but we will not give uncritical backing to parties or individuals. We will also engage with and publish voices from the right. In an age of tumultuous change, nobody has a monopoly on good ideas. But our guiding focus, especially in countries such as Britain, the US and Australia, will be to challenge the economic assumptions of the past three decades, which have extended market values such as competition and self-interest far beyond their natural sphere and seized the public realm.

> Katherine Viner, 'A mission for journalism in a time of crisis', *Guardian*, 16 November 2017

The *Daily Mail* world-view

The Mail supports a free market economy, and British traditions such as the royal family, the church, the army and democracy.

In 2013, Paul Dacre, the then *Daily Mail* editor, argued that the Mail stands up for its readers, 'with their dreams (mostly unfulfilled) of a decent education and health service they can trust, their belief in the family, patriotism, self-reliance, and their over-riding suspicion of the state and the People Who Know Best'. They are sceptical 'over the European Union and a human rights court that seems to care more about the criminal than the victim ... [and] while tolerant, fret that the country's schools and hospitals can't cope with mass immigration'. He adds:

> I am proud that our Dignity For The Elderly Campaign has for years stood up for Britain's most neglected community. Proud that we have fought for justice for Stephen Lawrence, Gary McKinnon and the relatives of the victims of the Omagh bombing, for those who have seen loved ones suffer because of MRSA and the Liverpool Care Pathway. I am proud that we have led great popular campaigns for the NSPCC and Alzheimer's Society on the dangers of paedophilia and the agonies of dementia. And I'm proud of our war against round-the-clock drinking, casinos, plastic bags, internet pornography and secret courts.

> Paul Dacre, 'Why is the left obsessed by the Daily Mail?', *Guardian*, 12 October 2013

Note: the *Mail Online*, though sharing material with the *Daily Mail*, is edited separately to the print newspaper and has a much more internationalist outlook, especially in its social media feeds.

Let's analyse the following two tweets from the *Guardian* and the *Daily Mail Online* in terms of selection and combination in the light of these different world-views.

Revision activity

How do these two statements suggest different ideologies? Which is more collectivist and which more individualist? Which is more internationalist and which more nationalist?

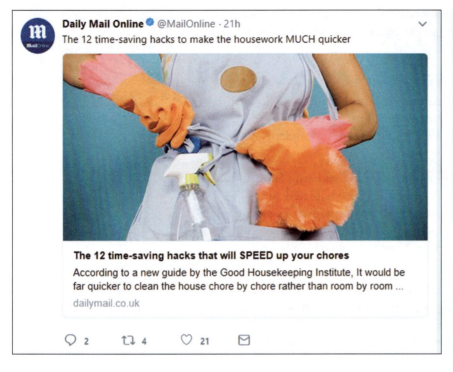

Figure 1.3 Daily Mail Online Twitter post

The *Mail* tweet has chosen to combine the headline for an article on housework with an image of a woman putting on an apron. The two elements fit together within patriarchal ideology as they reinforce the representation of housework as a feminine activity. This can be seen as fitting into the *Daily Mail* world-view insofar as complaints about sexist stereotyping may be seen as interference from Paul Dacre's 'People Who Know Best'.

Figure 1.3 *Guardian* Twitter post

The *Guardian* has chosen to combine a feminist headline about (gender) inequality with an image – which looks like a patriarchal promotional image for an airline – showing a woman serving a man. The two

Revision activity

Find articles from your set products (the *Guardian* and the *Daily Mail*) that exemplify these contrasting world-views. The *Daily Mail* changed editor in 2018 after decades under Paul Dacre; check if the current newspaper still follows the same world-view as that outlined above.

Exam tip

You may be asked to analyse representations in newspapers other than the two set products. In this case a general familiarity with the political position of each newspaper as in the table above should suffice, though the more familiar you are with a range of newspapers the better.

elements carry very different representational meanings in order to raise questions about gender inequality, so fitting the *Guardian's* world-view as a progressive newspaper.

News: realism and constructing reality

Most media products make some claim to realism but news works within particularly stringent rules of realism, as the controversy over 'fake news' illustrates. News in its purest form will adhere to standards of truthfulness, of fact.

News is traditionally separated from editorial, the first being factual, the second being opinion. Both should be clearly demarcated from advertising. These boundaries are established by journalistic and editorial practice and professional ethics, by self-regulation, and by the laws of libel (which mean that a newspaper has to prove the facts to be true to successfully defend a libel case).

It is easier to maintain these standards in the quality national press, where audiences are paying for high-quality journalism. In lower-status newspapers, such as local papers, advertisers can more easily succeed in their aim to blur the boundary between journalism and advertising. In such cases what may be presented as factual journalism may simply be persuasive content from media relations and public relations personnel. The *Daily Mail* and the *Guardian*, by contrast, would aim to maintain that boundary by attributing sources and clearly labelling advertising or sponsored material.

We would expect the *Guardian* and the *Daily Mail* to construct different versions of reality, within the constraints of the news of the day, to match the different world-views coming primarily, but not exclusively, from their editors. These might be expressed as binary oppositions, as used by Levi-Strauss, as in the table below (the '*Daily Mail* reality' column is based on the newspaper under Dacre up to August 2018).

Daily Mail reality	*Guardian* reality
Many problems are caused by the ruling liberal elites and the nanny state.	Many problems are caused by uncontrolled free markets.
Problems are best solved by allowing the free market to operate and minimising bureaucratic interference.	Problems are best solved by public control in the public interest.
We should look after our own people before we look after foreigners.	As a rich country we have a duty to help others in the world.
Ordinary people are rightly proud to be British.	Some patriotism is associated with xenophobia and racism; we should be both internationalist and proud to be British.
We should respect great British institutions such as the monarchy.	We should recognise where institutions need to improve.
Catching criminals is more important than protecting human rights.	Protecting human rights is the cornerstone of a free society.
Brexit is a fantastic opportunity.	Brexit is a disaster.

The two newspapers differ in how definite they are about their version of reality. Looking again at the two tweets on page 19, it is clear that the *Mail* tweet is trying to represent an unproblematic version of reality whereas the *Guardian* tweet suggests there is a problem caused by a difference between the image and the reality. Though both newspapers have their own moral certainties, the *Daily Mail* represents a more definite world, the *Guardian* a more questioned world. As we shall see later, this may be because the *Daily Mail*, in Hall's terms, is providing a more dominant representation of events (the view of the world embodied in traditional ideologies of Britishness), whereas the *Guardian* is providing a more negotiated representation of events, one that accepts aspects of how society is organised and criticises other aspects.

Narrative is important in the construction of reality. The world of 'spin doctors', for example, is to create a suitable narrative around news events. News stories are constant disruptions of Todorov's **narrative equilibrium** in that most news stories are 'bad news' – a disruption of the previous state of affairs and a drive towards a restoration of a new equilibrium. Like dramatic narratives, a good news story will keep the audience wanting resolution by at first delaying it, creating desire in the audience to know what happens next, then giving them resolution before they lose interest. Some news stories cannot offer resolution (e.g. will climate change be remedied?) and are inherently less satisfactory. Examples of much more satisfactory resolutions include stories about people falling down wells when the narrative is resolved by a successful rescue. For example, a news story about a baby who was rescued after 58 hours trapped in a well in 1987 was famous enough to be revisited by the *Mail Online* in 2017 in an article about 'baby Jessica' from the 'miracle rescue' 30 years on.

> **Narrative equilibrium**: The state of stasis before the narrative disruption occurs. This is often inadequate in some way, so that the resolution leads to an improved equilibrium. The transformation from the initial to the final equilibrium suggests the key values or ideology of the narrative.

The competing narratives around Brexit are a good example of different constructed realities. Coverage of this issue reflects the different narratives the two newspapers have created up to Summer 2018 around the process, as illustrated below using Todorov's categories.

	Guardian	Daily Mail
Original equilibrium	EU membership offers substantial benefits and commits Britain to internationalism.	EU membership means Britain has to accept laws from a European super-state, cannot control immigration or make its own trade deals.
Disruption	Deciding to leave the EU liberates xenophobic and nationalistic forces and threatens Britain's economy.	Brussels bureaucrats and Remainers try to thwart the liberation of the British people to be sovereign and make their own way in the world.
Desired new equilibrium	Brexit is reversed or made as undamaging as possible.	A clean Brexit – Britain breaks away as completely as possible from the EU.

It may be useful to analyse news stories in this way if asked about the construction of reality – what are the narratives that the different newspapers are trying to construct around this event and how do they differ?

Representation: the news industry and contexts

Media industry

The two different social realities represented by the *Guardian* and the *Daily Mail* reflect their very different traditions and ownership.

The *Guardian* originated in 1821 as the radical *Manchester Guardian*, devoted to enlightenment values, liberty, reform and justice. Its most important editor, C. P. Scott, was a radical Liberal (this was 1872, before the founding of the Labour Party) and party activist who cared greatly about social justice, welfare and pacifism. In an essay of 1921 he laid out some core principles for the newspaper: 'honesty, cleanness [integrity], courage, fairness, a sense of duty to the reader and a sense of duty to the community'. This adoption of what the *Daily Mail* might see as smug moral superiority has meant that the *Guardian* has embraced many controversial positions, such as being the only newspaper to pursue the phone-hacking scandal that led to the closure of the *News of the World* and the Leveson Inquiry (see below for details in Question 3). The *Guardian* is owned by an independent trust whose aims are to protect its editorial freedom and promote liberal values.

The *Daily Mail* was established by Harold Harmsworth, 1st Viscount Rothermere, and his elder brother, Alfred Harmsworth, 1st Viscount Northcliffe, and the company that owns the newspaper and its online sister is run by the present Viscount Rothermere, who is a majority shareholder. The newspaper was founded in 1896 as mass-market newspapers took off with increasing levels of literacy and spending power among the general public, rapidly becoming very successful with a mix of imperialist, patriotic news stories and human-interest material. This has proved a winning approach with its readers, meaning that the newspaper is still profitable today. The *Mail*'s strongly opinionated and right-wing stance briefly allowed its owner in the early 1930s to praise fascism, for example. It is strongly nationalist and conservative, but unafraid to criticise the British state or Tory Party policies when it disagrees with them.

Note, however, that media ownership is not a sure predictor of the representations in a newspaper. Newspapers owned by News International – the *Sun* and *The Times*, for example – have taken very different political positions over events, despite their shared ownership. The *Daily Mail* took a different view to its sister newspaper the *Mail on Sunday* over Brexit.

Media contexts

Consumerism counts as a social, cultural, economic and even political context, as it affects all these areas of society. It affects representation in a number of subtle ways.

Treating audiences as consumers leads to a different view of politics, for example. The term 'retail politics' describes the way that politicians now feel the need to sell their policies to voters through the mass media, and newspaper coverage of politics may emphasise the popularity of policies (e.g. through opinion polls) rather than their effectiveness or moral worth.

Treating audiences as consumers influences:
- the quantity of lifestyle content in newspapers such as the *Guardian* and the *Mail*
- the celebration of celebrity culture as a lure to fickle consumers, particularly in online editions of newspapers, such as the *Mail Online*
- the representation of audiences themselves, whether by letters to the editor in the print editions, or comments in the online editions and social media, or articles about readers in the membership section of the *Guardian*.

Celebrity culture is a social, cultural and even political context that affects representation in newspapers by enabling coverage of celebrities,

Revision activity

Revisit the representations in your set products – the *Guardian* and the *Mail* print and online editions and use of social media – and note how they constructed realities. The *Daily Mail* changed editor in 2018, check if this has changed its construction of reality from that outlined above (e.g. the new editor comes from the anti-Brexit *Mail on Sunday*).

Revision activity

Find two examples of recent stories that exemplify the differing ethos of the *Daily Mail* and the *Guardian*.

celebrity events and celebrity politicians such as Donald Trump, Boris Johnson and Vladimir Putin. Celebrities including those from show business and the monarchy feature heavily in the *Mail Online*, for example, especially in the 'sidebar of shame' in the right-hand column of the website. Celebrity events are perhaps clearest in sport, with the near-universal dominance of Premier League, Champion's League and World Cup football and the world of entertainment, with universal coverage of the Oscars, for example.

Multiculturalism is a social and cultural context that will affect representation in newspapers. This is perhaps best illustrated by comparing the routinely all-White representations in newspapers in the 1960s to those today. When Black and minority ethnic (BAME) people were represented in the 1960s, it would be most often in the context of a story about race; today the representations are more varied and less self-conscious. Any example of this kind of representation would count as the influence of multiculturalism. For example, a photostory in the *Mail Online* (7 March 2018) about creative parenting includes an image of two Black kids being made to wear a 'get along' T-shirt for two and their inclusion is not commented upon. However, writers such as Gilroy and hooks point out that racism is far from eradicated and assumptions of White superiority persist in the modern world.

The impact of **feminism** is a social, cultural and political context, which means that many more media producers are women, many more powerful people in the world are women, and the media are more aware of the perils of sexist stereotyping. So any example of deliberately avoiding stereotyping or covering feminist issues may be seen as an example of the influence of this context, as might coverage of female leaders such as Theresa May or Angela Merkel. However, feminists such as Van Zoonen and hooks argue that patriarchy persists in the modern world and that sexism is far from eradicated.

Changing attitudes to **sexualities** is a social, cultural and even political context – which means that different sexualities and genders are now far less closeted than in the past, and that gay, lesbian, trans and other queer issues are now represented in the mainstream media. Unsurprisingly, this is more evident in the *Guardian* than the *Mail* – for example, a headline in the online *Guardian* edition (7 March 2018) asking 'Why hasn't the gay community had a #MeToo moment?' Any representation except for homophobic ones may be seen as examples of the influence of this context.

Political contexts that influence representations include, in 2018:
- the fight against sexual harassment, violence and gender income inequality
- the aftermath of the economic crises of 2008, including the rise of populist movements and disillusionment with mainstream politics
- increasing international tension, e.g. conflict with North Korea and Russia
- global warming
- Brexit.

Positive and negative uses of stereotyping

The power of media representation lies in repetition. When some representations are constantly repeated they can result in stereotyping. Note that while 'stereotype' implies something real and unchanging,

Revision activity

What are the political issues influencing the news this year? Which of the list on the left are no longer relevant?

Revision activity

Revisit the representations in your set products – the *Guardian* and the *Mail* print and online editions and use of social media – and note how they reflected media contexts and media industries.

calling a representation stereotypical is probably best seen as a judgement with which others might disagree rather than a hard-and-fast fact.

A stereotype suggests that all the members of a group of people or events are covered by the judgement. A stereotype may be based in reality but still inaccurate because of this 'catch-all' quality. Stereotypical judgements can be positive or negative, though both may be inaccurate. 'All Italians are passionate' is an example of a positive stereotype; 'All Americans are fat' is an example of a negative stereotype.

Let's look at the two tweets above from the *Guardian* and *Mail Online*. The *Mail's* tweet about housework uses a sexist stereotype of housework being women's responsibility. This stereotype may have been used in an unthinking way, as part of the *Mail's* traditional world-view or it may have been a conscious decision that the story was about advice from a women's magazine and that this would address women. In this case it is the traditional division of labour where women took responsibility for housework and men for earnings that has generated both the representation and the magazine from which the story originated. The *Mail* prides itself on its robust, 'no-nonsense' style, which means that it may not be overly concerned about gender stereotyping.

The *Guardian's* tweet also uses a stereotypical image of a woman serving a man. However, in this case the use of the stereotype is clearly deliberate, as it illustrates the issue of gender inequality in airlines that the article explores. Here a stereotype is being deconstructed, as Hall suggests progressive texts should do, by attention being drawn to its stereotypical nature. Stereotypes work by drawing on our assumptions, by our unthinking acceptance that a representation is normal and natural, so drawing attention to the artificiality of the stereotype does serve to undermine it. However, at the same time, a feminist might argue that the *Guardian* has still decorated its Twitter feed with an image of a conventionally attractive woman, reinforcing the ideology that women are there to be looked at (and men are to do the looking).

Stereotyping is more likely in media products, such as newspaper headlines or photographs that have to generate meaning quickly and do not have the time to portray subtle and nuanced representations. Stereotyping is also more likely to occur in products such as tabloid newspapers that rely on a 'matey' mode of address – an informality that suggests a warm personal relationship with the reader. Here the use of a stereotype may imply a set of feelings and understandings shared with the reader.

Under-represented or misrepresented groups

Under-representation and misrepresentation are both highly loaded terms. The term 'under-representation' implies that there is some kind of mathematically correct proportion of representations that each social group should receive. The term 'misrepresentation' implies that there is some kind of truthful representation from which actual representations deviate. However, we can never know the correct numbers of representations or the nature of the most accurate representations as we never have access to all the reality that is being represented. Accusations of misrepresentation, in particular, are always judgements.

This means, in practical terms, that analysing under-representation and misrepresentation in any media product is best boiled down to factors such as:

Exam tip

It is hard to make judgements about diversity if there are few representations in a source – and therefore harder to analyse a social media post than a complete front page or home page, for example. So we might expect exam questions on this topic to use a source with multiple representations.

Do not rush to judgement on the reasons why minority groups may not be represented: consider whether the absence of a social group is due to **conscious bias**, **unconscious bias** or the effect of exclusion in the real world that is being represented.

Bias: Treating people differently because of social differences and labels. **Conscious bias** is when the biased person or institution is aware of what they are doing. **Unconscious bias** is when they are not.

- use of stereotyping
- diversity of representations
- opportunities for self-representation.

Diversity combats under-representation by increasing the number of representations of different social groups. In turn, alleviating under-representation should help combat misrepresentation as the more representations of a group are present the more possibility there is for a range of representations rather than simple stereotypes or limited representations. For example, the actor who played an out gay character – Colin in *EastEnders* – in the 1980s, when this was exceptional for a British soap opera, complained that his one character had to represent the whole of the gay community. This is always the problem with tokenism – the inclusion of one token minority character to 'tick the box' of diversity.

The issue of who is doing the representing is also key, though not always easy to analyse in an unseen print media product. It is a fair assumption that self-representations are less likely to be misrepresentations than those created by outsiders.

Under-represented and misrepresented social groups are often groups defined by ideologies of exclusion; traditionally these include the groups listed below.

Group	Ideology of exclusion
Any group defined in terms of '**race**'	Racism
Women	Sexism
LGBT people	Homophobia/transphobia
Old people	Ageism
People with disabilities	Disablism
Foreigners and 'other' cultures	Xenophobia/**ethnocentrism**

However, many of these ideologies of exclusion are, at the very least, contested in contemporary Britain and we would expect self-representations from all of these groups within the mainstream media, especially newspapers such as the *Guardian*. For example, the exclusion of people with disabilities once passed largely unnoticed in the British media (and many prominent people with disabilities, such as political leaders, would hide them). The increasing visibility of people with disabilities – the representation of the Paralympic Games, for example – means that this under-representation is no longer normalised.

Certain people, on the other hand, will be defined as complete 'outsiders' and their point of view will be consciously excluded from media products. These groups include people such as terrorists, child sex offenders and violent racists. On the international level, some countries are seen as outside the world order and will never have their point of view represented, unless it is to be represented as an unacceptable 'other' – North Korea, for example.

Beliefs, attitudes, values, discourses, ideologies and positioning

These terms all overlap but have different meanings.

Beliefs are consciously held sets of ideas about the world. Similarly, attitudes refer to an individual's ideas and feelings about something,

Race and ethnicity: **Race** is a system of exclusion (marking people as 'other'). It may or may not be based on characteristics such as skin colour. **Ethnicity** refers to inclusion – the culture to which people feel they belong (e.g. they share a language). Where an ethnic group is subject to racism or excluded people form a common culture the two overlap, so the terms are often used together.

A common error is to confuse ethnicity and ethnic minorities; for example, to state 'there is no ethnicity' in a representation when there are no visible ethnic minorities present. Anybody can be ethnic and either a majority or a minority. For example, to be British is an ethnicity (this is complicated by national identities within Britishness, such as the English, Scots, Welsh and Northern Irish). When British people in Spain retain their native language and customs and fail to integrate into the ethnic majority (Spanish) culture then they are an ethnic minority.

Ethnocentrism: Belief that your own culture is natural and normal, and that other cultures are inferior and strange

which affect their behaviour. A person's values are the things that person thinks and feels are important.

These three might be shared. Shared beliefs, attitudes and values might be consciously held. For example, political beliefs, attitudes and values might be held in common with others and opposed to other beliefs, attitudes and values. However, if beliefs, attitudes and values are so widely shared that they may be taken for granted and never questioned, then they become part of an ideology by which people live their lives. Ideologies are usually seen as reinforcing the position of the powerful in society: feminists such as Van Zoonen and hooks see men as benefiting from patriarchal ideology, Gilroy and hooks would see White people as benefiting from racist ideology, Marxists see capitalists as benefiting from capitalist (or 'Bourgeois') ideology.

Ideologies often only become evident when they are contested, when there is ideological conflict. In Britain today we can suggest evidence of ideological conflict between:
- nationalism and internationalism in the Brexit debate
- democracy and authoritarianism in the conflict with states such as North Korea and Russia
- consumerism and fundamentalist religion in the conflict with so-called religious terrorism.

Discourses, unlike ideology, do not serve the interests of powerful social groups, except perhaps the professionals who administer them. For example, commonly invoked discourses in journalism include those about education and medicine, both successfully promoted by their practitioners as 'good' in themselves and embedded in well-funded public institutions. The growth of a managerial discourse – viewing problems as 'challenges' to be managed in a positive manner – can be found in journalistic articles about wide-ranging topics such as politics and lifestyles. In politics, covering how government manages any problem or event and calling them to account when they fail to do so; in lifestyle journalism, covering how we should manage our diet, exercise or spiritual development.

Audience positioning refers to the way that representations attempt to place the audience in a certain position, although this may be resisted by actual audiences in practice. For example, UK viewers are positioned as Americans when watching US television or Hollywood films. They may embrace or resist this if they are not Americans, but are so used to this process that sometimes they don't even notice. Audiences may be positioned to think, feel and have a sense of belonging in products with a strong audience positioning strategy – such as cinema or video games – but newspapers tend to invite more negotiation of the meaning by audiences.

Take, for example, the headline from the *Daily Mail* cited earlier: 'Fury over plot to let 1.5m Turks into Britain'. The strategy is to position the audience as furious, as suspicious of plots, as not wanting more Turks in Britain, and as British. Each of these could be contested by an audience reading the headline – the positioning works only if the audience already agree with the assumptions embedded in the headline. This is quite different from the strong positioning created by identification with characters in film narratives, which is where this concept originated.

However, the concept is still a useful one in analysing other media products, including newspapers.

Audience positioning works best where both the media product and the audience share the same ideology, the same system of values, beliefs and attitudes, as in the *Daily Mail* headline above. Let's now take a headline from the *Guardian*: 'Hedy Lamarr: the 1940s "bombshell" who invented wifi' (8 March 2018). This positions the audience as familiar with classic Hollywood of the 1940s, as having a feminist sensibility that would be offended by the use of the sexually objectifying term 'bombshell' without quotation marks but would recognise it as authentically 1940s, as intrigued by the combination of film stardom and invention. The headline will work in an unproblematic manner if the audience shares the same liberal feminist ideology as the *Guardian*.

An ideology toolkit, like the one below is useful for representation analysis. The first three entries in the list are often considered the dominant ideologies of advanced capitalism. Ideologies usually but not always have an 'ism' attached to their name, as the last two entries prove. Add to this toolkit as you come across ideologies in your analyses.

Ideology 'toolkit'	
Ideology	**How it might influence the representations**
Materialism	Expressed in news stories about wealth, income and material goods (rather than spiritual values, for example)
Consumerism	Expressed in news stories or lifestyle articles about brands, lifestyle and identity choices, and self-fulfilment through buying goods and services
Individualism	Expressed by stories celebrating individuals – whether celebrities or 'ordinary' – especially when they are standing up to big organisations Individualism is closely linked to the idea of freedom – the freedom of the individual being a core value – so stories celebrating freedom usually express individualism too
Sexism/patriarchal ideology	Expressed through unchallenged sexist stereotyping, sexually objectified representations of women
Feminism	Expressed by support for women's struggle for equality, representations of women with agency and power, exposing and criticising sexism
Racism	Expressed through unchallenged racist stereotyping or representations that imply racist beliefs
Anti-racism or multiculturalism	Represented by respect for different cultures, support of minority groups in their struggle for equality, exposing and criticising racism
Ethnocentrism	Expressed by representations that prioritise British lifestyle and culture over others (e.g. little coverage of foreign news), or represent other cultures from the point of view of a superior outsider
Liberal democracy	Expressed by representations of political leaders, other decision-makers, and political issues References to 'the will of the people' expressed through voting or opinion polls, representations of the rule of law (or its opposite, such as terrorism), freedom of expression (or its opposite, such as censorship and propaganda)
Belief in welfare	Expressed by representations of welfare state issues, such as benefits, education or the NHS, or of 'ordinary people' needing or offering collective help
Internationalism	Expressed by respectful coverage of foreign news and celebration of international cooperation

Representation: audience response and contexts

Audience interpretation of newspaper representations might depend on a number of differences:

- gender
- sexuality
- race/ethnicity and nationality
- age
- class
- region
- political affiliation
- a wide range of other individual factors and social/cultural contexts.

Hall suggests a typology of audience responses and interpretations depending on the position taken with regard to ideology:

- the dominant reading – the audience understands and agrees with the representation as both the product and the audience share the same ideology
- the negotiated reading – the audience share the same basic ideological assumptions but disagree with some aspects of the representation
- the oppositional reading – the audience opposes the ideology of the product and has a critical reading.

We would expect, for example, a diehard *Guardian* reader to have an oppositional reading of much of the *Daily Mail* and vice versa, as both newspapers propagate different world-views. This would be most true of opinion pieces, which clearly reflect the differences between the two newspapers.

However, where there is little ideological difference in news stories, such as the news story about nerve gas poisoning of a Russian ex-spy in rural England, then the reading might be more negotiated. A *Guardian* reader might see the use of barely relevant sexually objectifying photographs of a so-called 'femme fatale' in the *Mail*'s story (8 March 2018) as typical sexist stereotyping. In contrast, *Mail* readers might find the *Guardian*'s coverage comparatively po-faced and untitillating.

The influence of historical contexts on audience interpretation might be investigated by looking at copies of newspapers from the 1950s or 1960s as these reflect changing audience expectations. The 1950s and 1960s were an era of media scarcity compared to today, and media representations were much more White, male, middle class and (apparently) straight than they are today.

Applying the representation theories

See the Academic Theories section at **www.hoddereducation.co.uk/ myrevisionnotesdownloads** for a list of what you have to know about these theorists.

We saw above how **Hall**'s approach to representation can be used in suggesting possible readings of a representation. It is possible to apply this idea to analysing an unseen product, but only the preferred meaning would be a quality of the product itself, whereas the other two readings would depend on the specific audiences and their responses.

Gauntlett's analysis that the media offer many diverse and contradictory media messages that individuals can use to think through their identities and ways of expressing themselves may be applied by analysing contradictory representations in media products, whether within or between two products.

28

Exam tip

You are unlikely to be asked a question about audience response in the analysis part of Questions 1 and 2, as this is not a quality of the media product. However, you could be asked about this in the first bullet point of Question 2.

Revision activity

Access the newspaper front pages from 1960s editions of the *Observer* at: **www. ocr.org.uk/qualifications/ gcse-media-studies-j200- from-2017/assessment**. Make brief notes on what these pages tell us about changing audience expectations of newspapers between the 1960s and today.

Butler's theory of **gender performativity** could be applied by analysing how representations of masculinity, femininity, or identities that lie outside these categories, reveal the work of performing gender: for example, how 'feminine beauty' or 'masculine activity' are represented in products.

Van Zoonen's argument that in patriarchal culture the way women's bodies are represented as objects is different to the representation of male bodies as spectacle may be applied by analysing how patriarchy shapes representations of gender in products.

The stress in the work of **hooks** on 'Intersectionality' – the intersections of gender, race, class and sexuality to create a 'White supremacist capitalist patriarchy', whose ideologies dominate media representations – may be applied by analysing such intersections in media products.

Gilroy's concept of 'postcolonial melancholia', which expresses itself in criminalising immigrants and an 'us and them' approach to the world founded on the belief in the inherent superiority of White western civilisation, may be applied by analysing the absence of Black and post-colonial culture in media products or, if present, how they are represented as 'other'.

> **Gender performativity**: The idea that gender roles are constituted in their performance ('we are what we do') and thus, for example, that there is no essential masculinity or femininity. The opposite theory is that which sees gender as grounded in biology.

Case study: newspaper analysis

Let us compare two newspapers not yet covered – the *Daily Telegraph* and the *Daily Express*.

Example

Figure 1.4 *Daily Express* **front page, 8 March 2018**

Headlines (and standfirst):
- Corrie star Bill: my heartbreak
- (Actor's anguish over daughter's sudden death)

Skylines:
- Russian spy buys lottery scratchcards days before poison attack
- Will you fall victim to Britain's pension timebomb?

Figure 1.5 *Daily Telegraph* **front page, 8 March 2018**

Headlines (and standfirst):
- Policeman poisoned by Russian spy nerve agent
- (Use of rare chemical raises pressure on UK to take tough steps against Kremlin)
- Battle to raise cash holding back female entrepreneurs
- Tube bomb suspect 'trained to kill by Isil'
- Hammond accused of betraying fishermen
- US shares fall after Trump adviser quits
- Juventus conquer Spurs at Wembley

Skyline:
- International Women's Day: Join the *Telegraph* campaign backing Britain's female entrepreneurs

Media language analysis	*Daily Telegraph*	*Daily Express*
The combination of elements to create meaning	The ordered six-column layout with a mix of headlines connotes detail and comprehensiveness. The gothic font used for the masthead connotes tradition and formality. The language use, such as in the main headline, connotes formality and objectivity – there is little use of direct address other than the exhortation in the skyline to 'Join the *Telegraph*'s campaign' and in some of the small photos of women.	The layout dominated by a banner headline connotes immediacy and urgency. The serif font used for the masthead also connotes formality but in a modern style. The use of slang ('Corrie') in the headline connotes a greater informality and shared experience with the reader – there is use of direct address in both the photography and the question to 'you' in the skyline.
The generic conventions of print and online newspapers, looking at variations, change over time and hybridity	Consistently uses broadsheet conventions: serif fonts; sentence-case headlines; a black-on-white traditional masthead; restrained use of colour; multiple stories on the front page; an objective and formal language register; a focus on hard news. There is some hybridity/variation: the use of a colourful skyline with direct address to the audience; irregularly laid-out images of women that break up the formality of the layout.	Hybrid throughout: uses tabloid capitalised headlines but in a broadsheet-style serif font; uses a broadsheet-style black-on-white serif masthead but the sans-serif white on red 'exclusive' is more tabloid; has a tabloid soft main news focus on a human-interest story about a celebrity.
The relationship between media language and technology	The broadsheet paper size and the expectations of a print readership enable the newspaper to lay out far more copy on the front page than is possible on a webpage and still create an attractive and easily navigated page with a large photograph providing focus.	The tabloid paper size and hybrid generic conventions mean that the newspaper does not provide detail, but these do allow the banner headline to dominate the layout in order to sell the story to potential readers.
Intertextuality	There is little use of intertextuality except, perhaps, for the images of celebrity women in the skyline.	There is some explicit use of intertextuality in reference to 'Corrie' and a 'STREET LEGEND'.
The way media language incorporates viewpoints and ideologies	The *Telegraph*'s Conservative free market ideology is reflected in its choice of the term 'entrepreneurs' and the pun 'women mean business', which both carry positive connotations of business, as does the headline about how they are 'held back'.	The *Daily Express* is also a Conservative newspaper but use of emotive language suggests a more populist alignment with 'ordinary people' rather than business people – 'will you fall victim', 'heartbreak', 'anguish'. The more closely cropped image of the woman when compared to the more loosely cropped image of her father reflects perhaps the patriarchal view that women are to be looked at, with her features in greater close-up.

Media language analysis	Daily Telegraph	Daily Express
Barthes	(See row 1 on the previous page for connotations.) The expression 'Russian spy nerve agent' alongside a photograph of someone in protective clothing suggests the Cold War myth of the Russian Spy – sinister, cunning and deadly. The ideological effect of this may be to reinforce a sense of national unity in the face of external enemies.	(See row 1 on the previous page for connotations.) The grief suggested by language such as 'heartbreak', 'anguish', 'tearful' and 'shock' suggests the ideology of the family as the pre-eminent social unit.
Levi-Strauss	Binary oppositions that could be used to analyse the main story. policeman : Russians law and order : lawlessness to be praised : to be punished	Binary oppositions that could be used to analyse the main story. father : star actor grief : fame like us : not like us
Neale	Newspaper generic conventions are both maintained and subtly changed over time with each new edition of different newspapers. The *Telegraph* is maintaining traditional broadsheet conventions, as befits its conservative base, but varies these slightly (e.g. in the innovative skyline) to create variety. The *Express* is maintaining middle-market tabloid conventions that are in themselves already hybrids.	
Baudrillard	It is possible to argue that 'Russian spy nerve agents' are hyperreal texts in that they refer to previous news stories about nerve agents and countless media narratives about Russian spies.	It is possible to argue that 'Bill Roache' is a hyperreal text. 'He' is a signifier of other signifiers. This is narrative about a man who is known through other narratives (a soap opera and related media stories).
Media contexts	The positive media language used to cover International Women's Day in a conservative newspaper shows the influence of the impact of feminism on newspapers.	That the layout is dominated by a story about a soap star's loss shows the influence of celebrity culture on newspapers, particularly the tabloids.

Representation analysis	Daily Telegraph	Daily Express
How selection and combination create representations of events, issues, individuals and social groups	The image selection of a person in a protective suit combined with the headline represents a severe disruption of normality – an event that tears at the social fabric. To balance this, the images of women looking confident and colourful alongside the International Women's Day coverage shows Britain as also full of positivity and resourcefulness, a representation reinforced by the choice of a closely cropped photograph of the person in the protective suit that emphasises their apparently calm demeanour. The selection and combination of a number of news stories on the front page reinforces a representation of control, inviting the audience to survey the day's events as if from a comfortable distance.	The selection of the three news stories on the front page – threat to pensions, a poisoned spy, a dad's heartbreak – combines to represent the world as a dark and threatening place in which normality is constantly disrupted. The inclusion of the (ethnocentric) image of a crusader in the masthead represents the newspaper as perhaps a protector against these disruptions. This may be reinforced by the use of direct address and the sense of addressing the readers' lifestyles (as lottery players, future pensioners, family members, soap opera fans). There is no reference to International Women's Day.

Representation analysis	Daily Telegraph	Daily Express
How news makes claims about realism and constructs versions of reality	Broadsheet conventions of the *Telegraph* make extra claims to realism as they connote objectivity; this is matched by the high standards of journalistic ethics expected in the quality press. The *Telegraph* version of reality fits its conservative stance: law and order must be maintained, women should gain equality by becoming more entrepreneurial, and Brexiteers, such as Hammond, may be 'betraying' the country.	Tabloid conventions of the *Express*, while still claiming truthfulness, suggest a more 'gossipy' version of realism and an emotional focus in soft news such as the human-interest story on the front page. The *Express* version of reality implies this is a difficult and scary world for people who take out pensions, for stars who are also ordinary in having daughters and for Russian spies who do ordinary things like buy scratch cards before assassination attempts on their life.
The impact of the media industry and social, cultural and historical contexts on how producers choose to represent events, issues, individuals and social groups	**Media industry** The *Telegraph* has a long tradition of conservatism and is a successful newspaper that targets a traditionally conservative, older, middle-class audience. This influences its representation of International Women's Day in terms of a campaign for more women's businesses. **Media contexts** The impact of feminism has influenced this front-page coverage of International Women's day. The dominance of celebrity culture is reflected in the choice of photographs to illustrate International Women's Day. Historical conflict with Russia is reflected in the wording of the headline about the poisoning. The political and historical context of Brexit has influenced the Hammond headline. The historical context of the rise of international terrorism is reflected in the story about the tube bomber.	**Media industry** The *Express* is a struggling newspaper that has had several recent owners and loses out in competition with the *Daily Mail*. The choice to run 'an exclusive' about a soap star's grief may reflect this competition for audiences more than consideration of news values. **Media contexts** The dominance of celebrity culture is reflected in the choice of front-page lead article.
Positive and negative uses of stereotyping	There is use of deliberate anti-stereotyping in the 'Women mean business' campaign in an attempt to create a positive stereotype of women as successful business leaders. The images of women used to illustrate this appear to be only of White women, suggesting a stereotypical equation of fame and success with Whiteness. Several of the women are smiling at the camera – in more stereotypically passive poses.	The main story outlines an event – the death of a daughter – stereotypically, in order to fit 'common sense' and render it easily understandable. 'Corrie star Bill' is represented as both different to ordinary people, as a 'legend' and as an ordinary person, suffering heartbreak. This fits the positive stereotype of celebrities as both 'like us' but 'not like us'. Ironically, this turns out to be true of Russian spies, too. The pension story puts a negative stereotype on pensioners as victims by equating old age with weakness.

Representation analysis	*Daily Telegraph*	*Daily Express*
How social groups may be under-represented or misrepresented	There is under-representation of any groups in the photographs other than adult White people.	There is under-representation of any groups in the photographs other than adult White people.
How representations, particularly those that systematically reinforce values, attitudes and beliefs about the world across many representations, invoke discourses and ideologies and position audiences	The focus on the policeman who has been poisoned reinforces individualism, in concentrating on the effects of the event on individuals.

The prominence given to the crime reinforces the democratic ideology of the rule of law, in that this is a big news event due to the extreme law-breaking and the victimhood of an agent of the law.

The illustration of International Women's Day by images of British celebrity women reinforces both ethnocentrism and consumerism (in celebrating celebrity).

Ethnocentrism is also reinforced by the fact that there is only one foreign news story on the front page.

Positioning

The front page positions the reader as British, shocked and concerned about threats to social order, interested in women's equality, and a football fan. | Individualism is reinforced by all the stories on the front page – all concern individuals, including possibly the reader.

The reference to the poisoning story similarly reinforces the democratic ideology of the rule of law.

The prominence given to a celebrity story reinforces consumerism, drawing upon the consumption of a media product – *Coronation Street*.

The front page reinforces ethnocentrism by featuring only British news stories.

The lead story about the soap star draws upon ideologies of welfare insofar as it assumes that the population should care for the needy – in this case the care is merely sympathy.

Lack of references to International Women's Day may reflect sexist ideology, also suggested by only one woman being represented and this because of her personal link to a famous man.

Positioning

The front page positions readers as British, fans of soap opera on television, worried about their standard of living in old age. |
| How audience response and interpretation reflect social, cultural and historical circumstances | A positive audience response to this front page might reflect that gender equality has become a mainstream issue so is acceptable in the *Telegraph*.

Older audiences who remember the Cold War might interpret the poisoning events through the lens of this historical experience.

A negotiated or oppositional reading might be made by Russians, by anti-capitalists, by anti-Brexiteers or by Spurs fans.

Anti-racist activists might oppose the all-White representation on the front page. | A positive audience response to this front page might reflect the acceptance of celebrity culture in British society.

A negotiated or oppositional reading might be made by followers of high culture who look down on soap opera.

Anti-racist activists might oppose the all-White representation on the front page. |

Representation analysis	*Daily Telegraph*	*Daily Express*
Hall	'Preferred meanings' include the validation of free market capitalism in the story about entrepreneurs, of the democratic ideology of the rule of law, and of British ethnocentrism.	'Preferred meanings' include the validation of celebrity culture, of family values, of the rule of law, and of British ethnocentrism.
Gauntlett	Diverse and contradictory media messages include: Men are represented in a contradictory way in that the ex-spy is photographed shopping, mixing stereotypically feminine and masculine private and public roles. Women are represented as entrepreneurs, which is a diverse message as it goes against stereotypes.	Diverse and contradictory media messages include: The diverse representation of masculinity – a positive representation of an older man in terms of his occupation, plus his heartbreak and tearfulness, both go against stereotypes of masculinity. The woman is not represented in a sexually objectifying way, which defies stereotypes of femininity in many tabloid newspapers.
Van Zoonen	Patriarchy is influencing the representations of gender: the women in the skyline are in stereotypically passive poses and the article about helping female entrepreneurs reflects male dominance in business.	Patriarchy is influencing the representations of gender: the man is defined by his occupation, the woman by her relationship to the man.
hooks	Evidence of intersectionality in the gender difference in representation, the all-White representation and the middle-class bias of the stress on entrepreneurs in solving gender inequality (which ignores the international dimension of gender inequality).	Intersectionality is in evidence through the gender difference in representation, the all-White representation and the possible middle-class bias of concerns about pensions.
Butler	Gender performativity is shown in the costume, make-up and hairdressing of the women in the images.	Gender performativity is shown in the more obvious make-up of the woman in the photo compared to the man who, if made up, has been made to look natural.
Gilroy	Race, ethnicity and the colonial legacy are marked by their apparent absence from this front page, as befits a nation that failed to mourn its loss of empire.	Race, ethnicity and the colonial legacy are marked by their apparent absence from this front page, as befits a nation that failed to mourn its loss of empire.

Now test yourself

TESTED

1 What is the difference between denotation and connotation?
2 What are the connotations of the gothic font as used in the *Daily Mail* masthead?
3 What are the generic conventions for tabloid and broadsheet headlines?
4 What do the *Daily Mail* and *Daily Express* have in common in terms of genre?
5 How are both tabloid and broadsheet conventions adapted for online editions?
6 Why might newspapers use intertextuality?
7 List the ideologies you might use in your 'toolkit' for analysing products.
8 Why is audience positioning fairly weak in newspapers?
9 Name Hall's three possible audience readings of representations.
10 A media product you are analysing only represents White people. Whose theories could you apply here?

Answers on p. 205

How to prepare for the exam

Questions 1 and 2 are analysis questions, so you must practise analysing a range of print and online news sources.

You should compare:
- front pages from the print tabloids – the *Sun*, *Star*, *Mirror*, *Mail*, *Express* – with front pages from the quality press – the *Telegraph*, *The Times*, *Guardian*, *Financial Times*
- the home page and other pages from online newspapers, again comparing the *Sun*, *Mirror*, *Star*, *Mail Online* or *Express* with the *Guardian*, *Independent*, *The Times*, *Telegraph*, *Financial Times*
- tweets from a range of newspapers
- Instagram feeds from a range of newspapers
- Facebook feeds from a range of newspapers.

Concentrate on media language and representation, but note how audience and industries may affect language and representation.

Practise using concepts from the theories in your analysis.

Exam tip

Be prepared to use the coverage of the role of media contexts in media language and representations (in the section on Questions 1 and 2) in your revision for Question 3 too. Question 3 could ask about the influence of contexts on any area of the theoretical framework – media language, representations, audiences and industries.

Exam practice

Try answering exam practice Questions 1 and 2 on page 3 and compare your answers to the sample answers online.

ONLINE

Question 3

What this question involves

REVISED

The following information is based on the specimen assessment materials produced by OCR. These are likely to be the format of exam questions in the live exam papers, but OCR reserves the right to make changes to this format if this turns out to be necessary.

This question is a knowledge and understanding question on the influence of media contexts on newspapers. This question will be about the media form as a whole, but if you are instructed to give particular examples these will be from the set products – the *Guardian* and *Mail* print newspapers, online editions and social media feeds.

Timing

REVISED

Question 3 will probably be a 10-mark question, so you should spend about 17 minutes answering this question.

What the examiner is looking for

In exam practice Question 3 below, examiners are looking for:

- how accurate, comprehensive and detailed your knowledge and understanding are of–
  - ○ the relevant media contexts – in this case political contexts
  - ○ the influence of these contexts – in this case, on ownership and regulation
- the detail and accuracy of your references to the set products.

Revision activity

Past papers and practice papers are published on the OCR Interchange – ask your teacher to access these so you can check whether the format for Question 3 has changed over time.

Exam practice

Question 3

Explain how the political context in which newspapers are produced influences their ownership and regulation. Refer to the *Guardian* and the *Daily Mail* newspapers you have studied to support your answer. **[10]**

Sample answer available online

Recommended revision for this question

For media **industries** you should know:

- how news is shaped by how it is **produced, distributed and circulated**
- the ownership and control of news
- economic factors such as funding for news
- how news industries maintain audiences nationally and globally (this is covered under audiences)
- the impact of technological change, especially digital convergent media platforms, on news
- the role of regulation in news and the impact of digital technologies on regulation
- the effect of individual producers on news
- the ideas of Curran and Seaton, Livingstone and Lunt, and Hesmondhalgh on industries.

For media **audiences** you should know:

- how audiences are categorised by news industries
- how news producers target, attract, reach, address and potentially construct audiences through content and marketing
- the interrelationship between media technologies and news consumption and response
- how audiences interpret the news, interact with the news, and can be actively involved in news production
- the way in which different interpretations reflect social, cultural and historical circumstances
- the different ways audiences defined by **demographics**, identity and **cultural capital** use the news
- the different needs of mass and specialised audiences and their significance to the news
- how specialised audiences can be reached through different technologies and platforms, nationally and globally
- the ideas of Bandura, Gerbner, Hall, Jenkins and Shirky on audience.

Production, distribution and circulation: Production is the making of the product, distribution is getting the product to the retailer, circulation is how the product is consumed.

Demographics: Measuring audiences in terms of social characteristics, such as age, gender, class, region, nation, race and ethnicity.

Cultural capital: Capital is wealth you can invest to make more money. Cultural capital refers to aspects of culture such as education that help a person progress in society. Media literacy (a knowledge and understanding of media forms) is part of cultural capital in modern society.

For media **contexts** you should know:

- social contexts: how media products reflect their society – the social anxieties, the agreements, conflicts and inequalities between social groups (including ideologies)
- cultural contexts: how media products reflect their surrounding culture – the way of life, the arts and the popular culture: including cultural change, conflicts and ideologies
- political contexts: the political system and forces within which the media operate and which they influence, particularly the effect of these on ownership and control and regulation
- economic contexts: the influence of the economic system on media, including on funding, the profit motive and competition between producers
- historical contexts: how media products reflect historical events and historical changes in the other contexts.

Newspapers: media industries

REVISED

News production, distribution and circulation

In print news:

- the **production** of news is in the hands of the newspaper journalists, editors and printers
- **distribution** of news is by the organisations that send newspapers to newsagents, who have some control over which publications get distributed, but no control over content
- newsagents and other retailers sell the newspapers (**circulation**)
- it is the producers who control the news content.

In online news, the situation is less clear. Distribution and circulation are combined in websites or social media. There may be many more news producers, including amateurs, whose news may be distributed by social media such as Facebook, who have a great deal of control over which audiences see which news stories, as well as by traditional newspapers operating online.

Hesmondhalgh argues that cultural industries follow the normal capitalist pattern of increasing concentration and integration – cultural production is owned and controlled by a few conglomerates (concentration) who integrate across a range of media to reduce business risk.

News is a particularly risky area as its shelf life is so short. News exclusives were traditionally used to sell news, but these have become less valuable as the news cycle has shortened with online news where your exclusive can be picked up by the competition and recycled instantly. Instead, news organisations are relying on formats such as gossip, lifestyle journalism, opinion sections and sports journalism to minimise risk.

As Seaton has pointed out, news in the online era is still controlled by powerful news organisations which have successfully defended their oligarchy, meaning that the mainstream media still control news, giving it a centrist political bias, about which both right-wing and left-wing political activists complain.

The growing importance of social media in the distribution and circulation of news means that the social media companies are now crucial news gatekeepers, but their lack of editorial control – they claim to be platforms rather than publishers – means that fake news and clickbait as well as authentic citizen journalism can proliferate.

News circulated via social media is more likely to be image driven than traditional news. For example, the *Guardian* Instagram feed carries more soft news stories than either the Twitter feed or the online edition of the newspaper. The *Mail Online* Twitter feed carries more international soft news and animal stories than the *Daily Mail* Twitter feed, reflecting the different agendas of these two versions of the *Mail*.

Influence of contexts

The economic context of print and online journalism is that all such journalism is driven by the profit motive (apart from that produced by the BBC). The flight of advertising revenue from print journalism to online media (where most is spent on Facebook and Google) has starved journalism of funds. This has led to a decline in expensive journalism such as international news and investigative reporting and a rise in the cheaper alternative, be it opinion, reporting celebrities and public relations events, lifestyle journalism and sport. Marketing departments are much more powerful in all newspapers as profits decline, as they attempt to boost areas that attract advertising (such as travel journalism).

The ownership and control of news

Curran and Seaton argue that media industries follow the normal capitalist pattern of increasing concentration of ownership in fewer and fewer hands. This leads to a narrowing of the range of opinions represented and a pursuit of profit at the expense of quality or creativity.

We can see from the table below, (the daily circulation figures are rounded up to 2 significant figures), that three owners control more than 80 per cent of print circulation, so ownership is concentrated. Newspapers are different from other industries in that they are not usually profitable, but are seen as a means of gaining political and social influence. This means they are more likely than other media forms to be owned by rich individuals rather than conglomerates. News businesses tend to specialise in newspaper (and sometimes magazine) publishing rather than a range of media:

- News International is part of a media conglomerate (publishing newspapers, books and radio), which has only recently separated from 21st Century Fox.
- The *Mail* and *Metro* newspapers and some magazines are the only mass media interest of the Daily Mail and General Trust.
- Reach plc mostly runs national and regional newspapers.
- The Telegraph Group is a private company that runs the *Telegraph* and the *Spectator* magazine – both seen as 'house journals' for the Conservative Party.
- Nikkei is a Japanese financial newspaper publisher who own the *Financial Times*.

Newspaper groups	National daily titles owned	Daily circulation (average per issue) August 2018 in millions
News International	*Sun, The Times*	1.9
Daily Mail and General Trust	*Daily Mail*	1.3
Reach plc.	*Daily Express, Daily Star, Daily Mirror*	1.3
Telegraph Group	*Daily Telegraph*	0.37
Johnston Press	*i*	0.24
Nikkei	*Financial Times*	0.18
Guardian Media Group	*Guardian*	0.13

(Source: www.abc.org.uk)

While there are internet-only news providers such as Buzzfeed, traditional newspapers and broadcasters such as the BBC dominate online news by the power of their authoritative brands.

Influence of contexts

Concentration of ownership is limited by regulators such as the Competition and Markets Authority which exist to prevent anti-competitive business monopolies. This is a political and economic context: the government has set up this agency as free markets require competition to work effectively. Media plurality is a live political issue in Britain today; for example, Labour Party policy is to try to increase the number of newspaper owners and help create more diverse voices.

The political context of the role of press freedom in the running of democracy gives opportunities but also places limits on the control exercised by owners of newspapers. Newspapers are permitted to be opinionated and politically biased, but newspaper editors invariably insist in public that the owner never interferes with the content of the newspaper. Rupert Murdoch, who owns much of News International, has expressed strong views about the European Union, yet his newspapers – *The Times*, *Sunday Times* and *Sun* – took different positions in the Brexit referendum. The Harmsworths – who own the *Daily Mail* – are known to be Europhiles, yet the *Daily Mail* was strongly anti-EU under the editorship of Paul Dacre. Direct interference might destroy the credibility of the newspaper and will be resisted by editors and journalists. This is because the free press cannot be seen to be simply organs of propaganda.

The *Guardian* enshrines the independence of the newspaper in its ownership model. The Scott Trust – named after a famous liberal editor of the *Manchester Guardian* – was set up in the 1930s to protect the editorial independence of the *Guardian* and to safeguard journalistic freedom and the newspaper's liberal values. Staff on the paper are given a voice in its editorial stance – on which party it will support at elections, for example – and the newspaper carries a range of political views.

However, the Leveson Inquiry into the press found that politicians of all parties had 'developed too close a relationship with the press in a way that has not been in the public interest', and that politicians' relationships with newspaper owners, managers and editors (i.e. not just editors) were not clear and open. This suggests that newspaper ownership does give a certain degree of political leverage. British politicians have routinely met with Rupert Murdoch before elections, presumably to seek his support in the expectation that this might result in more favourable press coverage. For example, the Labour Prime Minister Tony Blair, who visited Murdoch before he was elected in 1997, received far more favourable coverage than his Conservative predecessor, John Major, who reportedly did not 'do a deal' with Murdoch.

The *Daily Mail* has had a strong and consistent political viewpoint, which comes primarily from its editor but also its long-established ethos. The editor of the *Guardian* is appointed by the Scott Trust explicitly to carry out liberal journalism. Appointing the editor is one form of indirect power that an owner wields, even if they never interfere with the editorial content.

News industries: funding

Traditionally, newspapers depended on circulation and advertising for revenue. Tabloid newspapers had larger circulations but their working-class audiences were less attractive to advertisers, so the tabloids relied more on cover price. Broadsheet newspapers had the reverse – smaller circulations but attractive upmarket audiences – and relied more on advertising.

Newspapers now have a wider range of funding sources, which they need, given the continuing fall in print advertising revenues:

- Circulation – subscription or over-the-counter sales. The *Daily Mail* keeps the cover price low at 65p (£1 on Saturdays) to boost circulation in order to attract advertising; the *Guardian* has a much higher cover price at £2 (£2.90 on Saturdays) to raise revenue. The Saturday editions of both newspapers are much fuller than the weekday ones – the *Guardian* sells twice as many papers on this day. Some newspapers, such as the *Daily Mail*'s national stablemate *Metro* and many local newspapers, are given away free to boost circulation and attract advertising.
- Paywalls – paying to access online content, e.g. at *The Times* website. The *Sun* has just discontinued this option as it reduced online readership.
- Membership – the *Guardian* is experimenting with this model for protecting free online content. It announced that it had reached 800,000 paying supporters (members, subscribers and supporters) worldwide in October 2017 and that the income from these now exceeded that from advertising.
- Print and online advertising – print is traditionally much more lucrative than online advertising but has drastically reduced in recent years. However, concerns over advertising being placed next to inappropriate online content by Google and Facebook, for example, may boost print advertising, though online newspapers have the ability to reach a global audience.
- Sponsored content – this blurs the boundaries between advertising and editorial that journalists prize but advertisers/brand managers wish to blur, e.g. in the *Guardian*, 'Cricket has no boundaries' was paid for and controlled by the bank NatWest and 'Connecting Britain' was editorially independent content 'supported by' Alstrom, the train company.
- Events – the *Guardian* frequently runs courses (e.g. on journalism or literature), meetings and conferences.
- Sales – the *Guardian* sells holidays and books, for example, linked to its review and travel sections; the *Mail Finance* advertises financial products with 'trusted partners'.

Influence of contexts

The rise of the internet as an economic context gives problems and opportunities for news industries to make money. Online audiences can be global as much as national so may be much larger than print audiences, but online advertising seldom pays as much as print advertising and newspapers have struggled to 'monetise' their online content. News sites that charge to access their content attract far fewer audiences unless, like the *Financial Times*, for example, they have a very niche audience that is willing to pay for specialist content.

The social and cultural context of audience expectations of free online content is an important factor in this. Online audiences resist paying for content – the anarchistic self-governing ethos of the early internet encouraged this attitude.

The battle between independent journalism and brand marketing reflects competing contexts:

- the economic context of pressure from advertisers and public relations professionals to insert brands into editorial content
- the cultural context of the rules and ethics of journalism (as illustrated by media representations of heroic journalism).

The cultural context of the prestige given to print journalism means that all newspapers (except, at the time of writing, the *Independent*) have maintained print editions despite the adverse cost–benefit ratio of lower circulations (higher costs and lower incomes). Some newspapers are near the 100,000 circulation point where print newspapers become uneconomic, but it is possible that most will continue print editions for the prestige this brings of being a 'proper newspaper'.

The political context of the desire to preserve journalism in the face of economic pressures had led to debates about whether the state should subsidise news or social media companies be made to pay for news. A small start has been made with the BBC funding court reporters in local newspapers as this reporting is seen as a vital local news function.

The impact of technological change on news

Printing underwent a technological revolution in the 1980s with the replacement of expensive inflexible printing processes. This enabled newspapers to remain profitable with smaller print runs and more extensive use of photography and colour. It also accelerated the hybridisation of newspaper genres.

Digitally convergent platforms may be either the use of social media or the production of online editions by traditional print newspapers to be read on PCs, tablets or mobile phones. Their impact on news includes:

- the opportunities for audience interactivity
- the growth of citizen journalism, with extensive use of mobile phone footage by mainstream media news outlets
- the rapid speeding up of the news cycle, from a 24-hour rhythm to constant updating of news
- the way certain types of news are prioritised in different online iterations – especially soft news and news with attractive visuals
- how online news offers opportunities as well as new competition for news producers
- how the lack of online regulation and editorial ownership leads to problems of fake news, clickbait and propaganda produced by bots
- how the funding of news production may have to be revolutionised in order for news to survive.

When newspapers operate online there is technological and cultural convergence of media forms. Online newspapers will use the traditional media language of newspapers – headlines, copy, photography and so on – but also that of television through embedded video, and that of social media through readers' comments on blogs, or one another's comments. Online versions of newspapers often take on more online attributes (such as 'clickbait'). The *Mail Online*, for example, is much more celebrity and gossip focused than the print newspaper. The *Guardian* online recognisably follows the structure of the print edition, but with greater prominence for the lifestyle, food and sport sections that are kept out of the main section of the print newspaper, plus a much higher proportion of photography and headlines to copy on the home page.

Influence of contexts

The social/cultural context of the authority of an established newspaper has enabled print newspapers to extend their brand online – both the *Guardian* and the *Mail* are hugely successful as online newspapers because they each carry a strong, established brand identity, which stands out in the cornucopia of online content. Convergence has brought **synergy** between print and online platforms: the print edition brings the authoritative brand; the online editions bring immediacy and interactivity.

The role of regulation in news

The press in Britain is self-regulating. Newspapers may join either the Independent Press Standards Organisation (IPSO) or IMPRESS (see page 43) or, like the *Guardian*, refuse to join either. Online newspapers may choose to join either of the self-regulators. Newspapers such as the *Guardian* try to offer a trusted brand online by applying the same ethics and journalistic practices as the print newspapers, and by actively moderating readers' comments to filter out inappropriate comments.

The libel law provides additional legal constraint. Journalists argue that Britain has particularly onerous libel laws – journalists have to *prove* that what they allege is true to win cases (unless they can demonstrate that the story is in the public interest). Cases like that of Jimmy Savile – who was first investigated by journalists in 1967 but not publicly exposed until after his death – show the ability of those with the financial means to hire expensive libel lawyers to silence the press.

Online news is not regulated at all, unless online newspapers choose to sign up to a regulator such as IPSO. The issue of 'fake news' came to special prominence during and after the 2016 US presidential election. A special counsel was appointed to investigate Russian interference in the election, which included extensive use of false news reports on social media. Facebook appointed its first content reviewers in 2017 to try to address this problem. This constitutes a retreat from the social media company's previous position (common to all social media companies) that it was not a media company but an IT company offering a platform for other people's content, an extreme 'freedom of speech' position it hoped would absolve it from journalistic ethics or regulation.

UK libel law does still apply to online news and social media, however, even if a post has been deleted.

Influence of contexts

The key context is the political context, but this has social and cultural ramifications.

Newspapers were the main form of mass communication at the time when Britain was becoming a fuller democracy, when more adults gained the vote. A free press was seen as crucial to democracy, so censorship was abolished and press freedom held up as a precious ideal to be defended at

Synergy: A relationship in which both parties benefit so the whole is greater than the sum of its parts.

all costs. Anyone must be free to set up a newspaper and newspapers must be allowed to publish whatever they want without interference from the government or other authorities.

This ideal of press freedom remains very much alive today and is the reason why newspapers and magazines are not regulated by a body set up by the government (like Ofcom, which regulates television). In practice, the idea of press freedom means that the press are the most opinionated of all the 'old' media. Newspapers can campaign on political issues and journalists are expected to be highly critical of those in power. The same journalistic ideals apply to magazines, but it is newspapers that are treated as being the more important opinion-formers in society.

The 'red top' or 'tabloid' press offer a brash, no-nonsense style that addresses the passions of their target audience to retain their loyalty. This style, however, has led to regular concerns about issues such as invasion of privacy and cheque-book journalism. In the 1990s the government threatened to create a regulatory body to enforce a code of practice, so the press set up the Press Complaints Commission in 1991. This proved ineffective. Matters came to a head in 2011 when the *News of the World* was exposed, after a long campaign by the *Guardian*, as having hacked the voicemails of a young murder victim in such a way that her parents thought she was still alive. This 'hacking scandal' led to the Leveson Inquiry into the 'culture, practices and ethics of the press'. The inquiry recommended that the press should regulate itself with a body that could levy substantial fines, but that this body would have to be recognised by another body set up by parliament. In response, most of the press joined a new regulator named IPSO, which refused to apply to the recognition body as it saw this as unwarranted state interference in the free press. A rival regulator – IMPRESS – was recognised by the recognition body, but only covers a few local newspapers. The government has so far refused to invoke the 'stick' that Leveson proposed – having to pay libel expenses. Known as Section 40, this would encourage newspapers to join a compliant regulator. Labour Party policy is to introduce Section 40 and new controls on concentration of newspaper ownership.

Revision activity

Note examples illustrating the unregulated nature of newspapers from the set product editions of the *Guardian*, *Daily Mail* and *Mail Online*.

The effect of individual producers on news

The *Daily Mail* was edited by Paul Dacre until 2018 and its outlook was thought to reflect his views, with its consistent social and political attitudes. The *Guardian*, on the other hand, is considered more collegiate in allowing a range of views, whether or not the editor agrees with them. However, writers such as Max Hastings – an ex-Conservative cabinet minister – have written for both newspapers, suggesting that they both allow some divergence of views as Hastings is politically to the left of the *Mail* and to the right of the *Guardian*.

Columnists are often key personnel in setting the tone of a newspaper. This is particularly true of the *Daily Mail*, which in 2018 featured long-standing columnists such as:
- Peter Oborne, who typically offers trenchant right-wing views on politics
- Richard Littlejohn, who comments on politics and some social issues
- Amanda Platell, who comments on celebrities, the royals and social issues
- Bel Mooney, the 'agony aunt'.

Revision activity

Note the views expressed in articles by major columnists from the *Guardian*, *Daily Mail* and *Mail Online* editions that you have studied.

OCR A Level Media Studies 43

The *Guardian* tends to offer a wider range of comments from a larger group of columnists, which means that they set the tone of the newspaper less than those in the *Mail*. Whereas the *Mail* carries on the tradition of using male columnists for important issues such as politics, the *Guardian* has more of a gender balance.

Influence of contexts

The influence of **celebrity culture** can be seen in the celebrity of some columnists, who are given prominent by-lines and photographs in both newspapers. Many columnists, particularly political columnists, appear on television, which uses them for additional colour and strength of opinion.

The impact of **feminism** may be seen in the rise of women columnists, particularly in the *Guardian*. The development of **multiculturalism** is reflected in the increasing number of ethnic minority staff, though the editor has admitted that the paper's staff is not diverse enough because journalism was, for many years, dominated by White men.

Newspapers: media audiences

REVISED

How audiences are categorised by news industries

The Publishers Audience Measurement Company Ltd (PAMCo) is an organisation run by the newspaper and periodical publishers and advertisers. Their figures for newspapers include such demographic categories as age, gender, class and region. News industries will use these categories to sell their audiences to advertisers. Newsworks – www. newsworks.org.uk – is a useful website for looking at these statistics as it uses PAMCo data for readership and ABC (Audit Bureau of Circulation) data for circulation. Let's take the *Daily Mail* and the *Guardian* print editions as examples (data from October 2016 to September 2017).

A note on social class categories

The phrase 'AB adults', for example, refers to adults in social classes A and B. The detailed classes are as follows:

- Class A are upper-middle-class people such as higher managers and highly paid professionals.
- Class B are middle-middle-class people such as lower-paid professional (e.g. teachers) and middle managers – this is the second largest group.
- Class C1 are lower-middle-class people such as clerical workers – this is the largest group.
- Class C2 are skilled manual workers – this is the third largest group.
- Class D are semi-skilled manual workers.
- Class E are unskilled manual workers.

Students are defined by the occupation of their head of household, usually a parent.

These categories can be combined to make up the middle and working classes, as below:

Categories	General social class	Proportion of UK population
A, B, C1	Middle class	54%
C2, D, E	Working class	46%

Let's apply the demographic categories to the two newspapers:

Print audience	Daily Mail	Guardian
Circulation	1.3 million	0.15 million
Readership	2.9 million	0.9 million
% Men	48	51
% Women	52	49
% 15–34	10	27
% 35–54	15	30
% 55+	75	41
% AB adults	27	62
% C1C2 adults	56	31 (22% C1)
% DE adults	17	7
% London	26	40
% Midlands	19	17
% South and South East	15	12
% North West	12	11

These clearly show that the *Guardian* readership is much younger, more upmarket (more middle class), much more London-based and slightly more male than the *Daily Mail* readership. We can clearly see the *Mail*'s middle market bias in the high proportion of C1C2 readers and its reach into both the AB and E categories, making its audience more evenly spread than the *Guardian*'s.

Although the differences in the audiences for the print newspaper are huge, they are much less for the online editions.

The *Mail*'s online audience is, compared to the *Guardian*'s:
- only very slightly less upmarket
- only slightly older
- only slightly more female
- slightly less London-based.

Influence of contexts

Social and cultural contexts will influence how audiences are categorised. Class has become a much less significant predictive factor in how people behave, including which brands they buy, compared to, say, the 1930s. This is due to social and cultural change. This means that, though news industries still sell audiences to advertisers in terms of class, they are more likely to use psychographic categories (categories based on psychological traits, taste and lifestyle, the sort of material Facebook is very useful for analysing). The *Guardian*, for example, sells its audience profile using the following terms:
- a progressive audience (forward looking and curious, embracing change)
- active fashion and tech consumers
- well travelled
- finance savvy
- highly affluent and well educated
- engaged, influential and well connected
- with a passion for food, art and culture.

> **Revision activity**
>
> Look up the latest figures for the *Daily Mail and Guardian*'s UK online audience monthly readership at pamco.co.uk.

A postmodern culture in which people are encouraged to define their own identity may accelerate the tendency for old labels to become obsolete.

How news targets and addresses audiences

Let's consider the different audiences for a wider range of newspapers.

Broadsheet newspapers	The *Guardian*, *Telegraph* and *Times* have markedly upmarket audiences and more London-based readers.
Red top tabloids	The *Sun* and the *Mirror* have markedly downmarket audiences and fewest London-based readers.
Guardian	Has the most London-based audience, but also has a North-West audience reflecting its Manchester roots – both are strongly Labour-supporting areas. It has the youngest audience of all these newspapers and the most female audience of the broadsheets.
Daily Mail	Has the most female and the oldest audience of all newspapers, and the most evenly spread readers in terms of social class.
Sun	Is the most male newspaper and has the youngest audience of the tabloids.
Mirror	Is the most northern newspaper, perhaps reflecting its working-class audience and support for the Labour Party.
Daily Telegraph	Has the oldest audience of the broadsheets.

The content of the newspapers will reflect the social make-up of their audiences as the newspaper tries to reach and address that audience. The *Daily Mail*, for example, has sections that reflect the lifestyle of its audience. The *Femail* section on Thursdays, which has a tab in the *Mail Online*, addresses its female audience with topics similar to women's lifestyle magazines – fashion, food, beauty and babies. Health issues feature heavily in the newspaper, including a 'Good Health' section on a Tuesday and a Health tab in the *Mail Online*. The newspaper reflects its social class mix by including both sensationalist celebrity coverage and a fairly detailed business section including share price listings. These are reproduced online within 'Money' and 'TV & Showbiz' tabs. The 'Travel' section attracts advertisers aiming at the time-rich older audience, with a bias towards adverts for cruises.

> **Exam tip**
>
> Be prepared: you may need some knowledge of the audience base of any newspaper for Questions 1 or 2.

The *Guardian* attempts to engage and address its upmarket, younger audience by extensive coverage of the high culture that is largely missing from the *Daily Mail* as well as the popular culture that is covered by the tabloids. The Saturday *Guardian*, for example, includes a 'Review' supplement dedicated to literature, as well as a 'Guide' supplement and a culture section in the main paper covering opera, classical music, art, dance, pop, film and television. The 'Culture' section on the website has its own gold colour scheme and culture items can appear throughout the home page. The *Guardian's* relatively high female readership is no longer served by a 'Women's Page' as this was deemed sexist. No parts of the weekday paper or website are obviously gendered, although there is a bias towards female fashion and beauty issues in the 'Weekend' magazine and male sport in the 'Sport' section. The business section in the *Guardian* concentrates more on issues affecting consumers than those for investors, perhaps addressing a more left-wing audience. The travel section tends to serve the more independent traveller, though the *Guardian* does offer a range of packages to suitably cultural destinations. The *Guardian* website tabs – News, Opinion, Sport, Culture, Lifestyle – suggest that the website is addressing a younger audience by giving the last three bigger prominence than in the print newspaper, but still retaining a broadsheet ethos.

The viewpoints of the *Mail* and *Guardian*, as discussed under Questions 1 and 2, also suggest engagement of different audiences. The *Mail*'s strongly populist viewpoint, supporting 'ordinary people' against a hostile world, may address the beliefs of an older, conservative audience with a sense of pessimism or grievance. The *Guardian*'s equally moralistic, but liberal, viewpoint may address the beliefs of a younger, more liberal and optimistic audience. The media language of the two newspapers also suggests attempts to address a more upmarket audience in the *Guardian* and more downmarket audience in the *Mail*, particularly in terms of language register and choice of photography.

The fact that the websites for the *Guardian* and *Mail Online* are so different in style and content, yet fairly similar in terms of audience make-up, might lead to the conclusion that:
- these differences in style and content are not so significant online as they are in print
- the online audience is less loyal to any one newspaper, possibly arriving at the website by a clickthrough from a social media feed.

The *Mail Online* addresses audiences quite differently to its print sister. The style is much younger, the content much more celebrity and gossip focused, and the international nature of the audience is reflected in more international stories and headlines that are more explanatory than those in the print newspaper.

The marketing of newspapers will also reflect their audiences. Red top tabloids used to advertise themselves (in the past when they had the budget for this) with special offers and slogans such as 'The Soaraway Sun' that summarised the breezy confidence of the brand and addressed a downmarket audience. Broadsheets typically used strategies that emphasised the seriousness of the brand. The *Guardian* ran a television campaign showing how easy it is to stereotype when you don't have all the facts. *The Telegraph*'s advertising emphasised its news coverage and its 'devilishly hard crossword' – addressing the audience as one that likes to be stretched intellectually.

The idea of 'constructing' an audience suggests that the newspaper can directly affect its audience. **Bandura** argues this case, that human values, judgement and conduct can be altered directly by media modelling. **Gerbner** argues that heavy users of television – the medium he studied – were more likely, for example, to develop 'mean world syndrome' – a cynical, mistrusting attitude towards others; if this applies to newspapers, then the *Mail*, for example, might be seen as constructing its audience in its own image.

Influence of contexts

The growth of **consumerism** means that newspaper audiences, like all media audiences, feel the media should serve them rather than being loyal to particular newspapers. This means that newspapers must work harder to address the needs of the full range of their audiences, including the demand for immediacy and interactivity in the online media.

The impact of **feminism** means that newspapers cannot patronise women readers by assuming they only occupy stereotypical roles and must address the requirements of women across a range of roles in society; for example, the *Guardian* losing its 'Women's Page' in favour of more integrated coverage.

The rise of **multiculturalism** means that newspapers can no longer reflect only White society and must increase their range of representation to address the diversity of ethnic groups in Britain. Even the *Daily Mail*, which could be viewed as a very White newspaper, has ethnic minority staff pictured in by-lines.

Changing attitudes to **sexualities** are clearly reflected, for example, in the *Guardian*'s coverage of LGBTQ issues (addressing both the LGBT and straight audience), if less so in the *Daily Mail*.

The **political** and **historical** context will influence the extent to which newspapers address and even construct different audiences. We have seen already that many traditionally Conservative-supporting newspapers switched to supporting the Labour Party in the context of Tony Blair's bid to win the middle ground of politics for that party. By contrast, the period of struggle over Brexit in 2017 and 2018 caused a great polarisation in British politics over this issue, which led Dacre's *Daily Mail* to attempt to construct its audience as ardent Leavers, with a succession of articles about the betrayal of Brexit, and the *Guardian* to try to construct its audience as ardent Remainers, with a succession of articles about the dangers and difficulties of Brexit.

Technologies, audience consumption and response

The clearest distinction here is between the consumption of print and online technologies. Print newspapers, especially the broadsheets, are designed for more detailed surveillance of the news, for enjoying impactful large photographs and being guided by print layout. The house style of the newspaper will be embedded in its design, plus audiences are likely to be more loyal to a print newspaper, so audience response may be conditioned by what the audience expect of that newspaper. For example, *Daily Mail* readers may discount a lurid headline (perhaps thinking that's just how that newspaper is) that would shock *Guardian* readers.

Online technologies for all newspapers offer a different kind of consumption, even with the same (the *Guardian*) or similar (*Daily Mail*) content. The websites, but even more so the social media feeds, offer immediacy and a 24-hour news cycle. They also provide instant choice, quick navigation and interactivity. This suggests much higher audience expectations of online news in that the bar seems to be lowered for what counts as news and thoughtful content, but raised for speed of response by the news organisation and its audience. **Sharky** calls this the move from 'filter then publish' print content to the 'publish then filter' attitude that is typical of online content.

Influence of contexts

The **social and cultural context** within which news technologies now operate includes rising audience expectations of choice, control and participation.

However, the **cultural** context of the authority given to print journalism – due to the social, cultural and political role that print newspapers have played in democracies – means that newspapers resist the economic temptation to follow the example of the *Independent* in 2016 and go solely online. This is because print newspapers carry a legitimacy and authority that it is feared would be lost if a newspaper became just another website. Even so, it may be that this sense of the advantage of the print form will fade away over time.

> **Revision activity**
>
> Note at least one example illustrating how different audiences are addressed from each of the *Guardian*, *Daily Mail* and *Mail Online* editions that you have studied.

The **economic** context of the flight of advertising revenue from traditional media forms to the online media, due to the latter's superior ability to **data mine** its audience, lies behind the growth of online news outlets. However, the fact that the vast majority of new online advertising revenue goes to Google and Facebook brings further problems, as the cost cutting at online news outlets such as Buzzfeed in 2017 demonstrated.

The economic success of different societies and the degree of authoritarianism in their political system will influence freedom of access to the internet. In authoritarian North Korea, for example, less than 10 per cent of citizens have access to the internet. This means that the state can closely control the print media without the fear that large numbers will be gaining alternative information online. The international telecommunications union estimated in 2014 that less than one-third of the population of developing countries used the internet.

Audience interaction and prosumers

Hall's typology of audience interpretations can now be tested by reading audience comments on news articles.

- The *dominant-hegemonic* position: a 'preferred reading' that accepts the text's messages and the ideological assumptions behind the messages. For example, the comments on an article in the *Mail Online* suggesting dissent with Jeremy Corbyn's position on Russia in the Labour ranks elicits a first comment saying 'Corbyn out? Yes please'. (The article can be found at: www.dailymail.co.uk/news/article-5508805/Labours-Keir-Starmer-contradicts-Corbyn-Salisbury.html#newcomment.)
- The *negotiated* position: the reader accepts the text's ideological assumptions, but disagrees with aspects of the messages; for example, the third comment on the above story, 'No evidence yet. Just hysteria', that engages with the argument in a critical way.
- The *oppositional* reading: the reader rejects both the overt message and its underlying ideological assumptions; for example, the second comment on the above story: 'Nope. We are BEING FED A NARRATIVE. Stop it MSM', which rejects the whole argument as illegitimate and concocted by the mainstream media (MSM).
- Online comments on news articles can be seen as (somewhat weak) forms of what **Jenkins** calls 'participatory culture', in which audiences are active and creative participants rather than passive consumers. Many threads develop their own lines of argument that may start from quite a different place to the original article. For example, a *Guardian* article about the representation of post-menopausal women in the media generated comments about other representations missed in the article, about women's experience of menopause, and about how women should or should not be defined and the role of the menopause in this. (The article can be found at: www.theguardian.com/commentisfree/2018/mar/15/menopausal-women-screen-glory-representation-menopause-popular-culture.) This illustrates **Sharky**'s argument that amateur producers have different motivations to those of professionals – they value autonomy, competence, membership and generosity – and that user-generated content creates emotional connection between people who care about something. In this case the discussion appears to be between women who care about feminism, the representation of women in the media and sharing experiences of getting older.

Data mine: The use of audience data gathered by online media platforms in order to attract advertisers. A free service is provided to the audience in exchange for this data being offered to advertisers to micro-target audiences based on their demographics, their tastes, their likes or their searches.

Revision activity

Give examples of the differences between print and online news in the editions of the *Guardian, Daily Mail* and *Mail Online* that you have studied in class.

Social, cultural and historical contexts

Several factors may influence the audience to actively interpret and interact with the news to a greater extent:

- the rise of consumerism created a decline in deference to one's 'betters' – and this has influenced our view that the public has a right to be heard and to argue with 'experts'
- a historical period that sees more political conflict (such as over Brexit, or increasing political polarisation) may accentuate active audience interpretation and interaction, as audiences may be clearer about their viewpoints during such times
- the impact of feminism has been to give women a more public voice
- the impact of multiculturalism has been to give ethnic minorities a more public voice
- changing attitudes to sexualities have given minority sexualities a more public voice
- a postmodern culture in which truth is a more relative concept may encourage the audience to dispute authority.

> **Revision activity**
>
> Note at least one example of audience participation from each of the online *Guardian* and *Mail Online* set products.

The ways different audiences use the news

There are many different audiences who use news differently as they have different needs. Various platforms exist to serve these audiences:

- Minority national, regional and local audiences use local and (the few remaining) regional newspapers, such as the *Yorkshire Post,* to sustain a sense of local/regional identity, to keep abreast of local news, and to access advertising for local services (e.g. estate agents and car dealerships).
- Religious audiences use the specialist religious press, such as the *Jewish Chronicle* or the *Catholic Herald,* to help maintain their religious identity and gain information about their community.
- Ethnic groups use the ethnic press, such as the *Voice* for Black groups, to help maintain their identity and gain information about their community.
- Business leaders and aspiring business people use the specialist financial press, such as the *Financial Times*, which provide detailed surveillance of businesses and the markets and target a global specialist audience.
- Audiences with significant cultural capital use the broadsheet press to maintain their identity as 'well educated and well read' and to gain surveillance over what is new and emerging in society and culture.
- Audiences lacking cultural capital use the tabloid press to maintain their identity as 'ordinary people' and to gain information, diversion from everyday life and entertainment.
- Highly specialised groups who are not served by newspapers may use social media groups as a way of reinforcing an identity, maintaining relationships and sharing information about the group.

Influence of contexts

The constitution of these specialist groups clearly depends on their social, cultural and historical context. The *Voice*, for example, exists because of the Black diaspora caused by the slave trade and the context of **Gilroy**'s 'Black Atlantic', a common culture based on transatlantic Black social experience, making being Black a form of ethnicity despite its racial origin. The existence of a vibrant Scottish press (newspapers such as the *Scotsman*), with no equivalent in Wales or Northern Ireland, reflects the political, historical and cultural contexts of Scottish nationhood and devolution.

> **Revision activity**
>
> Note at least two examples illustrating the different uses and gratifications offered by the set product editions of the *Guardian*, *Daily Mail* and *Mail Online*.

The economic context of competition for advertising revenue from the internet has influenced the ability of local and regional newspapers to survive, as their traditional reliance on classified advertising has been undermined by online competition.

Now test yourself

TESTED

1 Identify one economic context influencing the way news is produced.
2 How many news companies own more than 80 per cent of print circulation?
3 Why might newspapers offer different political views to that of their owners?
4 Identify three sources of funding for newspapers other than cover price or paywalls.
5 Identify the two newspaper self-regulators.
6 State three attributes of the *Daily Mail's* audience.
7 State three attributes of the *Guardian's* audience.
8 Give two examples of newspapers that address specialist audiences.

Answers on p. 205

Exam practice

Now try answering exam practice Question 3 on page 36 and compare your answer to the sample answer online.

ONLINE

How to prepare for the exam

You must revise what you have studied in class about the influence on print and online news of all the media contexts:

● social
● cultural
● economic
● political
● historical.

You may concentrate on the influence on media audiences and media industries (especially when considering economic contexts) but don't forget to revise their influence on representations and even media language.

Don't forget that the material in this section on media audiences and media industries might also be needed for part of Question 2.

Question 4

What this question involves

REVISED

This will be a question about evaluating one of the theories listed in the specification under the heading 'Academic ideas and arguments'. For the sake of brevity we will refer to these as 'theories'. In this question you will evaluate the usefulness of the theory in understanding either print newspapers or online news, or perhaps both.

You may be given a choice of theories to evaluate or the question may specify only one theory.

Revision activity

Past papers and practice papers are published on the OCR Interchange – ask your teacher to access these so you can check whether the format for Question 4 has changed over time.

Timing

REVISED

Question 4 will probably be a 10-mark question, so you should spend about 17 minutes answering this question.

What the examiner is looking for

REVISED

In the following exam practice Question 4, examiners are looking for:
- how comprehensive, detailed and accurate is your application of knowledge and understanding of media audiences to evaluate the theory
- how convincing, perceptive and accurate is your evaluation of the theory in understanding audiences for online newspapers.

In short, you are being rewarded for using what you know to *evaluate* the theory (not for explaining the theory).

Exam practice

Question 4

Evaluate the usefulness of one of the following in understanding audiences for online newspapers such as the *Guardian* and the *Mail Online*:

EITHER

Gerbner's cultivation theory

OR

Shirky's 'end of audience' theory.

[10]

Sample answer available online

ONLINE

Recommended revision for this question

REVISED

- The theories – these can be found on pages 53–59.
- In what ways each theory is useful in understanding print and online newspapers.
- The limitations of each theory in understanding print and online newspapers.

Newspapers: academic theories

Semiology – Barthes

How the theory is useful

- Can be applied to any sign, including language and image, to tease out connotations and ideology (see media language analysis under Questions 1 and 2 and media language analysis of the two newspaper front pages).
- Draws attention to the naturalising effect of ideology in any text – this applies particularly to newspapers, as headlines typically assume a shared view of the world with the readers (see media language analysis under Questions 1 and 2).

How the theory is limited

- Does not explain anything specific to newspapers as it is a general theory of signification.
- Does not say anything about the ownership and control of newspapers and the process of mediation that leads to the messages in newspapers.
- Does not reveal how audiences interpret newspapers and give meaning in different ways to the same signs.

Genre theory – Neale

How the theory is useful

- Can be applied to any generic media product, including newspapers, and links together media language, audiences and industries (see media language analysis of the newspaper front pages).
- The 'shared code' explains how genres can change, e.g. the quality press becoming more like tabloids, and hybridise, e.g. middle-market tabloids, such as the *Mail*, following both 'tabloid' and 'broadsheet' conventions (see media language analysis under Questions 1 and 2).
- Can be applied to online news insofar as the online version of the newspaper follows codes and conventions established in print version of newspapers or online news website conventions (see media language analysis under Questions 1 and 2).

How the theory is limited

- Developed primarily in relation to film products, where genre is an important marketing tool, unlike newspapers which appeal to audience loyalty or sell themselves by front-page splashes that emphasise individual difference rather than generic similarities.

Structuralism – Levi-Strauss

How the theory is useful

- Can be applied to any cultural product, including newspapers (see the media language analysis of the two newspaper front pages).
- Particularly applies to newspaper stories that set up an 'us' and 'them' opposition, in which the audience are invited to think of themselves as 'us' (see media language analysis under Questions 1 and 2).

How the theory is limited

- Does not explain anything specific to newspapers as it is an extremely high-level theory of culture.

- Does not say anything about the ownership and control of newspapers and the process of mediation that leads to the messages in newspapers.
- Does not reveal how audiences interpret newspapers and give meaning.

Narratology – Todorov

How the theory is useful

- Enables us to think of news stories as a series of 'disruptions', each implying an initial equilibrium and a possible resolution.

How the theory is limited

- Was not designed to explain news stories but narratives with resolutions, so does not fit most news stories that fade away without resolution.

Postmodernism – Baudrillard

How the theory is useful

- Can be applied to any cultural product, including newspapers (see the media language analysis of the two newspaper front pages).
- Particularly applies to news about news (e.g. stories about viral stories), or famous for being famous celebrities, where there is no clear sense of a 'reality' lying behind the hyperreality.

How the theory is limited

- Does not explain anything specific to newspapers as it is an extremely high-level theory of the postmodern world – the theory is unfalsifiable as it cannot be proved false or true.

Theories of representation – Hall

How the theory is useful

- Can be applied to any media product, including newspapers (see the representation analysis of the two newspaper front pages).
- Applies particularly to the way in which newspaper headlines and photos try to fix the meaning of a representation.
- Highlights the role of power in representations – both the general distribution of power in society and newspapers' institutional power – but also the audience's power to decode representations in different ways.

How the theory is limited

- Does not explain anything specific to newspapers as it is a general theory of representation.

Theories of identity – Gauntlett

How the theory is useful

- Can be applied to any media product, including newspapers (see media language analysis of the two newspaper front pages).
- Applies to the sense of identity that a newspaper can offer its readers, e.g. the identity of a liberal, progressive *Guardian* reader or a patriotic, hard-headed *Daily Mail* reader, or a celebrity-savvy *Mail Online* reader.
- Applies to the diverse and sometimes contradictory media messages provided to audiences in discrete newspaper sections, which offer a range of points of identification.

How the theory is limited

- Applies less to newspapers, as younger people, who are more likely to gain a sense of identity through self-expression in user-generated online media products, are less likely to use newspapers for this end.
- Assumes that audiences are powerful, active agents, and so may underestimate the power of media conglomerates to shape popular culture, tastes and identities (see Curran and Seaton).

Feminist theory – Van Zoonen

How the theory is useful

- Can be applied to any media product, including newspapers, especially representations of gender (see representation analysis of the two newspaper front pages).
- The concept of patriarchy may be applied to the ownership and control of newspapers, the recruitment and ethos of newspaper professionals, news values and the representation of gender in newspapers, especially the representation of women's bodies.

How the theory is limited

- Does not explain anything specific to newspapers as it is a general theory of patriarchy.
- In prioritising gender inequalities, the theory may not aid analysis of other forms of inequality in representation in newspapers.
- In stressing the influence of social conflict on representations, may underestimate the influence of social consensus on representations.

Feminist theory – hooks

How the theory is useful

- Can be applied to any media product, including newspapers, especially representations of gender (see the representation analysis of the two newspaper front pages).
- 'Intersectionality' draws attention to misrepresentations and stereotypes based on the interrelationship of gender, race, class and sexuality in any newspaper representations.

How the theory is limited

- Does not explain anything specific to newspapers as it is a general theory of patriarchy.
- In stressing the influence of social conflict on representations, may underestimate the influence of social consensus on representations.

Theories of gender performativity – Butler

How the theory is useful

- Can be applied to any media product, including newspapers, especially representations of gender (see representation analysis of the two newspaper front pages).
- Can be applied particularly to lifestyle sections of newspapers, where the performance of gender may be demonstrated in fashion and make-up advice, for example, and in articles about forms of 'gender trouble'.

How the theory is limited

- Does not explain anything specific to newspapers as it is a high-level theory of gender.
- The theory is unfalsifiable – it cannot be proved true or false.

Theories around ethnicity and post-colonial theory – Gilroy

How the theory is useful

- Can be applied to any media product, including newspapers, especially representations of race, ethnicity and the post-colonial world (see representation analysis of the two newspaper front pages).
- The concept of the 'Black Atlantic' draws attention to continuities in the culture created by the African diaspora across national boundaries.
- The concept of 'postcolonial melancholia' draws attention to the continuing role of colonial ideology – of the superiority of White western culture – across newspaper representations.

How the theory is limited

- Does not explain anything specific to newspapers as it is a general theory.
- In prioritising race and the post-colonial experience, may not aid analysis of other forms of inequality in representation in newspapers.
- In stressing the influence of social conflict on representations, may underestimate the influence of social consensus on representations.

Power and media industries – Curran and Seaton

How the theory is useful

- Studying newspapers as an industry draws attention to forms and effects of ownership and control, journalists' working practices, and issues of risk and profitability.
- Applies to the narrow range of political opinions expressed by British national newspapers, with a bias to pro-capitalism.
- Applies to the long history of 'press barons' owning newspapers in order to achieve status and wield political power.
- For online news, corrects over-optimistic views of the internet as an arena for freedom and unlimited creativity.

How the theory is limited

- In prioritising the effects of ownership and control on newspaper content, this theory may not aid in understanding how ideologies, audience choice (see Jenkins and Shirky) or media language conventions can determine media content.

Regulation – Livingstone and Lunt

Does not apply to newspapers.

Cultural industries – Hesmondhalgh

How the theory is useful

- Draws attention to newspapers as an industry – the forms and effects of ownership and control, journalists' working practices, and issues of risk and profitability.

- Applies particularly to the response of newspapers to competition for readers and advertising revenue from the 'new' media.
- For online news, corrects over-optimistic views of the internet as an arena for freedom and unlimited creativity.

How the theory is limited

- In prioritising the effects of ownership and control on newspaper content, this theory may not aid in understanding how ideologies, audience choice (see Jenkins and Shirky) or media language conventions can determine media content.

Media effects – Bandura

How the theory is useful

- May apply to a wide range of media products, including newspapers.
- Would most apply to newspaper messages that are delivered strongly and consistently across newspapers, e.g. about the wrongness of terrorism.
- Draws attention to the need to investigate the direct effects on individuals who consume newspapers.
- Supports the argument that newspapers should be regulated to avoid public harm.
- For online news, supports the argument that the internet should be regulated to avoid public harm, e.g. to remove fake news and terrorist propaganda.

How the theory is limited

- Originally developed to explain the effects of media with powerful audience positioning, such as television – newspaper representations of violence are less likely to produce imitative behaviour.
- Newspaper messages are likely to be contradicted by messages from politically and socially opposing newspapers (e.g. the *Guardian* and *Mail*).
- For online news, messages can be challenged by audiences in comments, tweets or other posts, reducing the effect of the original messages.
- Prioritising the effects of the media on the audience may mean that the effects of the audience on the media are underestimated (see Jenkins and Shirky).

Cultivation theory – Gerbner

How the theory is useful

- May apply to a wide range of media products, including newspapers, where content analysis is widely used to study consistency in messages.
- Would most apply to newspaper messages that are delivered strongly and consistently across newspapers, e.g. about the wrongness of terrorism.
- For online news, would most apply to audiences within a 'digital bubble' who consume messages from only a narrow range of sources that target their demographic and psychographic (e.g. news feeds on Facebook).
- Draws attention to the need to investigate the longer-term effects on audiences – violent representations in newspapers and news sites may create the belief that the world is an inherently dangerous place.
- Supports the argument that newspapers should be regulated to avoid public harm.

How the theory is limited

- The theory was developed to explain the power of television, so may be less applicable to newspapers, where media consumption is rarely as heavy.
- Newspaper messages are likely to be contradicted by messages from politically and socially opposing newspapers (e.g. the *Guardian* and *Mail*).
- The theory may be outdated for online news; for example, online newspaper messages will be challenged by audiences in comments, tweets or other posts, reducing the effect of the original messages.
- Prioritising the effects of the media on the audience may mean that the effects of the audience on the media are underestimated (see Jenkins and Shirky).

Reception theory – Hall

How the theory is useful

- May apply to a wide range of media products, including newspapers.
- Draws attention to the range of possible audience readings while acknowledging the role of ideological power in creating dominance within newspaper messages and values.

How the theory is limited

- Assumes that there is one dominant meaning to which the audience responds – does not fit messages with a multitude of different possible readings (e.g. deeply ironic messages).

Fandom – Jenkins

How the theory is useful

- Draws attention to the potentially revolutionary effect of online media on news and the threat this represents to traditional models of news gathering and distribution.
- Highlights how online newspapers increasingly rely on participatory media such as Facebook, Instagram and Twitter to disseminate news.
- Draws attention to the role of participatory culture in developing citizen journalism.

How the theory is limited

- Does not really apply to print newspapers due to their traditional, centralised production.
- Fandom and participatory culture are less likely to occur in relation to online newspapers than in other areas of the internet due to their content and the ethos of professional journalism.
- Its optimistic view of the power of online audiences may underestimate the power of media conglomerates to shape and control online content and the importance of journalistic professional practice (see Curran and Seaton, and Hesmondhalgh).
- May underestimate the effect of media products on audiences (see Bandura and Gerbner).

'End of audience' theory – Shirky

How the theory is useful

- Draws attention to the potentially revolutionary effect of online media on news, and the threat this represents to traditional models of news gathering and distribution.

- Highlights how online newspapers increasingly rely on participatory media such as Facebook, Instagram and Twitter to disseminate news.
- Draws attention to the role of amateur producers in citizen journalism.

How the theory is limited

- Does not really apply to print newspapers due to their traditional, centralised production.
- Applies less to online newspapers than to fully user-generated online content as online newspaper brands have not embraced the 'publish then filter' model of the new media.
- Its optimistic view of the power of amateur producers may underestimate the power of media conglomerates to shape and control online content and the importance of journalistic professional practice (see Curran and Seaton, and Hesmondhalgh).
- May underestimate the effect of media products on audiences (see Bandura and Gerbner).

Now test yourself

TESTED

1 What is the key concept in Levi-Strauss's theory and how is it useful in understanding newspapers?
2 A newspaper has a story about a celebrity's publicity stunt. Whose theory is most useful to explain this news item?
3 Which social groups are included in hooks' idea of 'intersectionality'?
4 Whose theory states that the media have direct effects on audiences?
5 Give one example of Jenkins' participatory culture operating in news.

Answers on p. 205

Exam practice

Try answering exam practice Question 4 on page 52 and compare your answer to the sample answers online.

ONLINE

How to prepare for the exam

- You will need to learn the advantages and limitations of each theory in understanding your two news in-depth studies.
- While it is tempting to try to guess which theories may be paired with which in-depth studies, this doesn't really narrow down the choice very much, so it would be safer to assume that any combination could be asked for (except for Livingstone and Lunt for newspapers).
- Learning all this is a big task, so try to note all the repeated limitations and advantages as you may be able to fall back on these.
- Remember that the exam will probably give you a choice of theories to evaluate.
- Practise applying the theories to your two news in-depth studies so you have some detailed examples of how they have been useful in your analysis that you can use in your exam answers.
- Access the published OCR exam papers and practise answering the questions, checking your answers against the mark scheme.

What you have to do

This section of the exam asks two questions on your study of media language and representation across three media forms:

- advertising and marketing
- magazines
- music videos.

Which areas of the theoretical framework must I study?	
Advertising and marketing	Media language
	Representations
	Social and cultural contexts
Magazines	Media language
	Representations
	Social, cultural and political contexts
Music videos	Media language
	Representations
	Social and cultural contexts

The two questions in Section B will be as follows:

Q5	10 marks	This will probably be a knowledge and understanding question about one of the three media forms you study for this section: • advertising and marketing • magazines • music videos. This short essay should take about 17 minutes to plan and write.
Q6	15 marks	This will probably be an analysis question about one of the three media forms you have studied for this section: • advertising and marketing • magazines • music videos. This question may ask you to analyse an unseen extract: this will be either advertisements that are not your set products or a front cover of *The Big Issue* magazine that you should not have studied. You may be asked to compare the set product advertisements you have studied with an unseen advertisement or advertisements. This essay should take about 25 minutes to plan and write, and should be well structured with a clear conclusion.

Questions 5 and 6

What these questions involve

Question 5 will probably ask you to demonstrate knowledge and understanding about media language and representations in one of the three media forms. It may further ask you to refer to the set product(s) you have studied.

Question 6 will probably ask you to analyse either of the following:
- a source in the exam – a front cover of *The Big Issue* or a/some print advertisement(s) for a soft drink, male grooming product or a charity
- one or both of the set product music videos you have studied, with no source in the exam.

At some point the exam must ask you to compare the media language in a charity advertisement that is outside the commercial mainstream to a more mainstream, commercial advertisement, but you cannot predict when this combination is going to occur.

Question 6 will probably ask for both:
- analysis of media language or representations
- judgements and conclusions.

> **Revision activity**
>
> Past papers and practice papers are published on the OCR Interchange – ask your teacher to access these so you can check whether the format for Questions 5 and 6 has changed over time.

Timing

REVISED

Question 5 will probably be worth 10 marks, so you should spend about 17 minutes answering this question.

Question 6 will probably be worth 15 marks, so you should spend about 25 minutes answering this question.

What the examiner is looking for

REVISED

In exam practice Question 5 below, examiners are looking for:
- how comprehensive, detailed and accurate is your knowledge of media language and/or representations in this media form
- the clarity, precision and balance of your explanations in answering the question
- the detail and accuracy of your references to the set product(s), if required.

Exam practice

Question 5

Explain how representations in music videos are chosen to promote the artist(s). Refer to **one** of the music videos you have studied to support your answer. [10]

Question 5

Explain how the media language in advertising incorporates the brand image the advertisers wish to convey. Refer to the advertisements for Old Spice and Lucozade you have studied to support your answer. [10]

Question 5

Explain how the representations in magazines reflect their contexts. Refer to *The Big Issue* covers you have studied to support your answer. [10]

Sample answers available online

ONLINE

In the following exam practice Question 6, examiners are looking for:

- how well you apply your knowledge of the area of the theoretical framework (e.g. media language, or representation) to analyse the two sources
- how convincingly, accurately and perceptively you analyse the sources, with logical connections and lines of reasoning
- the detail and accuracy of your references to the sources
- how accomplished and developed your judgements and conclusions are.

Please refer to the section on 'Making judgements and reaching conclusions' for Question 2.

Exam practice

Question 6

Analyse why *The Big Issue* magazine has used an intertextual approach to Brexit on its front cover.

In your answer you must:
- analyse the use of intertextuality to create meaning in the source
- make judgements and reach a conclusion about the advantages of this use of intertextuality on *The Big Issue* magazine cover. [15]

The source – Source C – for this question can be found in the sample assessment material on the OCR website at: www.ocr.org.uk/Images/316674-unit-h409-01-media-messages-sample-assessment-material.pdf.

Sample answer available online

ONLINE

Recommended revision for these questions

REVISED

For media **language**, you should analyse and explain:

- the combination of elements to create meaning using **semiotics**
- the **generic conventions** of the media forms looking at variations, change over time, generic **hybridity** and challenging/subverting conventions
- the relationship between media language and technology
- examples of **intertextuality**
- the way media language incorporates viewpoints and **ideologies**
- media language in the media forms in terms of media contexts.

For media **representations**, you should:

- analyse and explain how selection and combination create representations of events, issues, individuals and social groups
- analyse and explain how the media forms make claims about **realism** and construct versions of reality

Semiotics: The study of signs. (See Barthes in the Academic Theories section at: www.hoddereducation.co.uk/myrevisionnotesdownloads.)

Generic conventions: The shared understandings of what elements fit in which genres.

Genre hybridity: The stable mixing of different genres in one product. Many genres are commonly hybridised with romance, for example, to increase their audience appeal.

Intertextuality: Media products (texts) that refer to other media products.

Ideologies: Sets of beliefs, values and assumptions shared by a social group and embedded in social, cultural, political and economic institutions. Usually thought to reflect the interests of powerful groups. Consumerism, freedom, equality and individualism are often considered dominant ideologies in free market capitalist societies as they reflect the economic basis of these societies.

Realism: Realism is the set of conventions by which audiences accept a representation as 'real' or 'realistic'. There are different sets of rules for different genres and for different media forms, and there are many different forms of realism.

Positioning audiences: How products try to put their audiences in particular positions. This might be emotional positioning (e.g. making them feel fear or sympathy), cognitive positioning (how they think about representations in the products), social positioning (e.g. as males or females) or cultural positioning (e.g. being positioned as British or American).

> **Exam tip**
>
> These points have been taken from the subject content on pages 23–27 of the specification but condensed for clarity. Examiners may write their questions using the same wording as the subject content. So please read through the subject content to check you understand all the wording as well as revising the content below.

- analyse and explain the impact of social and cultural contexts (and political contexts for *The Big Issue*) on how producers chose to represent events, issues, individuals and social groups
- analyse and explain positive and negative uses of stereotyping
- analyse and explain how social groups may be under-represented or misrepresented
- analyse and explain how representations, particularly those that systematically reinforce values, attitudes and beliefs about the world across many representations, invoke discourses and ideologies and **position audiences**
- suggest how audience response and interpretation reflects social and cultural circumstances.

> **Exam tip**
>
> Note that this front cover relies on the audience having both knowledge of the appearance of politicians and the titles of Abba songs. As this knowledge is not considered part of Media Studies, this information is given alongside the source so that no students are disadvantaged.

Music videos

Music videos: media language

REVISED

Semiotics: combining media language elements

For an explanation of semiotics, see page 6 under Questions 1 and 2.

The media language elements for music videos are:
- camerawork
- editing
- mise-en-scène
- performance
- soundtrack.

Soundtrack is included as some videos, such as the 'Ya Mama' video, add **diegetic sound** to the soundtrack.

The media language used in a music video will generally do one or more of the following:
- reflect the tone of the song
- comment on the song
- reflect the public image of the artist
- reflect the style of the producers.

Whichever two videos you have studied from List A and B, the media language will contrast as detailed in the table below.

> **Diegetic sound**: Sound from within the fictional world (diegesis). In music videos, for example, diegetic sound may be used when there is no music playing.

List A videos	List B videos
Corinne Bailey Rae: 'Stop Where You Are' www.youtube.com/watch?v=KmFMwGycBd0	Fatboy Slim: 'Ya Mama' www.youtube.com/watch?v=d_SJfF6-JJ8
Massive Attack: 'Unfinished Sympathy' www.youtube.com/watch?v=ZWmrfgj0MZI	Radiohead: 'Burn the Witch' www.youtube.com/watch?v=yI2oS2hoL0k
Emeli Sande: 'Heaven' www.youtube.com/watch?v=883yQqdOaLg	David Guetta: 'Titanium' www.youtube.com/watch?v=JRfuAukYTKg
Camerawork, editing and mise-en-scène focus on the performer performing the song	Camerawork, editing and mise-en-scène focus on a parallel **linear narrative** in a fictional world that is related to but not driven by the song

List A videos	List B videos
Naturalistic mise-en-scène using real urban locations	Less naturalistic mise-en-scène – either animation (Radiohead), an exotic fictional location (Fatboy Slim), or period, cinematic fantasy mise-en-scène (Guetta)
Social realist media language focuses on the lives depicted in the videos	**Expressionist** media language focuses on the artificiality of the music video – shows influence of **postmodernism**

Naturalism: The opposite of expressionism. Media language that is self-effacing to suggest a transparent window on the world. Often linked to **social realism**.

Social realism: The set of conventions by which audiences accept a representation as reflecting real social conditions, especially the plight of the poor and powerless. The term may imply the depiction of a social group or social truth that is under-represented in other media products.

Linear narrative: A narrative with a beginning, middle and end in which earlier events cause later events. This causal chain is key – the narrative can use flashbacks and flash forwards to change the order in which events are narrated.

Expressionism: The opposite of naturalism. Media language that draws attention to itself, that expresses emotional states, e.g. harsh lighting might express alienation.

Postmodernism: A very general set of ideas about culture after modernism. If traditional art forms use traditional conventions (e.g. traditional architecture) and modernism broke with these by breaking conventions to create something pure and new (e.g. modernist glass and steel towers), postmodernism uses conventions in a playful and ironic way to create something new out of intertextuality (e.g. mixing up different styles). Media products tend to postmodernism by their very nature because most use existing genre conventions to create something different.The fact that postmodernism is difficult to pin down and define is itself quite postmodernist, as it reacted against the dogmatic ideals, truths and revolutionary breakthroughs that characterise modernism by adopting a certain fuzziness.

List A videos

Corinne Bailey Rae: 'Stop Where You Are'

This song's message is about enjoying the present and the video's media language connotes optimism within a theme of overcoming imprisonment.

The mise-en-scène creates a contrast between imprisoning concrete – grey and immobile – with the sky that it frames, the energy of the people in the video and the bright saturated red that Corinne wears as she sings. When the people are imprisoned within their environment they are shown in long shots heavily framed by the concrete, the scenes of transcendence when they escape their oppression are more often shot in close-up, emphasising their individuality.

The song's optimism is expressed in its sure-footed musical pace, with editing that reflects this via a stately editing pace throughout for a music video. This is reinforced by the use of slow motion during the song's choruses. The slow motion connotes the power of Corinne's message as the girls rush towards her, and the athleticism of the man who runs up the wall. The stateliness and soulfulness of the video is also connoted by the controlled use of camera movement throughout, the extensive use of medium shots on the performer rather than close-ups, and the restrained nature of her performance.

The narrative for this song is partly a performance montage and partly a linear narrative about urban paranoia being replaced by friendship and self-expression. The imprisoning mise-en-scène reinforces the connotations of threat which are overcome in the narrative by signifiers of community such as shared dog-stroking, offering a drink, dancing, smiling and laughing.

Massive Attack: 'Unfinished Sympathy'

This song's message is about loss, hurt and incompleteness. The video's media language reflects this by connoting gentleness and poignancy.

The lead singer – Shara Nelson – puts in a very restrained, intimate and sad performance, which sets the tone for the whole video. The camerawork follows this lead by the use of a single, gentle Steadicam shot for the whole video. This type of camerawork is usually considered bravura camerawork – many films are remembered for their famous lengthy shots – but in this case the camerawork does not draw attention to itself (despite the difficulty of the set up); apart for some clever use of a crane to take us from a close-up of some balls to Shara walking down the street, most of the camerawork simply shoots Shara from the front in medium shot, and occasionally medium close-up in the periods of emotional climax in the song.

Given the simplicity of the camerawork and lack of editing, the mise-en-scène has to produce most of the connotation. Shara walks at a steady pace that reflects the walking pace of the song through an urban landscape populated with members of the band, extras and the 'real' people who live on these streets (who include the street gang at the start); all the characters are dressed naturalistically to fit the environment and create a strong sense of social realism, a sense that this is what it is like to live on these streets. The video has been shot in a Californian low-income area at sunset; the golden lighting connotes a gentleness that reflects the song and projects a dignity around these lives.

The narrative of the video is constituted by the succession of people that Shara walks past, some of whom follow her. Thus, montage is created by the mise-en-scène instead of editing. The different character types – gang members, a boy with a toy, a man with amputated legs on a skateboard, a leafleteer, a man dressed as a Native American, women throwing vegetables, and so on – connote a cornucopia of lives, a richness in diversity.

Emeli Sande: 'Heaven'

This is a song of contrasts. First, the lyrics contrast the desire to be a better person ('Oh heaven!'), with the lure of temptation which leads to the character always letting people down. Second, the downbeat message of the lyrics contrasts with the upbeat nature of the music. The media language of the video reflects these contrasts in its mixture of gritty social realism, reflecting the downbeat message of the lyrics, and images of transcendence, which reflect the Heaven of the title and the upbeat music.

→

Emeli Sande: 'Heaven' (cont.)

The social realism is connoted through a range of media language techniques. The camerawork is largely handheld and not always in focus, which, especially when combined with the use of real East End of London locations and naturalistic-looking characters (who may be 'real people'), connotes documentary realism. Emeli Sande appears to be the exception in this video in that she is clearly wearing make-up; however, her portrayal in the opening singing in a forlorn manner looking out of a very ordinary-looking bedroom window hardly connotes glamour. Her performance, while energetic, does not include dancing, which would break the naturalism, and she quite often does not directly address the camera, implying that she may be a character in this drama rather than just the star performer. The editing style is very jumpy (though not jump cuts); as it cuts to different people, locations, time periods and moods it connotes a kaleidoscope of people and their experiences. One striking juxtaposition is from a low angle shot of a very ordinary-looking street to a statue of Christ on the cross to a young woman in a white dress.

The images of transcendence include a recurrent, low angle shot of Emeli on a rooftop that fills the frame with the sky, a long shot of clouds rolling in the sky, another of a flock of birds taking off, a medium shot of a man dancing ecstatically with his arms outstretched. These combine with the fast pace of the editing to bring connotations of joy and freedom to the video.

The narrative of the video is structured by a sense of **narrative disruption** caused by the wrong moves depicted in the song – this is shown visually in the shots of people looking let down. The video has an enigmatic ending that does not provide a satisfactory resolution – Emeli's character walks away from the man seen earlier waiting for her at the end of a tunnel. This lack of resolution fits the tone of the song, which is about internal conflict.

> **Narrative disruption**: The event(s) that disrupt an initial equilibrium and drive a narrative towards a resolution. For example, a murder can disrupt the peace of a community and cause investigation and solution.

List B videos

Radiohead: 'Burn the Witch'

This song with very edgy connotations is about persecution. The media language in the music video reflects these connotations and develops the theme of persecution which, in both the song and the video, is placed within the context of 'normal' society.

'Normality' is connoted in the video by the use of simple stop-motion animation with cheerful lighting and bright saturated colours – reminiscent of children's television and the safe world it projects. The media language emphasises a traditional setting whose mythical connotations of warmth and safety strikingly contradict the paranoia and persecution depicted in the video. The characters all wear traditional rural dress, such as smocks and folk costumes. The sets are designed to connote stability and tradition: town squares, white gates, the village fete laid out on tables. Our 'hero' arrives in what looks like a car from the 1950s, bearing a clipboard: the classic 50s signifier of bureaucracy. The editing pace is slow for a music video and the camerawork is primarily static, connoting theatricality. The video is shot in the 4:3 aspect ratio of pre-widescreen television.

The narrative follows a flawed protagonist being shown a series of events that become increasingly disturbing. We see a cross painted on a door, mini-doubles in a model village, children playing on a ducking stool, a group of 'deer-men' with swords, a bloody cow pie, flowered gallows, a 'happy' group of exploited fruit pickers. These reach a climax in the burning of the wicker man, followed by a coda in which we find that he has escaped.

Fatboy Slim: 'Ya Mama'

This is a track about exuberance – the energy in music – rather than anything external to the music. In a similar way, the video uses media language to create a self-contained fictional world that operates by its own self-consistent rules rather than referring to an external reality: a postmodern text about texts.

➜

Fatboy Slim: 'Ya Mama' (cont.)

The mise-en-scène – such as the use of music cassette tapes – suggests a time such as the 1980s, as does the old-fashioned 4:3 aspect ratio; the place, though shot in the Caribbean, is rather ambiguous. The early part of the video shows what appear to be poor White rural Americans sharing a house, but the market and police station scenes seem to contradict this, looking clearly set in the Caribbean. Despite this vagueness of time and place, the mise-en-scène is primarily naturalistic in that the characters are sweaty, wear little make-up and are cast for naturalism. The comedic acting and stunts undercut this with expressive outbursts of exaggeration when the music takes over, for example.

The camerawork and editing vary to create a sense of pace throughout the video and to reflect this balance between naturalism and expressionism. At the start the editing pace is rather slow for a music video and the camera is primarily static. As the action reaches the market the editing pace speeds up to connote a hectic busyness and this is reinforced by more expressive camerawork with more close-ups and a Dutch tilt as the man with the huge ghetto blaster arrives. The climax comes with a chase sequence with tracking handheld camerawork and very fast-paced edits.

To create the self-contained fictional world, the video has a very definite cyclical narrative construction. It starts with a postcard that is used to create the colour scheme for the painted ceramics and ends back at the same postcard at the same table but this time with a dancing man added. The arrival of the tape in the post is the event that causes the disruption of an initial equilibrium (the life in the house and order in the town). This disruption is played out on an increasing scale until the police try to restore order, but are defeated by the power of the music. The cyclic narrative ultimately refuses a resolution; instead the events may simply start again.

David Guetta: 'Titanium'

This is a track about resilience – being 'bulletproof' – and inner strength. The video uses media language to create a postmodern text about texts, a cinematic, self-contained fictional world that is structured around a similar theme of resilience, in this case the use of supernatural powers that protect the protagonist from restraint and control by others.

The camerawork and editing are more reminiscent of feature films than music videos. The opening features lengthy tracking shots following the boy's movements – in one shot the distinction between inside and outside the school is erased by camera movement. Only in one scene – the escape on the bike – does the editing pace and tracking speed increase to connote danger and excitement. The camerawork is mostly low angle or at the child's shoulder height to signify a child's view of the world.

The video is set in a historical time and place – the American suburbia of early Spielberg films – that is signified by the mostly naturalistic mise-en-scène in terms of:
● the setting (the white wooden suburban house, the empty suburban streets)
● the technology (a 4:3 cathode ray tube television, a boxy police car with chrome window linings, an old-fashioned landline handset)
● the costume (the boy wears an anorak and bobble hat, the joggers wear leg warmers, pastel jogging outfits and a sweat band)
● the set design (the stripped pine kitchen).

This filmic historical present is also signified through deliberate use of lens flare and shots of bright lights through the woods that are reminiscent of early Spielberg films.

The narrative expresses the theme of resilience through an enigma-resolution structure. After posing a series of enigmas (Who is this boy? Why is his school devastated? Why is his teacher afraid of him?), the remainder of the video depicts his attempts to escape from the forces of law and order. There are clues about his unusual powers (such as the floating toys), climaxing as, when cornered by a SWAT team, he releases a sphere of energy that knocks out all around him. The action narrative is unresolved but the enigma has been resolved, the audience now knows who has caused the devastation at the outset. The boy, though appearing small and vulnerable, is in fact 'bulletproof'.

Genre and music videos

Music videos are by definition a short form, so, although the form has developed some generic conventions since its rise in popularity from the mid-1980s onwards, genre is not as crucial to audiences and producers as it is in longer media forms such as television and film, where audiences need to know what to expect in terms of narrative, pleasures, and forms of realism or expressionism. A short form such as the music video can afford to surprise the audience – the List B videos are examples of videos that are unpredictable in content and form. On the other hand, the music video is essentially a commercial or promotional form, so the more mainstream music videos tend to follow generic conventions.

Performance videos, such as those on List A, are dominant in the genre; their conventions include such elements as:

- the soundtrack consists primarily or completely of the music track
- expressive camerawork and editing mirrors the tone of the song, but conventionally aims for movement, fast pace and excitement
- the mise-en-scène includes performance to camera – usually by the singer(s)
- costume, make-up, sets or locations are used to mirror the meaning of the song – these may be glamorous and sexualised or naturalistic and social realist, for example
- the narrative is driven by the structure of the song, especially verse and chorus, and often does not drive towards a resolution (reflecting the fact that music television channels in their heyday rarely showed videos through to the end).

A major sub-genre is the *narrative* video – which lacks performance to camera but constructs a diegesis (a self-contained fictional word) that either reflects or comments on the narrative of the song to which it runs parallel. List B videos are all narrative videos and the variation between the three videos demonstrates the loose set of conventions that govern this sub-genre, plus the expectation that certain artists or bands may produce videos that challenge and/or subvert conventions. These videos hybridise with other media forms, such as televisual narratives (e.g. Radiohead) or filmic narratives (e.g. David Guetta). But, further to this, the Radiohead and Fatboy Slim videos are characterised by **generic slippage**. There is no clear generic centre for these videos due to the incoherent mixture of elements of which they are constituted.

Many performance videos, including all the List A videos, contain at least some elements of narrative alongside that of the performance, so hybrids of the two sub-genres are extremely common:

> **Generic slippage**: Where products play with genre in such a way that the audience is surprised, e.g. by sudden changes in genre, or disorientated by uncertain or unreliable codes and expectations. Common in Bollywood film but considered postmodern in the West.

List A videos	Sub-genre	Elements of narrative
Corinne Bailey Rae	Performance	The little plots such as the teenage girls finding friendship, the man on the stairs being helped, the scary dog getting stroked.
Massive Attack	Performance	The succession of characters implying a world of different stories: the man window-shopping with his son, the person giving out leaflets, the drinkers, the kissers, the women throwing fruit.
Emeli Sande	Performance	The succession of characters implying a world of different stories: the sad people, the toddlers playing, the boy with angel-wing tattoos, the man in the scarf who dances.

While music videos for popular music have developed the above generic conventions, it should be noted that other musical genres may produce quite different videos. It is common, for example, for classical music videos to consist of one static shot of the orchestra playing a lengthy piece of music.

Media language and technology

The music video dates back as far as 1960s Beatles films (and the Beatles were instrumental in developing the form with their short films to accompany songs such as 'I Am the Walrus'). However, the form really took off with the arrival of music television (especially MTV) in the 1980s, which created much more demand for this content. The technology of cable and satellite television enabled a rapid growth in the number of channels available and thus the opportunity for music television. Early music videos were shot and edited on film, but it was the development of cheap and accessible digital editing that facilitated the music video industry, enabling the fast-paced editing style associated with the form, even if the video is shot on film. Similarly the advent of lightweight cameras has enabled the extensive use of locations, especially 'street' locations such as we see in the List A videos. In particular, the Massive Attack video relies on Steadicam technology to allow the camera person to shoot such a long continuous shot on the streets of Southern California.

Intertextuality in music videos

Music videos are highly likely to use intertextuality as they have to create meaning in a short period of time. Intertextuality allows them to 'borrow' already established meanings from other texts. For example, the use of bright flashlights in the woods at night in the David Guetta video carries meanings of innocence versus control established in Spielberg films such as *ET* and *Close Encounters of the Third Kind*.

Other uses of intertextuality include:
- to create humour
- to parody (criticise) the referred text or person
- to honour the referred text
- to flatter the audience – in that the product assumes that they are clever or well informed enough to understand the intertextual reference
- to attempt to transfer the value of the referred media product to the referring one
- to create a sense of shared experience with the audience.

Music videos have a long history of using intertextuality in order to address pop culture. Famous uses include two videos from the period of rapid growth of music videos: Madonna's 1984 'Material Girl' video, which was a pastiche of a musical number by Marilyn Monroe from the 1953 film *Gentlemen Prefer Blondes*, and Michael Jackson's 1983 'Thriller', which referenced horror films more generally.

Intertextuality in the set products

List A videos

These videos are not as rich in intertextual references as the List B videos. They do, however, use characters and settings that are familiar to the audience from other products and so are instantly recognisable, if not from particular media products as such.

Corinne Bailey Rae's video relies on ideas of 'the concrete jungle' established in film and television, and populates the video with familiar character types such as the bullying teenage girl gang or the working-class man with the dangerous dog.

The videos from Massive Attack and Emeli Sande rely on the idea of 'the street' established in film and television, and the idea of street life as rich in character and variety.

List B videos

Radiohead

This video is rich with explicit intertextual references from the first frame. The opening shot is a pastiche of the opening shot of David Lynch's *Blue Velvet* and carries, for those in the know, connotations from that film's narrative of an apparently happy, stable and conformist world hiding disturbingly dangerous social and sexual elements under its surface.

The narrative is a pastiche of the 1973 British film *The Wicker Man*, which, like the video, starts in apparent normality, becomes increasingly disturbing to its straight-laced anti-hero, and ends with his human sacrifice in a burning wicker man. Both the film and the video are implying that social solidarity and conformity can be based on horrific scapegoating of outsiders, and that this can happen in the most apparently cosy and safe communities. This theme was developed in other British 'folk horror' films such as *Witchfinder General* (1968) whose witch hunting is mirrored in the ducking stool found in the video.

The animation style of the video is an intertextual reference to the late 1960s children's television programmes *Trumpton* and *Camberwick Green*, stop-motion animation programmes that created a secure and predictable rural social world for small children. This style and its concomitant connotations contrasts with the dark narrative and, in doing so, accentuates its darkness.

The 'happily waving' workers in the greenhouse appear to be a reference to news reports of the plight of immigrant farm workers. The way they are ordered to wave by the man with the stick carries connotations of propaganda films such as Nazi films showing 'happy' inmates of 'civilised' concentration camps.

Fatboy Slim

This is a less intertextual video in that there is only one direct reference to another media product: the animated films of Tom and Jerry that were widely shown on children's television in Britain from the 1960s until 2000. The programme is heard for the first 36 seconds of the video and sampled intermittently after and briefly shown on the television. This connotes a childhood innocence, reinforced by the ceramic painting, contrasting with the appearance of the three young men, who look like types from film and television set in socially deprived America.

The reference to the Sony Walkman, the cassette tape and the ghetto blaster places the video some time in the 1980s.

The use of the Caribbean as a location may reference its use in films such as the Bond series, in which it connotes exoticism and pleasure.

The police are recognisable types from film and television. The hard-boiled police chief is a staple of the police drama, as are elements used of police procedure, such as bagging evidence.

David Guetta

There are references to both the early films of Spielberg but also to the film *Super 8*, which is itself an homage to those early Spielberg films – the protagonist in the music video is played by an actor from that film. Though you are not required to apply theory in this part of the exam, the video is a nice example of Baudrillard's concept of hyperreality – texts that simply refer to other texts.

Trademark Spielberg tropes that this video references include:
- the 'ordinary' boy hero
- adult misunderstanding of the children's world (the scared teacher)
- the American suburban setting
- use of enigma to delay narrative resolution (how and why has the school been devastated?)
- the bicycle as a symbol of childhood freedom and adventure
- the theme of loneliness (the boy must fight alone)
- families under strain (suggested by the mess in the house)
- menace is suggested rather than shown (the silhouette of a gun at the door, the bright lights in the woods)
- use of special effects or visual effects to create a climax.

Viewpoints and ideologies in media language

Music video	Viewpoints and ideologies	How the media language incorporates these
Corinne Bailey Rae	A celebration of everyday life	Social realist media language depicts the downbeat problems of everyday life; then the narrative depicts how the characters transcend these problems.
Massive Attack	A celebration of 'the street'	Social realist media language depicts the squalor of the streets but the sunset light and the sequential narrative, in which a kaleidoscope of characters come and go, depicts the beauty in the street.
Emeli Sande	Celebrates the desire to be better, possibly a religious message	Social realist media language depicts the sorrows caused by temptation but also suggests the power of redemption.
Radiohead	A critical viewpoint opposed to enforcing community and solidarity by exclusion and exploitation	Incongruity in the media language – the disparity between the narrative and the mise-en-scène – tries to create a sense of shock to establish critical distance from the fictional world.
Fatboy Slim	A celebration of the anarchistic power of music	The media language creates humour via the energy and absurdity of the narrative, its undermining of authority, and its creation of an exotic but safe fictional world.
David Guetta	Celebrates survival	An immersive world is created by high production values and narrative construction that encourages identification with the lead character and his quest to survive.

Revision activity

Apply the ideology 'toolkit' on page 14 under Questions 1 and 2 to your two chosen music videos.

Revision activity

Make notes on how far other contexts – consumerism, multiculturalism, feminism and changing attitudes to sexualities – may have influenced the media language in your two chosen music videos.

Exam tip

There is overlap between the media language and media representation areas of the framework – for both 'viewpoints and ideologies' and 'contexts'. So long as you adapt the points to answer the question, you may use ideas from either the media language or the representation analyses.

Media contexts reflected in media language

Music video	Contexts	How the media language incorporates these
Corinne Bailey Rae	Celebrity culture	The video focuses on the celebrity singer
Massive Attack	Celebrity culture	The video focuses on the celebrity singer
Emeli Sande	Celebrity culture	The video focuses on the celebrity singer
Radiohead	Postmodernism; social anxieties about immigration and national identity	Use of intertextuality and generic slippage The narrative of the video criticises scapegoating that is used to create a sense of identity
Fatboy Slim	Postmodernism	Use of intertextuality and generic slippage
David Guetta	Postmodernism	Use of intertextuality, especially pastiche

Now test yourself

TESTED

1 Why might music video producers choose a particular style of media language?
2 Which of the set product music videos use naturalistic media language to create social realism?
3 Which of the set product music videos use expressionist media language in a linear narrative?
4 Name the two types of music video.
5 What developments in technology helped the growth of the music video as a media form?
6 Which two contexts most clearly have influenced the media language in your two chosen videos?

Answers on p. 205

Music videos: media representations

REVISED

Representation: selection and combination

Corinne Bailey Rae

This video celebrates the underdog – whether defined by class, gender, race or age.

Social class is represented through location choice, the casting and the costume. The location suggests a council estate (although it is, in fact, an arts centre), as does the cast of characters with the exception of the middle-class man in a suit and the singer herself, who seems to exist beyond class in this world – she is both expensively dressed and also seems to belong (eventually) in this social setting.

Gender is represented through the selection of characters and the representation of the singer. Corinne's representation suggests a conventional view of femininity: her costume and make-up imply this as does the first shot of her high heels. Initially, this contrasts with the negative representation of the girl gang and the woman sitting on the stairs who are represented as aggressive and unhappy, as well as deviating from Corinne's standards of femininity. However, the celebration of their happiness by the end of the video softens this representation.

Masculinity is represented as initially threatening: two men disturb Corinne – the man who dances looms out of the shadows towards her and the tattooed man with the threatening dog – though they turn out to be full of balletic self-expression and care, respectively.

Age is represented through the vulnerability of the sad young girl in the blue hoodie who receives reassurance from the older woman. The video features mostly young people, with Corinne appearing to have a 'motherly' role in relation to her characters.

Racial integration is represented as a fact of life through the mixed-race casting and Corinne's own mixed-race heritage.

The narrative represents issues of paranoia and solidarity throughout, moving from a sense of threat (of attack, or suicide in the case of the dancer) to a sense of solidarity expressed through kindness and/or shared smiles.

Massive Attack

This video celebrates the underdog – whether defined by class, gender, race, disability or age.

Social class and/or poverty is represented through the location in low-income Los Angeles, with littered streets, graffiti and cheap shops. The inhabitants of this social world, however, are represented as diverse in terms of age, gender, race and ethnicity by creating a sequence of different social types, none of whom are judged by the narrative but presented as a matter of fact.

Race and ethnicity are represented in the first few seconds through a mixed collection of social types: a Latino gang, a mixed-race boy with a toy, the black British singer, a White couple, and an African-American man with his son window-shopping. Later we see a man dressed as a Native American.

Gender is represented by a mix of types. The woman and the men are of all ages, body shapes, and both able-bodied and with disability. The singer is not sexualised and the male members of the band follow after her, usually out of focus, suggesting that she has the agency in this narrative. Women are shown to be as active as men – distributing leaflets or acting out aggression with vegetables, for example.

At least one person with visible disabilities is represented as an integral part of this social world, picking up and reading a leaflet before going on his way.

Older people are included in a range of roles – as drinkers, as listening to a ghetto blaster – and middle-aged people make up many of the characters, including a pair kissing.

This deliberate celebration of often maligned groups of people – the urban poor – represents the issue of social inequality. The choice of a location in the USA for a band based in Bristol suggests that inequality is an international issue.

Emeli Sande

This video represents the negative consequences of giving in to temptation and at the same time celebrates street life.

The consequences of temptation are represented by a succession of sad faces, Black and White, male and female, reflecting the video's inclusive representation strategy in terms of gender, race and ethnicity, and class.

Street life is represented in a montage of people, places and events shot in a traditionally working-class district of East London. This represents youth as the norm – nearly all the characters are young adults or children, with the odd exception, such as the two old men (one with the 'interesting' face). However, there is no clearly dominant race or ethnicity, with a mix of Black, White and mixed-race people and a man in an Arab head scarf.

Temptation is represented early in the video by a shot of a woman in a red dress – this is a rare sexualised image of women in the video as, for example, Emeli is not represented in this manner. There are two further images of women who appear to be 'giving in to temptation' making the video ambiguous as to sexuality. This ambiguity suggests the representation of sexualities as fluid and not fixed.

Class is represented in terms of the 'ordinariness' of the location; the video is celebrating urban working-class life. Emeli Sande is represented as belonging in this world, as suggested by her unglamourised costume, location and performance style.

The video represents everyday life as a struggle.

Radiohead

This video uses the representation of a rural utopia to highlight exclusion and exploitation.

The traditional ideal British village – quaint, White and bound into a tight-knit community – is represented by the initial mise-en-scène. The outsider is represented as a bureaucrat by his suit and clipboard, a man who represents urbanism and central authority in opposition to the 'time-honoured ways' of rural communities. The insider is represented by the Mayor, a man of traditional authority. As befits a traditional community, no women are in charge – powerful women become the 'witch' of the song's title – instead they dress in traditional costume and have submissive roles such as being tied to a tree, serving food and dressing with flowers a structure that turns out to be the hanging gallows.

➡

Radiohead (cont.)

Exploitation of foreign workers is represented by the polytunnels full of tomato pickers who appear to be different and do not feature in the planning of the visit – instead they are made to wave cheerily by the drunken man with the stick.

Social exclusion is represented by the painting of a red cross on a front door, the traditional sign of a plague victim, followed by a cheery wave to the person trapped inside, by the deliberate fooling of the man in the suit, by the reference to witch hunting in the ducking stool that the children play on, by the ominous gallows and by the final wicker man ceremony in which the community is brought together in harmony over a brutal attempted murder. Exclusion is represented as normalised in this community, suggesting the darkness that lies underneath traditional notions of White Englishness.

Fatboy Slim

This video creates a mythical world by combining disparate elements. What appear to be two poor White Americans and one Latino are living on an unnamed Caribbean Island some time in the past. This world is represented as naive: the rednecks watch *Tom and Jerry* on television and make a living from painting ornaments. A traditional market carries signs such as 'This could be your cake' and 'For a brighter day put drugs away'. The police station is spelled 'Polis Stazion' and the police chief sits before a wall of photos of 'Problem People'.

This is a primarily male world. The trio, the police, the stall holders and those who are taken over by the music are all male. The few women shoppers in the market have no agency, except perhaps, the bossy girl heard in the *Tom and Jerry* programme. However, those women who are present appear to be serious 'grown-ups' in comparison to the men, who mostly act like children.

The White men end up being branded criminals and the only authority figure in the video is the Black police chief, perhaps deliberately reversing traditional roles. However, the chief's authority is undermined when he too is taken over by the music, allowing his men to laugh at him.

One indicator of the trio's low-class status is their pin-up of a sexualised image of a woman amongst the mess and clutter of their dilapidated house.

The representations in this video have been selected more for their absurdity and comic value than for the purpose of representing an issue. This is, perhaps, a touristic view of the Caribbean – a place of charm, idiosyncrasy and laid-back culture – so is a representation of a representation rather than an attempt at realistic representation.

David Guetta

This video represents Spielbergian Americana. That is, it is a representation of a representation. The social world represented in Spielberg films such as *ET* or *Close Encounters of the Third Kind* is a specific evocation of American suburbia that harks back to the small-town America evoked in classic Hollywood films.

This America is White – in the video the only Black characters are outsiders, the SWAT team sent in to deal with the situation. It is suburban, represented by wide roads connecting home and school, and on the edge of wild spaces, in this case the woods. It is 'classless' inasmuch as a fairly well-off White community might think of itself as classless. This world should be safe and secure, but is disrupted by powerful forces from outside, whether those of law and order, such as the SWAT team, or science fiction forces, such as the energy the boy retains.

Gender is represented as traditionally defined: the police are male, the teacher is female. The hero is male, the comedic joggers are female.

The forces of law and order are represented with a human face. They are startled by events despite their apparent power. They are trying to control events they do not understand and so they show fear.

The video represents in allegorical form the issues of growing up, of finding your identity, of finding out your power. It is, like the song, a representation of resilience.

Music videos: realism and constructing reality

List A videos

Music videos are, in the first instance, forms of marketing, and prioritise entertainment over realism. However, musical artists often wish to make statements about the world they live in and wish to use social realist techniques to make a claim of realism for their representations. For example, Beyoncé has made a series of famous videos about gender issues, such as 'If I Were a Boy', which try to construct a sympathetic exploration of the pressures on women today.

All the List A videos make claims to social realism. This means that, although fictional, they represent real social issues and social groups. They do this by following social realist conventions:

- exploration of social issues
- use of real locations
- use of non-actors
- an authentic performance style
- use of continuity editing and naturalistic mise-en-scène in order not to draw attention to the artificiality of the video
- use of documentary conventions such as handheld camera and montage (by editing in the case of Corinne Bailey Rae and Emeli Sande, by mise-en-scène in the case of Massive Attack)
- a realist narrative with consistent, identifiable characters and a plausible chain of cause and effect.

The versions of reality these videos construct are similar: inferring that life on 'the street' is difficult but conferring a dignity upon those who struggle for their existence.

The List B videos may be exploring social issues – the Radiohead video in particular – but do not conform to all the conventions of social realism to do so.

All three construct realist narratives with consistent, identifiable characters and a chain of cause and effect, but these are less plausible except within the conventions of fictional genres:

- horror (Radiohead)
- comedy (Fatboy Slim)
- science fiction/fantasy (David Guetta).

All three use continuity editing and conventional camerawork, but the use of mise-en-scène is expressive, especially in the Radiohead video, as befits the horror genre.

The versions of reality in List B videos are very different.

- Radiohead: a sinister, paranoid fictional reality that parallels and comments on real social issues.
- Fatboy Slim: a comedic pastiche of representations that constructs a surreal world.
- David Guetta: a pastiche of representations that constructs an intertextual world.

Social and cultural contexts

The primacy of the music video reflects changes in the cultural context of popular music. Before the internet, pop music was consumed by buying records or attending concerts. The relative scarcity of pop music

– you had to go out and spend money to access it – encouraged fandom, especially of cult bands (for aficionados) and the latest pop sensations (for mass audiences of young fans). Now the most popular means of accessing popular music is via YouTube, where music videos are freely accessible. Replacing relative previous scarcity with this plentiful choice is changing the role of pop music in people's lives and developments in pop music genres in ways that are still not entirely clear.

The List A videos share some similar contextual influences in showing the influence of:

- **celebrity culture** in the primacy accorded to the performer in the representations
- **multiculturalism** in the natural way in which race and ethnicities are mixed in the representations (though some groups, such as Asians, are still lacking)
- **feminism** in featuring women singers who also wrote the material and their lack of sexual objectification in the videos
- **changing attitudes to sexualities** to some extent at least in the range of gender identities on offer in the videos.

The List B videos all have in common the influence of **postmodernism**. They all combine existing elements to create something new in the combination:

- Radiohead's video plays with genres to create generic slippage – neither horror nor children's animation nor a stable combination of the two (hybridity), and so disorientating
- Fatboy Slim's video creates a witty, implausible social world out of cultural snippets – rednecks, police procedurals, images of the Caribbean – to create an intertextual, surreal world
- David Guetta's video uses a loving pastiche (an homage) of older films in order to create a self-contained fictional world that relates only in theme to the song it accompanies.

Each List B video also reflects a specific social and/or cultural context:

- Radiohead's video reflects liberal and left-wing concern about what they see as growing xenophobia and social exclusion in society, expressed in demands to reduce immigration
- Fatboy Slim's video reflects the touristic view of the Caribbean in Britain as a quaint and amusing playground
- David Guetta's video reflects the cultural prestige given to Hollywood film and the respect given to the film director in European, especially French, culture.

Stereotyping, under- and misrepresentation

We have seen already on pages 24 and 25 (under Questions 1 and 2) that analysing under-representation and misrepresentation in any media product entails concentrating on:

- use of stereotyping
- diversity of representations
- opportunities for self-representation.

For this reason stereotyping and mis/under-representation are best treated together in this context.

Music videos, as short media forms, have to establish meaning rapidly and so are likely to use stereotyping to achieve this. However, socially aware artists will try to avoid crass stereotyping or to explore and undermine stereotypes from within. Moreover, the crucial role of African–American musical culture in the formation of popular music means that many music videos honour that heritage and will make conscious attempts to avoid negative racial stereotypes.

Music videos may attempt to offer greater diversity in representations, but opportunities for self-representation by otherwise marginal groups (the working class, for example) are limited by the fact that many videos are produced by media professionals for successful artists.

Corinne Bailey Rae

The video deliberately uses, then attempts to deconstruct, negative stereotypes. A number of types often stereotyped as aggressive and uncaring – the girl gang, the businessman, tattooed males with scary dogs – are all shown to be supportive and caring. A negatively stereotyped location – the concrete jungle – is shown to be full of life and energy.

The young, conventionally attractive and glamorously dressed female singer is stereotyped positively as bringing happiness to people's lives. Concurrently, the association of a mixed-race artist with the urban is itself stereotypical, though it is unclear whether this is positive or negative.

The video attempts diversity of representation, though with a bias to the young, the energetic (suggesting able-bodied) and the working class. These may be over-represented in the video as an attempt to counter bias in the mainstream media.

This is not a self-representation, except perhaps for the representation of the singer.

Massive Attack

This video builds upon the positive stereotype established within popular culture of the authenticity of 'the street', perhaps reflecting the band's association with street art. This notion of authenticity is linked to a positive view of ethnic and racial diversity. Groups that are often negatively stereotyped are here represented in a neutral fashion: the street gang, people with disabilities, the homeless, all are recognisable as types, but without obvious positive or negative connotations. Obvious stereotypes are avoided – the small child window-shopping is with what appears to be his father, not his mother, the man with disabilities shows engagement rather than passivity in taking and reading a leaflet.

This is a deliberate attempt to represent under-represented groups and, for a music video, this is exceptionally diverse in terms of ages and body types, as it eschews glamour in favour of realism.

This is clearly not a self-representation – the group and the director are British – though the racial mix reflects in part that of the group members.

Emeli Sande

This video builds upon the positive stereotype established within popular culture of the authenticity of 'the street', a notion linked to a positive view of ethnic and racial diversity.

The video's montage of people and places requires rapid identification, so a number of clichés or stereotypes are used, such as:
- a woman in a red dress signifying sexuality
- innocent children playing
- mothers caring for children
- the carefree young woman in the white dress
- the ordinary street and the tower block as signifiers of urban working classness.

This quick montage suggests a neutral or positive representation.

The video is deliberately diverse in terms of ethnicity and gender in the range of people who appear hurt, though the age range is narrow.

This is not a self-representation, except perhaps for the representation of the singer.

Radiohead

This video deliberately uses positive stereotypes, as did the film *The Wicker Man*, to create a false sense of safety and security, then counters these with negative stereotypes. The village is represented positively at first as a happy tight-knit community, all agreeing with the patriarchal mayor in the village square meeting and honouring traditional signs of Englishness or Britishness (painting the red post box, decorating what appears to be a maypole, playing in the village band). All these are touristic stereotypes of village life. These stereotypes are then undermined by revelations: the red paint is used to mark a door, the maypole is a gallows, the band is playing at a fete where the centrepiece is a wicker man. Negative stereotypes of historic rural Britain are evoked, as a place of plague and xenophobic violence.

The video eschews diversity in representing the dangers of a cohesive monoculture held together by xenophobia and social exclusion of others who are seen as a threat.

As a fully fictional piece, this counts as a self-representation of Britain by British artists, but does not claim to be a self-representation of village life by villagers, as the village is metaphorical.

Fatboy Slim

This video uses stereotypes, but in an unfamiliar setting, which undermines them, as does the humour of the piece. The rural market (at first) uses a positive touristic stereotype of the Caribbean: sunny, full of character and authenticity. Likewise the police are represented as mostly childlike and unthreatening, a patronising positive representation of the Caribbean, perhaps. The rednecks in the house are established as readily identifiable types, but the usual negative stereotypes of violence, sexism and racism, though suggested, are undercut by elements of their domestic life – watching *Tom and Jerry* and painting ceramics – to destabilise the representation.

The video does contain diverse aspects, but this is definitely not a self-representation of the Caribbean but the creation of a mythical time and place by outsiders (a Swedish film collective).

David Guetta

This video knowingly uses stereotypes in an intertextual manner. Childhood is stereotyped as a time of uncertainty and new discoveries in a mostly uncomprehending adult world – a sympathetic stereotype. School is negatively stereotyped as a place of constraint – our hero has 'exploded' there – which mirrors the negative stereotypical representation of the forces of law and order.

By contrast, cycling is positively stereotyped as a moment of freedom – the one time the child escapes the restrictions of adults, illustrated as he sails past the joggers. These are all stereotypes reflecting a child's view of the world. The gender stereotypes – the female teacher and male police officers – reflect the 1980s world in which the video is set. The racial stereotyping – the only Black face is among the outsiders, the SWAT team, again reflects the image of White American suburbia.

Diversity is hardly attempted due to intertextual references. It cannot be a self-representation.

Discourses, ideologies and audience positioning

For explanation of these terms, see page 5 or the online glossary.

Music videos, as part of celebrity culture, are by their nature expressions of individualism and consumerism. They project the identity of the individual artist(s) and offer images of identity to their audiences for their consumption. Music videos encourage their audiences to define themselves by musical taste and the messages and values of the videos.

Certain genres emphasise materialism in their videos, an approach alluded to by the title of a video, 'Cash Money Millionaires: Bling Bling', that features expensive cars and pots of cash. The List A videos are materialistic in an opposing way in that they all feature representations of low-income life, suggesting the ideology of welfare – that society should help the less fortunate – by showing these characters as unique individuals rather than as statistics.

Corinne Bailey Rae

Tries to position the audience as identifying with Corinne and her optimistic view of the 'good in everyone'. This video suggests a quasi-religious discourse, that all are worthy of redemption, that all should learn to live in the moment, that people should help one another, a discourse that fits a left-leaning ideology. The video is anti-racist in its assumption of multiculturalism.

Massive Attack

Tries to position the audience as identifying with Shara and her journey through the streets of Los Angeles, to see these streets as a place where people belong rather than a social issue. The video invokes a left-leaning ideology by suggesting sympathy with outsiders and underdogs. It is anti-racist in its assumption of multiculturalism.

Emeli Sande

Tries to position the audience as identifying with Emeli and her struggles to cope with the pain she feels she inflicts on others. This video suggests a quasi-religious discourse, that the world is full of temptation that harms others, but also innocence and richness. The video invokes a left-leaning ideology by suggesting sympathy with outsiders and underdogs. It is anti-racist in its assumption of multiculturalism.

Radiohead

Tries to position the audience as seeing the parallels between the fictional world and modern society, invoking a left-leaning ideology of concern about the social exclusion and exploitation of minorities and the powerless.

Fatboy Slim

Tries to position the audience as maintaining a critical distance from the whole cast of characters in order to generate humour. The celebration of the power of music to disrupt social conventions and authority invokes an anarchist ideology that prefers self-governance to external authority.

David Guetta

Tries to position the audience as identifying with the boy and his attempt to escape the frightening forces around him. The video's sympathy with the underdog hero invokes ideologies of welfare, especially care for children.

Representation: audience response and contexts

Audience response and interpretation cannot be read from the product itself, so you will need to have undertaken some audience research on this topic, if only among your fellow students.

Audience interpretation of music video representations might depend on a number of differences:

- fandom and musical preference
- gender
- sexuality
- race/ethnicity and nationality
- age
- class
- region
- political affiliation
- a wide range of other individual factors and social/cultural contexts.

These will affect whether audiences accept the meanings intended for the representations or decode them quite differently. For example, individuals with right-wing leanings might not accept the left-wing representations in most of the set videos, reading them as yet more evidence of the liberal sympathies of the metropolitan elite.

Advertising and marketing

The three set products for this media form are these:

> **A poster advertisement for Lucozade – a soft drink brand**
>
> https://www.facebook.com/LucozadeSport/photos/a.57643721237130
> 1.149800.576388689042820/720272364654451/?type=3&theater
>
> Slogan: 'IN A DIFFERENT LEAGUE'/LUCOZADE YES

> **A poster campaign for Shelter – a charity for the homeless**

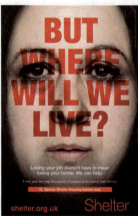

Figure 1.6 Shelter advert

Slogan: We can help

Copy:
- BUT WHERE WILL WE LIVE?
- Losing your job doesn't have to mean losing your home. We can help.
- Every year we help thousands of people avoid losing their homes.
- Search 'Shelter Housing Advice' now.

Copy:
- HE CAN'T DO THAT
- As a tenant it's hard to know where you stand. We can help.
- Every year we help thousands of people with difficult or rogue landlords.
- Search 'Shelter Housing Advice' now.
- To donate text *Home-40 £5* to 70070.

Copy:
- I CAN'T FACE IT
- Debt can seem too big to face, but if ignored can threaten your home. We can help.
- Every year we help thousands of people avoid losing their homes because of debt and other problems.
- Search 'Shelter Housing Advice' now.
- To donate text *Home-40 £5* to 70070.

A print advertisement for Old Spice – a men's grooming product brand

Figure 1.7 Old Spice advert

Slogan: None

Copy:
- OLD SPICE BAHAMAS SCENT COMES FROM AN ANTI-PERSPIRANT MINE IN THE BAHAMAS.
- THIS FACT HAS NOT BEEN FACT-CHECKED.

> **Exam tip**
>
> To prepare for the exam you need to have analysed the set products in detail and practised analysing similar adverts, noting their similarities and differences to the set products in terms of media language and representation.

You may be asked to:
- explain the use of media language and representation in advertising using examples from these set products
- analyse different unseen advert(s) in the exam – these will be for a soft drink, a men's grooming product or a charity for the homeless
- compare the adverts you have studied to the unseen adverts in the exam.

Advertising and marketing: media language

REVISED

Semiotics: combining media language elements

For an explanation of semiotics, see page 6.

Media language elements for print advertising and marketing are largely the same as for print newspapers:
- layout
- typography
- use of image
- use of language
- use of colour
- logo, slogan, brand identity.

Depending on the brand, advertising uses media language for a number of purposes. For example:
- to make the brand more memorable – establish brand awareness and brand identity
- to develop the brand image – promoting positive associations in the minds of the consumers
- to differentiate the brand from other brands
- to engage with the lifestyle of the brand's consumers
- to reassure existing users of the brand
- to persuade new users to try the brand.

Advertising outside the commercial mainstream, such as charity advertising, will have both similar and different purposes:
- to raise awareness of the charity's issue
- to build up the charity's brand image – promoting positive associations in the minds of the public
- to reassure existing supporters of the charity
- to persuade new supporters to donate to the charity.

Advertisers traditionally use the AIDA model – attention, interest, desire and action – to summarise what effect they wish to create. This can be seen at work in both the Lucozade and Shelter advertisements:

Effect on audience	Lucozade	Shelter
Attention	Use of celebrity	Use of faces
Interest	Claims of superiority	Issues the reader could face
Desire	To emulate the celebrity	To be helped or help
Action	Use the product to improve	Contact or donate

> **Serif and sans-serif typefaces/fonts**: Serifs are small ornaments on fonts, sans-serif fonts do not have these so look cleaner and more modern. A typeface is a family of fonts. Arial is a common sans-serif typeface. Times New Roman is a common serif typeface.

The Old Spice advert, on the other hand, uses a more modern technique that avoids overt persuasion in order to bypass a media-savvy audience's resistance to persuasive techniques.

Lucozade

Media language elements have been selected and combined to create a mix of science, aspiration and passion.

The myth of science is signified by:
● the use of high-contrast photography using a very white light
● the use of a cool blue background that matches one of the brand colours
● the use of scientific-looking pseudo data diagrams on the right-hand side
● the simple, uncluttered and formal layout, framed by the white key line
● the explicit claim that something – it is not made clear what – is 'scientifically proven'.

Aspiration is connoted by:
● the use of language such as 'In a Different League'
● the use of a celebrity role model with, as suggested by the data about him in the top right-hand corner, a record of sporting achievement
● Gareth Bale is posed and lit to emphasise his chiselled features and seriousness.

Passion is connoted by:
● the use of 'Lucozade Yes' as a slogan
● the seriousness and direct address of Gareth Bale's pose.

Brand identity is maintained through the use of the complementary blue and orange colour used in the packaging design and the use (though very small) of the Lucozade logo.

Shelter

Media language elements have been selected and combined to connote humanity, care and realism.

Humanity and care are signified as follows:
● the layout of each poster is dominated by a big close-up of a face to focus on the emotion – particularly anxiety – on each face
● the main copy, such as 'But where will we live?', relates to the individuals depicted, personalising the issues of poverty, debt and rogue landlords
● the repetition of 'We can help' across the campaign connotes care.

Realism is connoted by:
● the simple layout
● the use of plain language in a conversational tone
● the use of a no-nonsense capitalised **sans-serif font**
● the casting of unknown people rather than celebrities
● the lack of an obvious persuasive technique.

The brand identity is maintained through the use of the Shelter house colour (red) and the Shelter logo.

Old Spice

Media language elements have been selected and combined to signify surrealist humour and pleasure.

Surrealist humour is signified:
- first, by juxtaposition – surreal combinations such as a man who is wearing a beach, a man having a volcano head, and the beach featuring both peril (an attack by Neptune capsizing a boat, a crab menacing a man buried in the sand) and pleasure
- second, by using a naturalistic, brightly lit style of media language to depict these events
- third, by use of a comically absurd claim in the copy.

Pleasure is signified through the bright and colourful media language and the use of signifiers of pleasure (a woman sunbathes, a fisherman catches a shark, someone discovers a treasure chest in the surf). The pleasure would be conventionally aspirational, as would the use of an attractive ex-American football player, but both are undercut by the ludicrous nature of the surrealism.

Brand identity is maintained by the use of the Old Spice logo which, in its decorative italic font, contrasts with the no-nonsense sans-serif capitals of the copy, which itself contrasts ironically with the absurd claim the copy makes.

Genre and advertising

The two main genres of advertising that concern us here are charity and consumer brand advertising. These are primarily defined by their products, but also use different conventions to fit those products.

Advertising has also developed a number of different styles that rely on different advertising techniques.

USP (unique selling proposition) advertising

This establishes the product as somehow superior to other products; this 'hard sell' approach is often considered rather crude and old fashioned and has also been limited by regulation, which means that advertisers can no longer make unjustified claims about their products (as Lucozade found to its cost, when the Advertising Standards Authority ruled that it could not, in a previous version of its advert, claim its drink fuels and hydrates better than water). Note that Shelter has used this technique. The organisations paying for advertising often tend to insist on inserting some product message in order to feel that they are getting their money's worth.

Brand image advertising

This concentrates on the brand rather than the product and tries to build up brand values, often by the quality of the advertising. The Old Spice advertising is a good example of an advert that makes no claims about the product apart from an absurd one that parodies advertising itself; postmodern adverts like this one work by hoping to transfer the value of the advert – its wit and sophistication – to the brand itself, overcoming audience resistance by avoiding any obvious persuasive technique.

Revision activity

Practise analysing the media language elements of different soft drink, charity and men's grooming product advertisements. Note the ways these are similar or different to the set products.

Lifestyle advertising

This depicts or suggests the lifestyle of the consumers, in an aspirational or empathetic manner. The use in the Shelter advert of very 'ordinary' people just like the target audience who might be at risk of homelessness may count as an element of lifestyle advertising, but campaigns like the long-running one for Oxo featuring the 'Oxo family' are more classic examples.

Media language and technology in advertising

Print advertising often uses the advantages of print technology – especially its abilities to:
- convey detailed information
- create high-quality images (as in the Old Spice ad)
- use layout in striking ways, especially in large-scale works such as posters and billboards.

These help print advertising to create visual impact, particularly useful for connoting novelty, humour, and glamour or eroticism (hence the survival of upmarket glossy magazines supported by perfume and fashion advertising).

Magazines do offer targeting of audiences plus the major advantage of a safe environment for advertisers (unlike some online advertising). Posters and billboards offer geographical targeting and the opportunity to become part of the consumer's environment. The Shelter posters, for example, were displayed in six key locations where the risk of homelessness was highest. However, both these print forms are struggling against the lure of online **micro-targeting**.

Intertextuality in advertising media language

Advertisers routinely use intertextuality in order to establish meaning quickly, transfer the value of the referred product to the brand, and try to flatter their audiences. However, the set products do not clearly exhibit intertextuality, except that all campaigns work by clearly linking the different ads so each references the campaign as whole.

The Lucozade ad may be seen to reference the earlier campaign featuring the same image of Gareth Bale with the same layout, typography and colour scheme, which had to be discontinued due to the ruling from the Advertising Standards Authority.

The Shelter campaign can be used as three separate posters that will be recognised as three different people and problems photographed identically with the same layout, typography and colour scheme, and only minor changes in the copy.

The Old Spice campaign consisted of a series of television ads featuring the same actor/ex-footballer, but also referenced other print ads for different scents featuring the actor dressed as different tourist 'destinations'.

Viewpoints and ideologies in media language

We would expect certain ideologies and viewpoints to be incorporated into the media language of consumer brand and charity advertising.

Consumerism as an ideology might be expressed in media language that connotes quality, glamour or aspiration around a brand, as consumerism offers fulfilment and a sense of identity through consumer goods and services. Both the Lucozade and Old Spice adverts embody consumerism

Revision activity

Practise analysing the use of these techniques in different soft drink, charity and men's grooming product advertisements. Note the ways these are similar or different to the set products.

Micro-targeting: The very precise targeting of advertising messages to specialised audiences, facilitated by online platforms offering advertisers access to a database of personal information, obtained by data mining. Online advertising is viewed as more cost-effective as money is not wasted on targeting mass unfiltered audiences.

Revision activity

Practise analysing the use of intertextuality in soft drink, charity and men's grooming product advertisements. This might include reference either to other ads in the same campaigns or to other media products.

in this way. Coca-Cola's exhortation to 'choose happiness' expresses consumer 'choice' exactly.

Individualism as an ideology might be expressed in media language that emphasises the individual over the social group: Lucozade encourages individual sporting achievement; Shelter shows close-ups of individuals to bring a social issue to life; Old Spice features one individual who holds the campaign together.

The ideology of **welfare** is incorporated into the caring language of the Shelter charity advert, which repeats the slogan 'we can help'.

Media language and media contexts

Certain social and cultural contexts may influence much advertising.

Celebrity culture is apparent in the way the layout is dominated by sporting celebrities in the Lucozade campaign and, to a lesser extent, in the Old Spice campaign.

Some contexts are specific to particular adverts:

- Lucozade – shows the influence of the cultural dominance of football and the synergy between the internationalism of football (Bale is Welsh and plays in Spain) and global branding
- Shelter – shows the influence of originally religious discourses favouring charity
- Old Spice – shows the influence of postmodernism in its wit and reflexivity (playfully referring to the campaign as a whole and the practices of advertising).

> **Exam tip**
>
> You may wish to revisit the ideology toolkit for media language on page 14 under Questions 1 and 2.

> **Revision activity**
>
> Practise analysing the way media language incorporates viewpoints and ideologies in other examples of soft drink, charity and men's grooming product advertisements.

> **Revision activity**
>
> Practise analysing the influence of social and cultural contexts in soft drink, charity and men's grooming product advertisements.

Now test yourself

TESTED

1 What are the slogans for the two set product advertisements that have them?
2 What is the copy for the set Old Spice advertisement?
3 What are the key connotations for each of the set products?
4 Name the three different advertising techniques discussed.
5 What are the advantages of print as a technology for advertising?

Answers on p. 206

Advertising and marketing: media representations

REVISED

Representation: selection and combination

Representations in advertising are designed to reflect well on the brand. Advertisers will usually represent the world as a sunny, uplifting, glamorous or sensual place, or, in the case of charity advertising, as a place where harsh reality can be offset by care or donation.

The Lucozade advert represents sports people as dedicated, self-driven 'believers' who strive for excellence, through its combination of the image of a celebrity footballer and the slogan.

The Shelter posters represent people at risk of homelessness as 'ordinary' people who have had some bad luck by combining the copy with images of faces with conventional levels of make-up and grooming. By choosing two female faces and only one male face they are representing homelessness as non-gender-specific.

Old Spice's advert represents the world of Old Spice as an exotic, surreal playground by combining a series of 'tropical' elements from popular culture with a character already established in the campaign as a self-parodying trickster.

Advertising: realism and constructing reality

USP or 'reason-why' advertising (see the section on genre under media language above) relies on claims to realism in its messages about the product. Traditionally such claims were backed up by 'experts' such as 'scientists' or 'dentists', but increased self-regulation of advertising means that claims have to be honest and truthful and actors playing dentists, for example, have to state that they 'are not a dentist'. Many brands use formulations such as 'no other product is better' in order to avoid breaking the rules, or resort to vague wording that cannot be proved untrue. Thus, the Lucozade advert can state 'scientifically proven' so long as it does not actually specify what it is that has been 'scientifically proven'. The same campaign had previously claimed that the drink 'hydrates and fuels better than water'. This was based on officially agreed real health claims but the Advertising Standards Authority ruled that the adverts were still misleading and so could not be used. Hence the former claims were replaced by the slogan 'In a Different League'.

Brand image and lifestyle advertising has fewer such problems. Adverts that promote a brand's Italian-ness, Dolmio for example, can do so without breaking the rules (though they have to state where the product is made if not in Italy). Thus, the Old Spice advert can make a ludicrous claim about an 'anti-perspirant mine' – even though advertising is regulated in the USA by the Federal Trade Commission, which enforces truth-in-advertising laws – as the statement clearly makes no claim to realism.

Shelter's advert, like most charity advertising, relies on public trust in the realism of the charity's claims.

Representation and social/cultural contexts

Advertising is highly alert to social and cultural trends, and always aims to be at the forefront of new developments. However audience preferences, revealed by market research, play an important role in the design of advertisements and these have, in the past, acted as a brake on representations of minority groups or emergent trends. In the 1970s, for example, advertisers responded to criticisms about the stereotyping of women as housewives in adverts by arguing that research showed that female audiences objected to representations of men doing the housework as being 'unrealistic'. Similarly, advertising representations were very much Whiter in the 1970s, reflecting levels of racism in White culture, and any advertisements showing men enjoying male company had to eradicate any possibilities of gayness by, for example, showing three men entering a bar rather than two and never including anything that might suggest effeminacy (such as a pink shirt).

Changing attitudes to **sexualities** will thus be reflected in any advertisement that represents LGBT people or queers a representation by destabilising traditional gender roles. The Lucozade advert, for example, represents Gareth Bale in a potentially homoerotic manner. The equivalent advert from the 1970s would not have stressed his physical attractiveness and would have had him acting in a more 'manly', active way, such as kicking a ball.

Multiculturalism will be reflected in any advert that straightforwardly represents racial and ethnic diversity rather than as an issue or problem. In the Old Spice advert, the fact that the actor is an African-American is unproblematic. Though in this advert he is connected to a Caribbean island, in other ads in the series he is in a variety of locations. The Shelter posters feature ethnically ambiguous faces.

The impact of **feminism** may be reflected in deliberately avoiding stereotyping or covering feminist issues. The Shelter posters include two women as potentially homeless people to avoid the stereotype of the excluded homeless male.

Postmodernism has led to higher levels of irony in representation, complicating the representation process. Old Spice's advert shows the influence of postmodernism in its use of pastiche (reference) and bricolage (do-it-yourself assembly of disparate elements), its playful use of layout, and its lack of a coherent representational order. Postmodernism was a common technique in the 1990s but you may find fewer examples today.

Revision activity

View the Boddington's adverts from the 1990s as classic examples of parody in postmodernist advertising. Search for 'Boddington's Gondolas', 'Boddington's Face Cream', and 'Boddington's Crossing the Line'.

Stereotyping in advertising

Advertising relies on stereotyping, most often of the positive kind. Adverts are brief narratives and have to convey meaning rapidly. They rely on instant recognition and, it is hoped, emotional engagement as most audiences are resistant to advertising and have to be won over. Brand advertising wishes to transfer the positive associations of stereotypes to the brand itself. Dolmio, for example, showed a puppet Italian family to aim for value transference from the stereotypically warm, quirky and authentic family in their rural idyll to the brand (in fact, part of an American multinational conglomerate).

The Lucozade Sport advert uses positive stereotypes of sporting achievement, of science and of active masculinity.

Shelter's advert relies on a positive stereotype of people of mature age and conventional appearance as capable and self-directed – the ads work by generating surprise that such people could become homeless.

Old Spice's advert employs a positive stereotype of the Bahamas, as a place of exotic pleasure.

Under-represented or misrepresented groups

It is hard to analyse under-representation or misrepresentation in very short products with few groups represented. In general, advertising might be expected to fail to represent 'outsider' groups in society and to over-represent groups that are successful in terms of material wealth or in acting out important social values.

Most advertising is funded by the commercial mainstream so will reflect the interests of rich brands in its representations. Charity ads might be expected to demonstrate more sensitivity in their representations.

Industry reports from 2016–17 suggest that systematic under- and misrepresentation persists:
- Men are still over-represented in adverts compared to women and are more likely to be represented as leaders. Women are more likely to be younger, shown in revealing clothing and physically thin.

- People aged 20–40 are much more likely to be represented than older people.
- People with disabilities are extremely under-represented.
- Single parents are extremely under-represented.
- LGBT people are very under-represented.
- Black characters are often limited to roles such as sports person, musician or teacher.

The Lucozade advert reflects these trends in featuring a White, male footballer as the aspirational role model.

The Shelter campaign is unusual in deliberately representing young healthy adults – a socially central group – as part of a strategy to create surprise. Many charity ads would portray excluded or marginal groups as those needing their support.

The Old Spice advert creates diversity in the context of advertising as a whole by representing an African-American, albeit a rather stereotypical athletic ex-footballer.

Discourses, ideologies and audience positioning

All advertising tries to create very strong audience positioning. If advertising doesn't position its audience, the advertisers' money has been wasted. This positioning occurs despite the fact that advertising cannot emulate the immersive experience of feature films or serial television. In part, advertising tries to position audiences through its ubiquity – if a brand can appear everywhere then it may be seen as part of everyday life (hence the huge rise in product placement where logos, products or advertisements are included in television and film shots). In this sense, repetition of the message is key.

Brand advertising is in essence designed to invoke the ideology of **consumerism** – a dominant ideology in advanced capitalist countries. Advertising aims for the audience to have a relationship with brands and to link their sense of identity to their consumption of goods and services – where they live, what they wear, what they drive, how they eat, how they spend their leisure time, and so on. Brands are signifiers of consumerism; more than just products or services, they are either reliable reference points or signs of being at the cutting edge in a changing world.

Lucozade, for example, is selling the traditional status accorded to sporting excellence, as befits a brand that has been part of consumers' lives for a long time. Old Spice, though also long-lived as a brand, is selling itself as cutting edge. Two different techniques both giving the same underlying message: this brand is good, trust in it.

To this extent both adverts are positioning the audience as consumers, as people who care about brands. This ideology and positioning automatically relies on **materialism** and **individualism**: that people aspire to the best material goods; that people see themselves as individuals whose personal taste (in brands) defines who they are. Many adverts try to get around the 'nasty' associations of these ideologies by emphasising community, sharing and even spirituality in their advertising, as in the John Lewis Christmas adverts.

Charity advertising relies on pre-existing **discourses about charity** derived partly from religion. This is the idea that charity is a good in itself

> ### Exam tip
>
> See the explanations of these terms and the 'ideology toolkit' under Questions 1 and 2 on pages 14 and 27.

and that people should give to charity for moral reasons. It can also link in with the ideology of **welfare** – the belief that the state should share with and support the weak and vulnerable. In this way it moves away from the individualism of brand advertising. It retains the **materialism** of brand advertising in concern for other people's material well-being but also encourages some renunciation of material goods via the act of giving. All of this can be seen in the Shelter adverts, which attempt to position the audience as either concerned for the plight of people who could become homeless and willing to donate, or as recognising elements of their own social position in the representation offered by the posters and seeking help before it is too late.

Representation: audience response and contexts

Audience response to advertising is often to completely reject it. Those who are not part of the target audience may not engage or may develop an oppositional reading. Hence the saying 'Half the money I spend on advertising is wasted; the trouble is I don't know which half.' Google and Facebook have become very powerful on the basis of their offers to advertisers of micro-targeting and measuring of engagement (e.g. clicks and likes).

It is an old adage in advertising that men hate to be persuaded but women don't mind: there is a stereotypical association of masculinity with 'knowing your own mind'. Similarly, older people are considered more loyal to their existing brand preferences, so less useful to advertisers than younger people, whose brand preferences might not yet be so set.

For soft drink advertising it is possible that key factors such as parenthood and health awareness might lead to greater resistance to the advertising messages. For male grooming product advertising, such as Old Spice, it may be that different kinds of expression of masculinity linked to age or class or region or sexuality may play a major role. In charity advertising it may be that attitudes to social issues such as 'tough' and 'tender' orientations are key in audience interpretations, as will be proximity to people suffering from problems linked to the charity's cause.

> **Revision activity**
>
> Practise analysing how advertisements for charities and for consumer brands try to position their audiences. Note how far the positioning strategy is similar and different for these two types of advertisements.

Now test yourself

TESTED

1 Which of the three set product advertisements makes the least claim to realism?
2 Which social and cultural contexts have influenced the representations in the Old Spice advertisement?
3 Are positive or negative stereotypes most common in advertising? Explain why.
4 Which groups are under-represented in advertising, according to research?
5 What is the key ideology expressed in brand advertising?

Answers on p. 206

Magazines

For this section you will need to be able to either:
- analyse the media language and representations in an unseen front cover from *The Big Issue* magazine, or
- explain how magazines use media language and/or representation using the two *Big Issue* front covers you have studied as examples.

We shall use two front covers as examples.

The Martin Luther King cover (2–8 April 2018) – referred to as 'MLK'

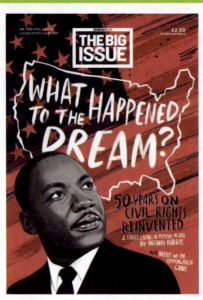

Figure 1.8 *The Big Issue*, **Martin Luther King cover, 2–8 April 2018**

Cover lines:
- 50 years on: civil rights reinvented & street living in Memphis in 2018 by Antonio Harris
- Plus Brexit and the Commonwealth gains [a pun on the Commonwealth Games that were then starting]

The David Tennant cover (19–25 February 2018) – referred to as 'DT'

Figure 1.9 *The Big Issue*, **David Tennant cover, 19–25 February 2018**

Cover lines:
- Meghan and Harry: coffee with *The Big Issue*
- *The Shape of Water* & a history of interspecies love [the film about a woman falling in love with an amphibian]
- A guide to Doggerland [about Dogger Bank in the North Sea]

Exam tip

You may be using two different front covers as your set products, but also practise analysing as many different front covers as possible in case an unseen front cover comes up to analyse in Question 6. You can refer to these covers, as examples, in Question 5 on magazines too.

Magazines: media language

Semiotics: combining media language elements

When analysing unseen front covers, you may wish to consider:

- layout (including the masthead, sell line, cover lines and cover image)
- typography
- image
- colour
- language use.

The Big Issue is unusual in its media language in that the front cover does not follow a house style as faithfully as more mainstream magazines. Layout varies from one edition to the next, though all front covers tend to the uncluttered with either one cover image or a montage with perhaps only three (MLK) or four (DT) cover lines. The masthead migrates across the top of the page from top left (DT) to centralised (MLK) to top right. It switches from white on background (DT and MLK) to black on white. Background colours vary from issue to issue, though tend to be fairly bright saturated colours as in the orange and red of our two examples. The typography, though usually sans-serif, again changes dramatically, as can be seen in the contrast between the retro connotations of the capitalised handwritten font of MLK and the more conventional font for DT. These variations connote idiosyncrasy, liveliness and a lack of pretension.

The masthead's capitals connote a no-nonsense solidity and political commitment, as does the sell line: 'A HAND UP NOT A HANDOUT' (top left). The lack of glamour extends to the photograph of David Tennant, which appears to have been shot using a single flash rather than professional lighting. By contrast, the stylised monochrome image of Martin Luther King connotes both the man's saintly cultural status and evokes the period of his death in 1968. Both covers also introduce a small element of humour to lighten the mix – the pun about the Commonwealth gains in the MLK cover, the cheeky reference to interspecies love in the DT cover.

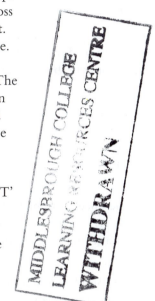

Genres and magazines

Magazines are categorised by audience as much as by genre. While there are clear genres of magazines such as consumer magazines, trade journals and scholarly journals, consumer magazines are often displayed by audience gender and publication frequency (women's weeklies, women's monthlies, etc.) rather than by genre.

The Big Issue is highly unusual in being defined by its distribution method: street sales by vendors. Thus, though it shares some content and style conventions of more mainstream magazines – especially lifestyle magazines, political magazines and entertainment magazines – it is free to challenge these and does not need to rely on being recognisable on retailers' shelves. This allows it to move its masthead around, not carry a barcode and completely change the style of front cover from one issue to the next. It still retains basic magazine conventions – a cover image, cover lines, a masthead, a sell line and date line, but its content is hybrid and unpredictable.

The David Tennant issue, for example, reflects how celebrities feature prominently in lifestyle or entertainment magazines. The Martin Luther King cover, on the other hand, reflects the presentation of issues in political magazines.

Media language and technology in magazines

Print technology offers the opportunity for the front cover to use visual impact to sell the magazine. A print front cover is generally simpler, less detailed and more coherent than a website home page, for example, with a clearly framed layout in which all the graphic design elements can be controlled. This enables the two front covers on page 90 to offer strikingly different designs – the retro feel of *The Big Issue* MLK cover contrasting with the quasi-documentary sparseness of the DT cover.

The layout of both front pages is dominated by the image, using print's advantage in allowing the image to be scrutinised and, if required, contain dense detail, as in some of the montage front covers celebrating street vendors.

Intertextuality in magazine media language

Both *Big Issue* front covers are intertextual, in order to quickly suggest a world of content to be discovered within its pages, to connote wit and sophistication, to connote shared experience with the audience, to flatter the audience.

The MLK cover does not make direct reference to other media products, but the image used suggests a media representation of the man – King as a cultural product as much as a real person, a product whose positive connotations of highly moral political activism the magazine might appropriate.

The DT cover references two media products directly:
- '*The Shape of Water*' – a newly released film
- 'The Doctor' – a reference to Tennant's role as Doctor Who on the BBC.

Both products are considered famous enough to require no explanation, suggesting a shared experience with a culturally aware audience and valuing both products culturally.

Viewpoints and ideologies in media language

The MLK cover uses media language via the dominant image of King and his dream to express support for his battle for civil rights and to question whether his legacy has been honoured. *The Big Issue* is rooted in campaigning, but also needs to appeal to as wide an audience as possible in order to support its vendors. So the choice of Martin Luther King (this was the fiftieth anniversary of his death) to depict the issue of civil rights is perhaps because of relative lack of controversy surrounding him. He is posed as if looking into the future with confidence, juxtaposed with symbols of America, next to language that uses a rhetorical question ('What happened to the dream?'), referencing his most famous speech. This almost religious imagery, representing King as a secular saint, further suggests that his righteous battle has not yet been won. This media language suggests both anti-racism and individualism – the former in the reference accorded to King, the latter in the focus of the cover layout on one man.

The DT cover incorporates individualism in its focus on the star individual. The media language suggests an almost casual acquaintance with members of the royal family ('Meghan and Harry: coffee with

Revision activity

Access the magazine archive at **www.bigissue.com/magazines** and find other examples of front covers that use intertextuality. For example, Issue 1258 from May–June 2017 references the cover of the 1960s Beatles album *Sergeant Pepper* in its design concept, though the cover makes no other reference to the album.

Exam tip

You may wish to refer to the ideology toolkit on page 14 under Questions 1 and 2 for analysis of unseen extracts from *The Big Issue*.

The Big Issue'), which connotes both a recognition and approval of these royals but also a lack of deference.

Media language and media contexts

Magazines commonly reflect **celebrity culture**, the influence of which can be seen in the layout of both *Big Issue* front covers. King is a celebrity political activist whose face is instantly recognisable; Tennant is a celebrity actor.

Magazines, such as this, that engage with current affairs, will reflect **political contexts**, especially political debates about the issue of homelessness. In the MLK front cover, the political authority given to the memory of Martin Luther King because of his commitment to non-violent protest is reflected in both the use of his image and the language chosen to discuss civil rights.

Now test yourself

TESTED

1 How can *The Big Issue* have a more varied front cover design than most magazines?
2 What is *The Big Issue*'s sell line?
3 How are magazines displayed in shops, if not by genre?
4 Which media context do you need to apply to magazines and not music videos and advertisements?

Answers on p. 206

Magazines: media representations

REVISED

Representation: selection and combination

Magazines select and combine to create representations that will reflect their brand and set the appropriate tone for the magazine as a whole. *The Big Issue*, for example, is a brand with a mixed tone. Its pitch to advertisers (**www.bigissue.com/advertising**) states that it offers 'provocative, independent journalism' and 'high-profile exclusive interviews' with celebrities.

The MLK cover, for example, chooses to combine icons of America – the stars and stripes and the outline of mainland USA – with a stylised image of Martin Luther King and a reference to his most famous inspirational speech from the 1960s. It positions the issue of civil rights in contemporary America within the context of a long political struggle. This suggests solidarity with civil rights protestors, an affiliation with the less powerful in society and a thoughtful, historically informed view of current events. All of this chimes nicely with the values of *The Big Issue* as a brand – 'to dismantle poverty by creating opportunity' (**www.bigissue. com/about**).

The DT cover chooses to combine an apparently unstaged photograph of a famous actor with language suggesting his vulnerability. This suggests both a conventional interest in the culture and entertainment industries and a concern with the authentic person behind the glossy appearances. Similarly, the magazine boasts of its association with royalty but does so in a down-to-earth way – 'Meghan and Harry: coffee with *The Big Issue*' – that avoids suggesting fawning over the monarchy.

Magazines: realism and constructing reality

Magazines are usually held to lower standards of realism than newspapers, depending on their genre, but magazines such as *The Big Issue* are governed by the professional ethics of journalism and aim to provide a truthful portrait of the world. *The Big Issue* has a slightly unusual perspective, often assuming the point of view of the homeless, as in the article linking Martin Luther King's quest for civil rights with the issue of street living today in the town where he was assassinated (Memphis). The magazine may well claim that this offers an extra dose of realism to its representations. The two other articles promoted by cover lines – on Brexit and the Commonwealth – both represent real-life issues raised by political debate on the one hand, and the Commonwealth Games, on the other.

The celebrity orientation of the David Tenant cover carries fewer claims to realism, but the seriousness of the magazine's approach is signified by a focus on the personal difficulties of fame. The cover lines do also include one referencing an informative article about Dogger Bank as well as two more entertainment-/celebrity-centred articles.

Social, cultural and political contexts

The front covers of magazines are like adverts for the magazine, so in the same way as with advertising they tend to reflect the influence of **consumerism**. This is particularly true of lifestyle magazines, where images and descriptions of lifestyles reflect our consumer society's ideals of a 'good life'. This is perhaps less true of *The Big Issue* branding, but some of its front covers do cover lifestyle issues such as Issue 1300's cover: 'How to be happy: Your essential guide in a world gone wrong'. However, even here a serious **political context** is referenced as the graphic includes a representation of North Korean intercontinental missiles to suggest a 'world gone wrong'.

The Big Issue exists to highlight and alleviate homelessness and poverty in what it sees as a **political context** in which neither are adequately addressed. Those who sleep on the streets have little power or status, so the magazine deliberately celebrates their individuality and achievements. In doing so, it hopes to challenge and shape public perceptions.

Celebrity culture is a major influence on the representation of David Tennant and Martin Luther King in the two covers sampled. The covers expect the audience to recognise and understand the cultural role of these two figures without explanation as they are both global celebrities.

Multiculturalism has influenced the representation of Martin Luther King insofar as the cover expects its audience to adopt the perspective of people of colour without difficulty. Liberal news sources in the 1960s would also have covered the events sympathetically, but from a far Whiter perspective.

Stereotyping in magazines

Front covers of magazines need to communicate messages rapidly so often resort to stereotyping. *The Big Issue* is less likely to need to use this tactic due to the way it is sold, but it is unlikely that any front cover could avoid stereotyping entirely.

The sell line on *The Big Issue* – 'A hand up not a hand out' – replaces the negative stereotypes of the 'hand out' (either as patronising charity

> **Exam tip**
>
> There is little evidence in two front covers of the impact of **feminism** or changing attitudes to **sexualities**, but these may influence unseen front covers you may be asked to analyse in the exam.

> **Revision activity**
>
> Access the magazine archive at **www.bigissue. com/magazines** and find examples of front covers that do reflect different contexts. For example, Issue 1293 celebrates 'A Suffragette Century' and issue 1279 featured the out gay musician George Michael.

or welfare for 'scroungers') with the positive stereotype of the 'hand up', suggesting aspiration and achievement.

The MLK cover uses positive stereotypes of Martin Luther King and the civil rights movement to signify the 'dream' of racial and ethnic equality. The images of America used – the stars and stripes, the outline of mainland USA – both activate stereotypes of America (seeing itself as the patriotic land of freedom), and Martin Luther King's far-seeing pose suggests positive stereotypes of political leadership.

The DT cover references a positive stereotype of Doctor Who as a culturally significant character role and of Harry as the caring prince.

Under-represented or misrepresented groups

The representation of homeless people and the issue of street living in *The Big Issue* is a deliberate attempt to remedy a systematic under-representation in the mainstream media. The magazine encourages writing by homeless people to provide a rare example of self-representation of this group, which acts to correct misrepresentation. At the same time, the magazine juxtaposes such representations with mainstream representations of celebrities from the world of entertainment. Such a juxtaposition further counters the representation of homeless people as 'outsiders' lacking dignity and self-respect by associating them with these more culturally central and successful people. For example, the MLK cover links the man's message about civil rights to the issue of street living in Memphis and the DT cover links homelessness to royalty in the cover line about Prince Harry.

Both these covers we have analysed feature men. A quick survey of the last 40 editions, in April 2018, shows that 18 feature men only on the cover and two feature women only, suggesting under-representation of women compared to men. The MLK cover is one of only two covers to feature a person of colour as the sole cover image, again suggesting under-representation of ethnic minority groups.

Discourses, ideologies and audience positioning

The MLK *Big Issue* cover positions the audience as concerned about political issues and current affairs, knowledgeable about King and the civil rights movement and sympathetic to their aims. It positions the audience as internationalists.

> **Exam tip**
>
> You may also use the 'ideology toolkit' on page 14 under Questions 1 and 2 to analyse covers.

The DT cover positions the audience as cinephiles (film-lovers), interested in entertainment news and the 'inner life' of actors, especially David Tennant, and familiar with the British royal family. The reference to 'Doggerland' may be deliberately enigmatic, and thus weak in its ideological positioning, in order to entice readers.

Both front covers embody **individualism** as a core ideology as both focus on individuals (though in the case of the MLK cover, this is done to illustrate a social and political issue). The DT cover is more **ethnocentric**, but the fact that the MLK cover is clearly internationalist suggests that this isn't a systematic bias on the part of the magazine.

The under-representation of women on the front covers shown in the figures above may suggest a systematic bias, which might reflect the influence of **sexism**, and the under-representation of people of colour may reflect the influence of **racism**. However, this does not have to be conscious racism and sexism on the part of the publishers, but may reflect either unconscious bias or a reflection of the effects of racial, ethnic and gender inequality in the world that is represented, rather than bias.

Representation: audience response and contexts

The Big Issue magazine can assume some empathy with the plight of the homeless on the part of its audience, but otherwise has to cater for a diverse audience. *Big Issue* readers are probably more likely to be left-wing and this is reflected in the tone of the magazine. This means that more right-wing readers might take exception to the representations and the magazine is less likely to find agreement among the politically apathetic.

The entertainment focus of *The Big Issue* is on popular entertainment, especially film and television. So cultural conservatives who value high culture over popular culture may reject these messages.

Now test yourself

TESTED

1 What is the key value of *The Big Issue*?
2 What is *The Big Issue*'s claim to realism?
3 How does *The Big Issue* address the misrepresentation and under-representation of homeless people?
4 Which groups are under-represented on *Big Issue* front covers?
5 Which groups are likely to interpret the representations in *The Big Issue* in an oppositional way?

Answers on p. 206

Exam practice

Try answering exam practice Questions 5 and 6 on pages 61 and 62 and compare your answers to the sample answers at the end of this guide.

ONLINE

How to prepare for the exam

Revise how media language and representations are used (and learn examples from the set products you have studied) in:
- advertising and marketing
- music videos
- magazines.

Practise analysing media language and representation in a range of examples of:
- soft drink adverts
- charity adverts
- male grooming product adverts
- *The Big Issue* front covers.

You should also practise comparing other adverts you have analysed to the three set product adverts.

Practise comparing and contrasting the media language and representations using detailed examples for the two music video set products you have studied.

What you have to do

This section of the exam asks two questions on your study of media industries and audiences across three media forms:

1 radio
2 video games
3 film (industries only).

Which areas of the theoretical framework must I study?	
Radio	Media industries Audiences Economic, political and cultural contexts
Video games	Media industries Audiences Economic and social contexts
Film	Media industries Economic and historical contexts

The two questions in Section A will be as follows:

Q1	15 marks	This will be a knowledge and understanding question about one of the three media forms you study for this section: ● radio ● video games ● film. It will probably include the influence of media contexts on this media form. This essay should take about 25 minutes to plan and write.
Q2	15 marks	This will be a knowledge and understanding question about one of the three media forms you have studied for this section: ● radio ● video games ● film. This essay should take about 25 minutes to plan and write.

Questions 1 and 2

What these questions involve

The following information is based on the specimen assessment materials produced by OCR. These are likely to be the format of exam questions in the live exam papers, but OCR reserves the right to make changes to this format if this turns out to be necessary.

These questions are knowledge and understanding questions on one of the three set media forms. You are likely to be instructed to give particular examples from the set products you have studied:

● *The BBC Radio 1 Breakfast Show* for radio
● *Minecraft* for video games
● the two *Jungle Book* films from 1967 and 2016 for film.

Both questions will cover media industries or audience, plus one of the questions, probably Question 1, will ask for the influence of media contexts on these.

Timing

Questions 1 and 2 will be worth 15 marks, so you should spend about 25 minutes answering each question.

What the examiner is looking for

In these three exam practice Question 1s, examiners are looking for:
- the accuracy, comprehensiveness and detail of your knowledge and understanding of the media form
- the clarity and precision of your explanation
- the detail and accuracy of your references to the set product(s)
- the accuracy, comprehensiveness and detail of your knowledge and understanding of a range of contexts and their influence.

There is nothing in the mark scheme to say that you *must* cover all the contexts mentioned in the question, but the term 'range' suggests you should attempt them all, though they don't have to be covered equally.

Exam practice

Question 1

Explain why popular music radio programmes struggle to gain recognition as Public Service Broadcasting. Refer to *The BBC Radio 1 Breakfast Show* to support your answer.

In your answer you must:
- explain how political, cultural and economic contexts influence the status of popular radio music programming. [15]

Question 1

Explain how the production and distribution of major Hollywood films have changed since the 1960s. Refer to the two versions of *The Jungle Book* to support your answer.

In your answer you must:
- explain how historical and economic contexts influence the production and distribution of major Hollywood films. [15]

Question 1

Explain how producers target, reach and engage audiences for video games through content and marketing. Refer to *Minecraft* to support your answer.

In your answer you must:
- explain how social and economic contexts influence how producers target, reach and engage audiences for video games. [15]

Sample answers available online

In the following three exam practice Question 2, examiners are looking for:

- the accuracy, comprehensiveness and detail of your knowledge and understanding of industries for the media form

- the clarity and precision and balance of your explanation
- the detail and accuracy of your references to the set product.

Exam practice

Question 2

Explain the impact of digitally convergent media platforms on video games production, distribution and consumption. Refer to *Minecraft* to support your answer.   [15]

Question 2

Explain how different audiences use radio differently. Refer to *The BBC Radio 1 Breakfast Show* to support your answer.   [15]

Question 2

Explain the effect of individual producers on films. Refer to the two versions of *The Jungle Book* to support your answer.   [15]

Sample answers available online

ONLINE

Recommended revision for this question

REVISED

For media **industries** you should know:
- how the media form is shaped by how it is **produced, distributed and circulated**
- the ownership and control of the media form
- economic factors such as funding for the media form
- how industries maintain audiences nationally and globally
- the impact of technological change, especially digital **convergent media platforms**, on the media form
- the role of regulation in the media form and the impact of digital technologies on regulation
- the effect of individual producers on the media form.

For media **audiences** you should know:
- how audiences are categorised by industries
- how producers target, attract, reach, address and potentially construct audiences through content and marketing
- the interrelationship between media technologies and consumption and response
- how audiences interpret the media form, interact with the media form, and can be actively involved in production
- the way in which different interpretations reflect social (for video games) and cultural (for radio) circumstances
- the different ways audiences defined by **demographics**, identity and **cultural capital** use the media form
- the different needs of mass and specialised audiences and their significance to the media form
- how specialised audiences can be reached through different technologies and platforms, nationally and globally.

Production, distribution and circulation: Production is the making of the product, distribution is getting the product to the retailer, circulation is how the product is consumed.

Convergent media platforms: Platforms, such as websites, that enable audiences to access previously distinct media forms (e.g. film, television, radio, newspapers, magazines).

Demographics: Measuring audiences in terms of social characteristics, such as age, gender, class, region, nation, race and ethnicity.

Cultural capital: Capital is wealth you can invest to make more money. Cultural capital refers to aspects of culture such as education that help a person progress in society. Media literacy (a knowledge and understanding of media forms) is part of cultural capital in modern society.

For media **contexts** you should know:

- social contexts: how **video games** reflect their society – the effects of social inequalities and differences on audiences and producers
- cultural contexts: how **radio** producers and audiences are influenced by the culture – the way of life, the arts and the popular culture – and cultural differences
- political contexts: the political system and forces within which **radio** operates and which it influences, particularly the effect of these on ownership and control and regulation
- economic contexts: the influence of the economic system on **radio**, **video games** and **film**, including on funding, the profit motive and competition between producers
- historical contexts: how **film** reflects its historical period in its production by media industries.

Exam tip

These points have been taken from the subject content on pages 23–27 of the specification but condensed for clarity. Examiners may write their questions using the same wording to the subject content. So please read through the subject content to check that you understand all the wording as well as revising the content below.

Film

Film: media industries

REVISED ☐

Film production, distribution and circulation

The processes production, distribution and circulation are known as production, distribution and exhibition in the film industry and are undertaken by separate companies. Films are usually produced by small production companies that may be so short-lived as to exist only to produce one film. Film distributors include the major Hollywood studios – the main power-brokers in the film industry. They often finance the films and they are responsible for marketing films and distributing them to cinemas. They are the most powerful agents in the chain as, without a distribution deal, it is very difficult to get a film financed. Traditionally, the exhibitors are the cinema chains, though DVD sales, television rights and streaming are alternative sources of revenue. Cinema exhibition is still important for gaining some of the prestige associated with film, such as film reviews and eligibility for film awards, even if a film is shown in only one or two cinemas. At one time the Hollywood studios were **vertically integrated** – owning the whole process from production studios, through film distribution to the cinemas themselves. This was outlawed in the USA in 1948.

The two versions of *The Jungle Book* were both produced and distributed by the Hollywood studios. The 2016 film was distributed by Buena Vista, the distribution arm of The Walt Disney Company; the 1967 film was produced by Walt Disney Productions, and the 2016 film by Walt Disney Pictures (the live-action branch of the studio). However, the visual effects for the animals and landscapes in the 2016 film were outsourced mostly to MPC, a British visual effects house.

Film is increasingly divided into two sectors: blockbusters and art house. The 1967 *Jungle Book* was produced before the advent of the blockbuster, though films were then rated in terms of their prestige and budget as 'A movies' and 'B movies'. The 2016 *Jungle Book* fits into the blockbuster category with its combination of a $175 million production budget and **saturation distribution**:

- in 4,028 cinemas in the USA (making more than $100 million box office) for the opening weekend

Vertical integration: Where a company owns the supply chain, for example, when Hollywood owned the studios that produced films and the cinemas in which they were exhibited.

More commonly, media conglomerates own companies that make related products such as film, television and video games. Technically, this is horizontal integration, but the principle is the same: to reduce risk by diversifying.

Saturation distribution: Filling all available cinemas simultaneously with a blockbuster film on its opening weekend in order to create a cultural event and crowd out other films.

- in 594 cinemas in the UK (making £10 million box office) for the opening weekend
- simultaneous release worldwide, except in Japan (August) and South Korea (June).

Blockbusters are films that rely on a combination of:
- big budgets
- use of the star system
- lower-risk formats such as franchises (only one non-franchise film has hit the number 1 slot for international box office this century – Disney's *Frozen*)
- extensive advertising using the film's unique selling features (stars, effects, locations, action, etc.)
- targeting a global mass audience in the film's form and content
- saturation distribution (filling a large number of cinema screens simultaneously).

The blockbuster aim is to become a cultural event – as much is spent on promotion as on production in order to ensure a huge opening weekend, trying to make the film a 'must-see'.

Art house cinema consists of films that:
- have smaller budgets (which reduces risk)
- offer character roles that can attract star actors seeking credibility or awards
- have one-off narratives that may be quirky, character-driven or experimental
- rely on reviews and film festival success to generate word of mouth
- target a more **cinephile** audience who are content to make sense of more difficult narratives (including subtitled foreign-language films)
- are mostly distributed to a small number of art house cinemas but may cross over into the mainstream.

> **Cinephile**: A lover of cinema, usually meant as a lover of art house or foreign language film.

Art house films aim to build word of mouth by recommendation from reviews or from audiences, so will usually have a smaller opening in cinemas and hope to be shown in more and more screens as they achieve success.

British film tends to be art house. An interesting contrast is that between the two films about Dunkirk released in 2017. The British film, *Their Finest* (BBC Films), was a character piece about a film company making a propaganda film about Dunkirk. It opened in a respectable number of cinemas and made nearly £1 million on its opening weekend as it was well reviewed, so achieved a degree of crossover success. In the USA, it opened in just four cinemas. It was never distributed to China. The Hollywood blockbuster *Dunkirk* (Warner Bros.) was a war film shot on an epic scale. It opened in more than 600 cinemas in the UK and made more than £10 million in its opening weekend. In the USA, it opened in nearly 4,000 cinemas. It made $50 million in China.

Economic contexts

Six Hollywood studios count as the 'majors' whose films dominate the box office:
1 Disney/Buena Vista
2 Sony/Columbia
3 20th Century Fox
4 Warner Bros.
5 Universal
6 Paramount.

One **mini-major**, Lionsgate, sometimes leapfrogs into the top six.

That these American studios dominate world cinema is a reflection of the economic context of the power of the American economy and its dominance in the entertainment industries. While US cinema is dwarfed by Indian and Chinese cinema in terms of the number of films made, Hollywood dwarfs cinema such as Bollywood in terms of global income.

> **Mini-major**: A Hollywood studio smaller than the big six 'majors' but big enough to compete with them.

Film industries and historical contexts

The increasing separation of art house low-budget and blockbuster high-budget film-making reflects the change brought by the blockbuster film in the 1970s and the development of saturation distribution to multiplex cinemas in the 1980s. At the time of the first *Jungle Book* film in 1967, there was a more gradual gradient from low-budget films to medium-budget to high-budget films and the high-budget films did not dominate cinema exhibition in the way they attempt to do now.

> **Revision activity**
>
> Look up the 'Studios' page under 'Indices' in 'Box Office Mojo' at **www.boxofficemojo. com/** to check whether the big six studios listed above still dominate.

The release strategies for the two versions of *The Jungle Book* reflect historical changes in distribution practices. In contemporary blockbuster-dominated cinema, summer and Christmas are the two key seasons as these are the peak periods for cinema attendance and the aim is to dominate a weekend in one of those key periods. The 1967 *Jungle Book* was released in the middle of October. It would have been released first in the USA then in Europe using the usual strategy of a few copies in major cities which then gradually toured the country in smaller and smaller venues until the audience (or the film stock) gave out. The 2016 *Jungle Book* was released in April, some time before the May opening to the summer season, but in a saturation release where world cinemas were flooded simultaneously.

The 1967 *Jungle Book* made much of its box office by being re-released in 1984 and again in 1990. This re-use of back catalogue has been rendered obsolete by, first, DVD sales and now streaming. Hence the emergent strategy of 're-imagining' old favourites, like remakes of 1960s films such as *The Jungle Book* and *Mary Poppins*. However, some editions of films are still 'vaulted' – taken off the DVD and download market – in order to try to preserve a sense of exclusivity around the product.

The ownership and control of film

We have seen that control of film-making is very much in the hands of the distributors, especially in the case of blockbusters where huge sums of money are being risked on a creative venture that can easily fail. Where art house directors have a track record of completing on time and not losing money on a small budget, there is more possibility of creative control, as was the case with Woody Allen films, for example.

Hollywood cinema is dominated by large media conglomerates. All the big six listed above are owned by global conglomerates. Much art house production is not truly independent but distributed by an art house division of one of the majors (e.g. Fox Searchlight). Big films such as *The Jungle Book* are thus produced on a risk-minimising basis for a global audience. For example, the 1967 film avoided any of the darkness in the original story to produce something light, fun and entertaining. By the time of the remake in 2016 audience tastes, as indicated by box office, seemed to have moved on, allowing an homage to the 1967 original that is slightly darker, but still maintains the Disney brand of family entertainment and profitability.

Indian cinema is a similarly free market to that of the USA, but with smaller budgets comes lower risk, a larger number of productions and less concentration in the hands of global conglomerates. Chinese film production is likely to be more strictly politically controlled, due to the role of the Chinese Communist Party in social institutions. The China Film Group Corporation controls about a third of all distribution in China and has a monopoly on distributing all foreign films (including Hollywood films) in China. Their film, *The Great Wall*, a Chinese/US co-production action film in English starring American actors may be a sign of ambition to access the global market. However, it was not very successful in the USA, though it covered its large production budget in China.

Economic contexts

Ownership and control in the USA and India reflect their economic context of **free market capitalism**: that anyone can set up a business and try to make a profit, driven by the belief that free competition and open markets promote efficiency. In China, by contrast, the monopoly given to The China Film Group Corporation reflects the context in which political control by the Communist Party is considered more important than free markets.

Economic factors such as funding for film

Film-making is a risky business. About nine out of every ten films make a loss. The Hollywood majors survive by operating on a large enough scale that their many losses are offset by large profits on a few films. The success of the 2016 *Jungle Book*, for example, offset the losses that Disney made that year on *The BFG*. Calculating profits is a dark art in Hollywood, but a rough rule of thumb is that a film has to make about two-and-a-half times its production budget to make a profit – this is to take into account the exhibitors' share and the distribution and promotional costs.

Historical contexts and funding

At the time of the 1967 *Jungle Book* there were fewer sources of income for film-makers. Merchandising was one means of increasing income – the *Jungle Book* record narrated the story of the film, included the original songs and achieved gold record status. However, Disney was most heavily reliant on box office for income, hence the strategy of re-releases.

The 1950s had been a disastrous period for cinema, with attendances falling rapidly due to competing forms of entertainment. This continued through to the 1980s. The film industry in this period was unsure whether or not it would survive, so Disney, like many other studios, had diversified into other areas such as television and theme parks.

By the time of the 2016 *Jungle Book*, film had become the prestige brand leader for complex marketing campaigns. These might include merchandising, such as *Jungle Book* clothing and toys, tie-ins such as Subway *Jungle Book* watches, a soundtrack album, and *Jungle Book* video games. DVD release and then downloads provided additional sources of

> **Free market capitalism**: An economic system where the free market delivers most goods and services as commodities (things the consumer pays for). The opposite is socialism, where the state runs the economy. Social democratic states have a mix of free market and state provision.

income for little additional expenditure. **Product placement** has become commonplace in film and this provides a source of income before the film is released. *The Jungle Book* doesn't really lend itself to product placement as brands would intrude, though it does serve to promote its own merchandising. While film is still a risky business, the role of the blockbuster as a global marketing event enables studios to diversify their sources of income to turn a profit.

Film industries and audiences

The main box office globally for the 2016 *Jungle Book* was earned thus:

USA	$364 million	India	$39 million	Japan	$23 million
China	$150 million	France	$28 million	Australia	$23 million
UK	$67 million	Mexico	$24 million	Russia	$20 million

(Table found at BoxOfficeMojo.com)

These figures don't completely reflect the size of the audience, as ticket prices vary by country, but they do show the global audience for blockbusters such as *The Jungle Book*. This success is built on a strategy of developing products with a simple clear narrative, offering a range of relatively undemanding audience pleasures, using cutting-edge technology that appeals to **technophiles**, offering a mix of the familiar and the novel, marketed with an emphasis on action elements that work well with a global audience.

Technophiles: Lovers of technology and shiny machines.

Exam tip

There is no need to learn these sales statistics – they are presented here to illustrate the global reach of Hollywood films.

The 2016 film was targeted at a variety of audiences, unlike the 1967 version which was primarily aimed at a family audience. The trailer for the 1967 version concentrates on the song and dance routines, humour, the warm characterisation of Baloo and of Bagheera and Baloo's double act, and the cavalcade of mostly comic characters. The 2016 trailers, by contrast, emphasise more adult pleasures. The **teaser trailer** focuses on the photorealist mise-en-scène, enigma (the voiceover starts by asking 'Are you alone out here?'), the action credentials of the studio and the director, conflict and spectacle and the star voice cast. The soundtrack follows the conventions of action films, not musical comedies. The only direct reference to the original film comes right at the end, when the voiceover turns out to be Kaa, the snake, who instructs Mowgli to 'Trust in me', a sinister reworking of the original character that suggests both novelty and continuity for older fans of the original. (This trailer can be found at: www.youtube.com/watch?v=HcgJRQWxKnw.) Later trailers added more characterisation and occasional humour, plus some reference to the song 'The Bare Necessities', but otherwise followed a similar strategy. This stress on action elements attracted a larger male audience than might be expected for the remake of a family film.

Teaser trailer: A trailer released early in the marketing campaign to elicit audience curiosity about a film.

The merchandising for the 1967 film, which included branded rides at Disney Theme Parks, was primarily aimed at children. The merchandising for the 2016 film, which included clothing from the designer Kenzo and an offer on treehouses from Airbnb, was aimed at a wider audience.

Figure 2.1 Film poster for the 1967 *Jungle Book* film

Figure 2.2 Film poster for the 2016 *Jungle Book* film

Historical economic contexts

The 2016 *Jungle Book* earned a higher proportion of its box office outside the US market (about two-thirds) than the 1967 version, illustrating the growth of globalisation in the intervening period. This was despite the fact that the 1967 version was more successful than the 2016 version when inflation in ticket prices is taken into account (the 1967 version comes number 32 in the all-time US sales chart – adjusted for inflation – where the 2016 version comes number 168).

The marketing for the contemporary film heavily involves social media, which did not exist in the 1960s. The 2016 *Jungle Book* used Facebook, Twitter and Instagram accounts to create a sense of a relationship between the film and its audience and to build up anticipation for the opening weekend, releasing teasers and 'making of' photos and videos in the months before the release. Disney uploaded an interactive film poster on Snapchat and users could apply a *Jungle Book* lens to turn their photos into images of Kaa, the snake.

The marketing for the 2016 film used television in a way that the 1967 film would not have done, as trailers in the 1960s were restricted to cinemas. This shows the historical development of a cross-media promotional strategy where paid television advertising and **covert promotion** on television (e.g. coverage of premieres and interviews with stars on chat shows) are a routine part of film distribution.

> **Covert promotion**: Promotion that aims to be within media products (unlike advertising, which is separate to the product). Includes sponsorship, product placement and promotional activities.

> **Revision activity**
>
> Make brief notes on how these two film posters reflect the different promotional strategies for the two films.

> **Revision activity**
>
> Watch the trailers for the 1967 and 2016 films and note how they target audiences. Explore examples of merchandising for both films.

The impact of technological change on film

Technological change has influenced all three of film production, distribution and exhibition.

Film production has been transformed by the development of visual effects, without which the mise-en-scène of the 2016 *Jungle Book* would not have been possible. The film was shot with the live actor and the animals added later. The scenes were shot in motion capture, then small sections of the sets were constructed with props and blue screen for the live action, using puppets or actors as the animal stand-ins – this could be edited live into the pre-visualised computer-generated imagery (CGI) set and the motion capture animals so the director could see a rough version of the finished product. Then the footage went into post-production for the fine-detail visual effects work.

Film distribution has been transformed by digital distribution. Contemporary film can be downloaded by the cinema, thus avoiding the expense of producing and sending out physical copies of the film. The advent of streaming means that some small independent films are simultaneously released on exhibition in one or two art house cinemas and as downloads. The marketing of films has been aided by digital convergence, as more opportunities now exist to create awareness of upcoming films via social media, film websites and the opportunities for fans to create online communities and their own versions of film products.

Exhibition has been changed by digital distribution. Cinemas can now show one-off screenings: for example, senior citizen screenings of acclaimed recent films that have finished their exhibition run (or never had one in that chain) are brought back for another screening. Theatre and opera can be streamed live – these events can reach the top ten for box office in the week they are shown. Blockbusters are available to all cinemas.

> **Revision activity**
>
> Look at local cinema listings and note examples of one-off screenings and live events.

Technologies such as IMAX and high-quality digital sound enable cinemas to offer a more immersive experience in order to compete with television and digital devices. Older attractions such as 3D have been reinvigorated with digital projection. The combination of 3D and talking animals in the 2016 *Jungle Book* was reportedly a major selling point in the Chinese market.

Historical technology context

None of the production CGI was possible in 1967. Computers were hugely expensive, unreliable and not used in film. The 1967 *Jungle Book* used copies of hand-drawn pictures on transparent cels. The studio used a multiplane camera to shoot a greater number of cels at different distances from the camera to create a more 3D effect than previously possible. The soundtrack is mono, as was common in the mid-1960s, as stereo sound was considered a luxury.

Distribution was slower in the 1960s. Expensive copies of the master film were made and physically delivered to the cinema. Fewer copies of the film were available and hence the slower roll-out across the country. Cinemas in the 1960s were old movie-palaces designed to hold large audiences for one film at a time, not the multiplexes of today. Audiences relied on cinema exhibition to see films – there was a long delay before they were available on television and, unlike today, there were no other outlets.

> **Revision activity**
>
> Ask people over 60 about their experience of cinema in the 1960s.

Regulation in the film industry

Film is a self-regulating medium. In order to avoid state regulation the film industry has policed itself. In the USA, self-regulation originally took the form of a production code that banned the representation of 'sex perversion' or profanity or nudity among other things. This code was still in force in the mid-1960s when the first *Jungle Book* was released, but largely ignored, so was replaced in 1968 by the Motion Picture Association of America (MPAA) film rating system. Under this system the 1967 *Jungle Book* on re-release was granted a G certificate, meaning it was suitable for 'General audiences' – all ages admitted. The 2016 *Jungle Book* earned a PG certificate for 'Parental guidance suggested' due to its violent action scenes and darker tone.

Certification in Britain is very similar and run by the British Board of Film Classification (BBFC). The 1967 film was a U certificate – suitable for all – and the 2016 film a PG. PG films may not be suitable for some children under 8 years of age.

Self-regulation relies on cinemas adhering to the age certification. For videos and DVDs, parents were expected to police the age limits. Individual consumption with streaming of films, possibly to mobile devices, renders this problematic.

Historical contexts

The production code embodied anxieties and intolerances from a previous historical period (the 1920s and 1930s) which would be considered ludicrous or offensive now. For example, the ban on depiction of miscegenation – a racist term for sexual relationships between the different 'races' – reflects a more racist society than that today. Similarly, the ban on ridiculing the clergy reflects a much more deferential and clerical society. The care to be taken over 'excessive or lustful kissing' meant that closed-mouth kissing was the order of the day in classic Hollywood in what would now be seen as a break with **realism**. On the other hand, smoking indoors around children was considered perfectly normal, though shockingly bad practice today.

The BBFC regularly surveys the public to discover what they find objectionable and wish to keep from children, as these attitudes change gradually over time and so do the boundaries between the certificates.

Economic contexts

The rising importance of the Chinese film market means that avoiding state censorship in China is increasingly important. The producers of the film *Red Dawn*, for example, changed the nationality of their villains from Chinese to North Koreans by removing dialogue and using visual effects to change flags, after criticism by a Chinese state-run newspaper.

The effect of individual producers on film

Film, or the 'motion picture *arts*', is still considered an art form and an arena for expression of the vision of the creators as well as a commercial product. For example, the 1967 *Jungle Book* is very much the product of Walt Disney himself (very few people could name the director). At the time, Disney was concerned about the drop in quality of his studio's animated films; the previous feature, *The Sword in the Stone*, was rather lacklustre and poorly received. He rejected the initial script for *The Jungle*

Realism: Realism is the set of conventions by which audiences accept a representation as 'real' or 'realistic'. If an Ancient Roman character in a period drama used a mobile phone this would break the rules of realism. If she or he spoke in English, a language not yet invented in Ancient Roman times, this would not break the rules. This suggests that, as with language or genre, the rules of realism are arbitrary, unwritten, and only noticed when broken. There are different sets of rules for different genres and for different media forms, and there are many different forms of realism. A very expressionist supernatural horror media product should still have emotional realism, for example, and should obey its own internal rules.

Revision activity

Check the BBFC website at **www.bbfc.co.uk** for any results of consultations on age ratings.

Book, changed the production team and took creative control. Disney cast and recorded the voices first – against standard industry practice – so that the characters and animations would reflect the personalities of the voice cast. Phil Harris, the voice of Baloo the bear, was so successful that his character became the film's co-star from what was at first a minor role. Walt Disney was reportedly responsible for the film's ending, where our boy hero sees a little girl and follows her back to the man-village.

Directors normally have less directorial control over a blockbuster film than they might over an art house project. The 2016 *Jungle Book* was directed by Jon Favreau who has a track record of directing blockbusters such as *Iron Man* with a certain flair that might derive from his independent film days (he first became famous for *Swingers*, which he wrote and in which he co-starred). He also has a credit as a producer, which gives him more decision-making powers. However, huge action films with extensive visual effects are essentially collaborative efforts.

Historical contexts

Disney's role in the 1967 film is perhaps the last gasp of the old-style studio head – the mogul – from the classic Hollywood era, when the studios controlled all aspects of production. As the Hollywood studios have become part of large media conglomerates the role of the studio head has changed and none is as famous as the old studio moguls. Walt Disney's rather conservative vision of the world has been replaced as Disney films now reflect multiculturalism (e.g. *Black Panther* or *Coco*), the impact of feminism (e.g. *Moana* or *Queen of Katwe*), and even changing attitudes to sexualities (e.g. the 2017 *Beauty and the Beast*).

Now test yourself
TESTED

1 For film, you study media industries and economic and historical contexts only. True or false?
2 In how many cinemas did the 2016 *Jungle Book* show in its opening weekend?
3 Name three features of a blockbuster film.
4 Name the key economic context of Hollywood film production.
5 Name the second largest national box office for the 2016 *Jungle Book* after the USA.
6 Explain how the 2016 *Jungle Book* was aimed at an older audience than the 1967 version.
7 Give one example of how changing technology has affected each of the following: film production, distribution and exhibition.
8 State the age rating of the two *Jungle Book* films.

Answers on p. 206

Video games

Video games: media industries
REVISED

Game production, distribution and circulation

The video games industry has production, distribution and circulation phases. Like the film industry, video game publishers, who market and distribute video games, were until recently the most powerful agents in the process, often producing the games in-house or financing and project managing the development of games by specialist production companies. Traditional retail sales in specialist shops have declined with the increase in online distribution gaming and free online gaming, especially on mobile phones. About one-quarter of the UK games market consists of physical games, about three-quarters are digital. The development of online retailers such as Apple's App store has weakened the power of publishers as developers can now upload direct to the App store. Mobile gaming is now the largest sector of the video games industry and the fastest growing.

The video games industry, like the film industry, is increasingly dominated by high-budget productions from mainstream producers that attempt to minimise the risk entailed by developing franchises and playing safe with content, which was traditionally designed to appeal to a core audience of young men. These games are developed by huge teams and are sold with high-budget and extensive marketing to mainstream gamers.

At the same time, the development of game design technology has allowed an independent sector to spring up, producing low-budget games with smaller teams that can afford to take more creative risks. For example, the 2018 Bafta video games award for best game went to *What Remains of Edith Finch*, a game with a female protagonist that explores narrative and characterisation, developed by small Californian studio Giant Sparrow.

Minecraft falls in between these two types of video games industries. It was developed by the independent Swedish company Mojang in 2009; but the company was taken over by Microsoft in 2014, due mostly to the success of *Minecraft,* which would give Microsoft access to a large audience. However, the game still retains elements of its independent origins:

- Although the sound and visuals have become much more sophisticated over time, the game retains an old-fashioned 'blocky' feel, which reflects its low-budget origins, which audiences appear to find comforting.
- The opportunity for user-generated modifications remains, which has been an important part of the success of the game and also reflects its indie roots in its choice of **open source software**. Mojang has recognised the importance of these 'mods' by creating 'The Marketplace', an in-game catalogue of user-generated content.
- The **sandbox** feature of the game, which allows players to log in and create a virtual world out of cubes, was considered not commercially viable until it turned out to be so.

Open source software: Software whose underlying code is published so it is available to be used and modified by others, promoting free exchange and participation.

Sandbox video game: An open-world game that enables the players to roam and create the virtual world at will rather than following a narrative progression set by the game.

In 2011, before the official launch, *Minecraft* had 16 million registered users and 4 million purchases, a popularity based on word of mouth as Mojang did not advertise. This success led to versions for mobiles (*Minecraft pocket edition*) in 2011, for Xbox consoles in 2012 (with multiplayer split screen), PlayStation in 2013, Nintendo in 2015, and 'cross play' in 2017, which allowed players using different consoles to play together. By early 2018, more than 144 million copies had been sold across all platforms, making it the second best-selling video game of all time. In its development *Minecraft* has become more mainstream, with modern versions such as 'Story Mode' following more mainstream game conventions such as narrative and tutorials on how to play the game.

Economic context

The tendency to large-scale production of commodities, as with the mainstream video games, is typical of free-market capitalist economies, as is the challenge to established companies by new and more dynamic companies. This leads to a constant tension between control of production by large companies and the wrestling away of this control by new competitors, who may in turn be bought up by the large conglomerates.

The ownership and control of video games

The relative novelty and rapid growth of the video games industry means that ownership is not as concentrated in the hands of a few multinational media conglomerates as it is in film, for example. The following list of the top video game publishers in 2017 shows the dominance of some diversified conglomerates, such as Tencent and Sony, but also the presence of companies specialising in video games such as Activision Blizzard and EA.

Publisher	Nationality	Publisher	Nationality
1 Tencent	China	**7** EA	USA
2 Sony	USA/Japan	**8** Google	USA
3 Activision Blizzard	USA	**9** Nintendo	Japan
4 Microsoft	USA	**10** Bandai Namco	Japan
5 Apple	USA	**11** Nexon	S. Korea
6 Netease	China	**12** Netmarble	S. Korea

Note that Tencent is growing rapidly and now dominates the game industry, with revenues roughly double those of its nearest rival, Sony.

Economic and social contexts

The video game industry is globalised, as can be seen from the countries on the above list. It is dominated by companies from the world's largest economies, the USA and China. Japan and South Korea also feature on the list as developed countries where gaming culture developed rapidly.

China is the world's most populous digital market and has the protection afforded by state censorship through the so-called Great Firewall – laws and technology to control the domestic internet and block some foreign websites. This has meant no competition from Facebook, Google, Twitter and Netflix, which has helped Tencent grow so that it is now the world's fifth largest company with 40 per cent of its income coming from gaming.

Economic factors such as funding for video games

Early video games were funded by the purchase price (and rentals to arcades). While the purchase price is still important to the industry, many online and mobile games are offered to consumers without a purchase price. Ways to monetise these games include:
- subscription
- freemium – players can play for free but pay for premium content
- advertising – seen as too invasive in console games, but more acceptable in free-to-play games
- microtransactions – selling virtual items (such as loot boxes) for small sums of money
- virtual currency – in-game virtual currency can be exchanged with real-world currency
- server-leasing – selling virtual space in the game
- merchandising outside the game
- offer walls – showing players a 'wall' of offers from 'partners' who pay for this access
- offering a game in exchange for a link a to a site – a common strategy
- donations from players, e.g. through PayPal.

Minecraft generates revenue through sale of the game – currently (April 2018) £17.95 for the Java edition for PC or Mac. However, there are some other sources of revenue: subscription to Minecraft Realms, a *Minecraft* film in production, a tie-in with Lego, which produces sets based on areas of the *Minecraft* world, an online merchandise shop on the *Minecraft* website, and a deal for children's books and magazines.

Economic and social contexts

Many internet users have a resistance to paying for content. This is partly due to the social make-up of much of the audience – young people, mostly males – and social expectations: so much of the internet is offering free content and consumer choice that the audience expect it all to be free, but may not mind paying for microtransactions, for example, if they feel they have a choice in the matter. Similarly, audiences object to advertising in paid-for games, but are happy to accept it in free games, presumably as this follows the model of commercial television.

The lack of state-funded video game industries, unlike television, for example, may reflect the novelty of this industry and the low social prestige given to video games as a media form. However, as with the film industry, there is some public support for UK games production. Video Games Tax Relief has been available for qualifying games companies to claim since April 2014. From 2014 to 2017 Video Game Tax Relief has provided £119 million to UK studios.

Video games industries and audiences

Marketing a high-budget video game follows a similar process to that for film. A series of teasers, trailers, adverts, opportunities for fan interaction and publicity stunts try to build up anticipation for the launch day. One way that marketing a game is different is that fans can be offered pre-orders: to buy a game before release in exchange for a guarantee to receive a copy of the game as soon as it is available and some additional reward, such as a special case, a discount on future games, extra downloadable content or an in-game advantage.

Marketing an independent game, as *Minecraft* was initially, is very different. *Minecraft* relied on word of mouth such as audiences sharing their own game footage and modifications ('mods') on web forums and video-sharing sites such as YouTube. These created a sense of ownership as fans could feed back on the game – this feedback was used actively from the start as both the alpha version (the first version, usually tested only by the producers) and the beta version (normally released for testing in the 'real world') were published, as well as a very early version that became known as *Minecraft Classic*.

Social contexts

Video gaming has created a gamer subculture among certain users – people who feel defined by their use of video games. This group is often the subject of moral panics, such as the fear of a link between gaming and violence. These may act to help bond gamers as a group. Most people who play games, however, do not self-identify as video gamers. People who play *Candy Crush* on their mobiles are less likely to identify as gamers than fans of particular games, especially those offering opportunities for fan interaction such as *Minecraft*.

Revision activity

Check the *Minecraft* website at https://minecraft.net/ for any other sources of income you can identify.

Revision activity

View the latest *Minecraft* videos at the 'TeamMojang' YouTube channel and note how the game attempts to maintain an audience.

Access the *Minecraft* wiki and note how fans express their relationship with the game.

Impact of technological change on video games

Video gaming relies on the development of computing but also feeds that development – improved features such as faster CPUs, 3D graphics and sound cards were prompted by the demands of video gaming. Games consoles, though now only a small part of the market, were crucial in driving take-up of video games. The development of the internet allows, for example, downloadable games (which save on distribution costs), global multiplayer games, monetising of games in play through microtransactions, for example, and fan forums. Smart phones and tablets have been crucial to the mobile games market. Virtual reality is a small but rapidly expanding portion of the video games market, creating new virtual, mixed reality and augmented reality games.

Minecraft used digitally convergent technologies to:
- enable testing of the game by players in the pre-alpha, alpha and beta phases
- enable game play across a range of consoles and mobile devices
- create online communities of *Minecraft* fans via the Minecraft wiki, for example
- encourage mods to the game by using open source software and cataloguing available mods in The Marketplace
- encourage audiences to download the game through cloud servers rather than hard copies, saving distribution costs, by offering downloadable versions some months before hard copies are available
- switch MineCon (the *Minecraft* convention) to live streaming rather than a physical meeting to reach a more global audience (the 2018 event is entitled MineCon Earth)
- set up servers, called Minecraft Realms, run by Mojang for paying users and their chosen friends to play in a more convenient way that is controlled by Mojang – in part a response to piracy.

> **Revision activity**
>
> See if you can add to the list of how *Minecraft* used digitally convergent technologies.

Economic context

The rapid and persistent fall in the cost of computing power is both a cause and effect of these technological developments in gaming.

Regulation in video games

Regulation of video games in the UK is undertaken by the Video Standards Council (VSC) Rating Board. As the designated authority for classifying physical games in the UK the VSC Rating Board must issue a certificate before any non-exempt game can be released.

The VSC Rating Board administers the Pan-European Game Information (PEGI) rating system, which is used in more than 35 countries throughout Europe. In 2012 the PEGI system was incorporated into UK law and the VSC was appointed as the **statutory body** responsible for the age rating of video games in the UK using the PEGI system. Games are rated by minimum age: 3, 7, 12, 16 and 18. The 3 rating means the game is suitable for all. Frightening scenes might put a game into the 7 rating. The 12 rating will be for games with some mild violence, mild swearing or nudity. Realistic violence or sex, swearing, the concept of alcohol and tobacco, and crime will all raise the rating to 16. Gross violence means an 18 rating.

In the UK, PEGI 12-, 16- and 18-rated games are legally enforceable and cannot be sold to anyone under those respective ages.

> **Statutory body**: A body established by law and charged with carrying out a duty for the state. Ofsted, which regulates radio and television, is a statutory body. IPSO and Impress, which regulate newspapers, are not.

> **Revision activity**
>
> Access the Video Standards Council at **https://videostandards.org.uk/RatingBoard/** to check for any information on updates or changes.

Most *Minecraft* versions are rated at 7 (because of the depiction of fantasy violence) but the *Minecraft Story Mode* spin-off was rated at 12 for bad language.

Social context

The regulation for video games is statutory rather than the self-regulation deemed acceptable for newspapers, magazines and film. This reflects social attitudes to video gaming, which may have been influenced by fears stoked up by other media, especially newspapers, about addiction, social isolation and the effects of violent representations. This regulation also reflects the fact that media aimed at young people are much more likely to be regulated as protection of the vulnerable.

Digital industries pose a challenge for regulators, as it is very difficult to regulate content that comes from outside the country the regulator is based in if it is distributed digitally. However, the type of society is an important context here. Authoritarian countries such as China attempt to control digital input from outside the country, for example, China's 'Great Firewall'. Several video games have been banned for 'smearing the image of China'.

The effect of individual producers on video games

The influence of the game's initial creator Markus 'Notch' Persson on the format of the game is clear. His earlier game had tried to create a world where audiences would have both instant gratification but also reward for hard work. This world-building concept was joined to the ideas, taken from the game *Infiniminer*, of a first-person game, the 'blocky' visual style and the block-building fundamentals. From then on, teamwork took over, not least when the classic version was placed as a developmental release on TIGSource forums in 2009. Feedback from this was crucial in later designs of the game.

Figure 2.3 *Minecraft* inventor, Markus Persson

Moreover, given the open world, sandbox nature of the game, in which the players are free to create whatever they like, the players themselves become producers, even before we take into account the role of modifications and the other user-generated content from video game **prosumers**. To this extent, *Minecraft* is not a top-down game reflecting its creator but a resource to be used in a myriad of ways.

> **Prosumers**: Consumers who are producers at the same time.

Video games: media audiences

REVISED

How the industry categorises game audiences

Age and gender are key demographic variables due to:
- the dominance of the games market by young audiences, including children
- the historic dominance of the physical games market by male audiences, meaning that most games were aimed at men
- the rise in female game audiences with mobile gaming, meaning that women are now seen as an important market
- the paucity of evidence about social class or race and ethnicity as variables.

Different types of game will appeal to audiences with different tastes, so **psychographics** will come into play. The audience research company

> **Psychographics**: Measuring audiences defined by tastes, attitudes and psychological traits. There is no agreed system of classification for this.

Quantix Foundry has published (at **https://quanticfoundry.com/audience-profiles**) a set of gamer motivations by which the psychographic profile of a game might be measured:

- Action: Destruction/Excitement
- Social: Competition/Community
- Mastery: Challenge/Strategy
- Achievement: Completion/Power
- Immersion: Fantasy/Story
- Creativity: Design/Discovery.

Minecraft, for example, will appeal to those seeking design, fantasy and community. Mojang is renowned for not collecting demographic data, which perhaps reflects its independent roots and the relatively universal appeal of *Minecraft*.

Social context

The UK interactive entertainment (ukie) industry organisation factsheet (**https://ukie.org.uk/research#fact_sheet**) includes a section on diversity, which shows the influence of feminism in that it focuses on gender, and particularly the role of women as audiences, representations and producers. This suggests that gender is now a prominent issue in the gaming industry and a key audience category.

Targeting and addressing video game audiences

The largest audience for video games is in the Asia-Pacific region, with China, Japan and South Korea accounting for nearly all this audience. China overtook the USA as the world's largest gaming market by 2016 and generated about one-quarter of the world's games revenues in 2017. This is mostly PC and mobile gaming, as consoles have only been available since 2014 and are controlled by the government. Tencent's most lucrative game in China, *Honour of Kings*, is a 3D, third-person, multiplayer online battle arena game, similar to *League of Legends*, the world's most popular PC game. This suggests that video games have a universal appeal and do not need to change format dramatically to appeal to different national audiences. However, it is adapted to the Chinese market by featuring Chinese characters and being specifically designed to play on mobiles. The western version, *Arena of Valour*, has westernised characters.

The marketing of video games will often use forms of **covert promotion** to attract the target audience and engage fan participation alongside traditional advertising. For example, the campaign for *Grand Theft Auto 5* leaked small amounts of information and put clues on the internet, set up Twitter accounts and websites from inside the fictional world of the game, offered exclusive material to key magazines and websites, incentives for pre-ordering, and pre-launch merchandise. Then Rockstar invited fans to New York to play the game on launch day in order to generate word of mouth through the fans' networks. Drawing on the fact that the game is the latest in a franchise with an existing fan community, the 'authenticity' of the campaign fitted the game.

Minecraft famously did not originally promote the game, which developed by word of mouth from humble beginnings. The audience was

> **Revision activity**
>
> Try applying the set of gamer motivations above to games with which you are familiar. Are there any other reasons for playing not covered by this list?

> **Covert promotion**: Promotion that aims to be within media products (unlike advertising, which is separate to the product). Includes sponsorship, product placement and promotional activities.

reached and engaged by the open source, sandbox quality of the game content, which encouraged creativity both in game play and in making modifications. The game's appeal was designed to be universal, as world-building games are attractive to female gamers as well as men. The game offered true collaboration in multiplayer mode: rather than two players working in isolation, the players could help each other with the same tasks, which is attractive to females as well as males and to older players as well as children. The rather abstract, 'blocky' visuals, while not attracting technophiles in the same way as shinier gadget-heavy games, were not age-specific. For example, it did not exhibit the rather teenage characteristics of much fantasy game play with women presented as sex objects and men as projections of male potency, which might alienate older players.

Minecraft trailers present gameplay to the audience, illustrating developments in the game and versions for consoles, such as the 2011 pocket edition trailer, the 2012 multiplayer split screen in Xbox trailer, the 2013 multiplayer in the pocket edition trailer, the 2014 PS3 trailer showing the two- or four-player split screen and the availability of up to eight online friends, and so on. Where there are multiplayers represented, at least one of them in the trailer is always female, though the majority are male, suggesting an appeal to female players within an assumption of predominantly male players.

The *Minecraft* home page at https://minecraft.net/ has an informal mode of address, suggesting a younger audience, but also offers a high level of detail, addressing an adult audience of reasonable sophistication as some of the items are quite technical.

Figure 2.4 *Minecraft* website home page

Social context

There is a gender dimension to how games reach audiences. Research in the UK suggests that women primarily discover games through friends and family, and secondly through social networks.

Men, on the other hand, are as likely to discover games through online video channels, review or game sites, and friends and family.

Both men and women do not rely on traditional advertising for information about games, perhaps reflecting modern audiences' resistance to advertising. The marketing for video games will work only if it generates word-of-mouth communication.

Figure 2.5 Sandbox features allow players to roam freely and create within the game.

Technologies, audience consumption and response

We have already discussed elements of the technology in and around *Minecraft* that are key to the audience experience:

- the open world or sandbox game elements that allow players to create their own worlds without rules or instructions
- the true collaboration possible in multiplayer mode due to the game design
- the very simple low-resolution block structure of the game that encourages interactivity
- the open source software used that allows prosumers to devise their own modifications to the game and alter textures, maps and craft kits
- the development of console and mobile versions that allow play over a variety of devices
- the development of cross play that allows players on different devices to play together
- the use of social media, video-sharing sites and web forums by fans to develop fan communities
- the use of the internet to live stream MineCon conferences to a global audience.

Economic context

The rapid decrease in the cost of computing power and storage, with the concomitant growth of the internet, has been crucial in allowing the rapid growth of the game and improved audience experience and interactivity.

Audience interaction and prosumers

Interactivity is key to video games, but different games offer different levels of interactivity.

Some games have a pre-existing narrative for the gamer to discover. For example, *What Remains of Edith Finch* is about a young woman who returns home to a mysterious, abandoned house, where she discovers unexpected and dark secrets. The game is structured as a series of a dozen or so short narratives, in which Edith accesses prohibited parts of the unusual house, finally learning the individual fates of her forebears by means of the fragments they left behind – diaries, letters, recordings and other mementos. In such games the interactivity is limited by the pre-existing narrative.

Some games set players tasks, creating a series that the player has to follow to complete, such as *Grand Theft Auto*, but even this can be played as a sandbox game, where the player simply inhabits the world, enjoying the environment.

World-building games such as *Minecraft* take interactivity further by simply providing an environment for the audience to work in without rules or objectives. Here players are in charge of what they do with the game, plus, as we have seen, how they share their gameplay with others, create and share modifications, and feed back to Mojang about the game design.

Economic context

The rapid decrease in the cost of computing power and storage, with the concomitant growth of the internet, has been crucial in allowing audience interactivity and their role as prosumers.

Audience interpretations and contexts

Audience expectations of participation are largely due to the social values embedded in the internet by its early producers, who saw the internet as an anarchistic self-governing community. This do-it-yourself ethos has encouraged user-generated content. Audiences brought up in a pre-internet age are more likely to feel at home in the 'old' media, with their top-down content, which possibly explains why older age groups use video games less than younger ones.

Different societies may experience video games differently, though strong evidence for this is lacking. Chinese players, for example, may have a different experience due to the state control of the internet and video games in China. For example, when Netease introduced a version of a South Korean 'Battle-Royale' game into the Chinese market called *Battle for Survival* it had to remove visible blood to evade the state censorship of violent games and incorporate Chinese Communist slogans (such as 'Safeguard national security and maintain world peace') into the game in order to exhibit 'socialist principles'. Apparently, this has caused some amusement among Chinese players.

The ways different audiences use video games

Commercial video games may be used very differently according to:
- the genre of game
- the **demographics**, especially the age and gender, of the players
- the commitment of the players to a 'gamer' identity
- the **cultural capital** of the users.

The most popular genre of video games in the UK, according to audience research, is the trivia/word/puzzle game, often played on mobile phones,

Revision activity

Pick one video game with which you are familiar and note:
- how different audiences might interpret it differently
- how audiences interact with the game
- how audiences can become producers of the game, or, if they can't, why not.

Revision activity

Conduct an informal survey among people you know who play the same game. Is there any pattern in their differences in interpretation? If so, might this pattern be linked to social characteristics such as gender, age, class, race and ethnicity, sexuality or fandom?

Demographics: Measuring audiences in terms of social characteristics, such as age, gender, class, region, nation, race and ethnicity.

Cultural capital: Capital is wealth you can invest to make more money. Cultural capital refers to aspects of culture such as education that help a person progress in society. Media literacy (a knowledge and understanding of media forms) is part of cultural capital in modern society.

and popular with female games players. This genre of game is usually free to use, may be played opportunistically as a time-filler, is unlikely to help the player feel part of a gamer community, and generally requires relatively little cultural capital, depending on the degree of difficulty of the game. Examples include *Angry Birds* and *Candy Crush Saga*. The major audience pleasure on offer is achievement on completion.

Action/adventure/shooter games are among the most time-consuming of video games, particularly online-focused titles like *Call of Duty*. The more immersive experience of these games and their multiplayer nature means that players are more likely to develop a 'gamer' identity and a sense of a gamer community. First-person shooter games offer pleasures such as action, competition, challenge and a sense of power, which, like their representations, tend to address a masculine audience.

Role-playing/strategy games, such as the massively multiplayer online role-playing game *World of Warcraft*, allow players to control a character avatar within a game world in third- or first-person view, explore the landscape, fight various monsters, complete quests, and interact with other players or non-player characters. Again, these games are multiplayer, highly immersive and considered 'core' gaming, so encourage a sense of a gamer identity. The pleasures on offer such as discovery, fantasy escapism, narrative pleasures, strategy, competition and cooperation address a feminine as well as masculine audience.

As more women play video games more games are designed to appeal to women. Games such as *Spiro* are based on a bright and colourful fantasy world with lovable characters and things to collect – all specifically designed to appeal to young female audiences.

Some games are designed to be fiendishly difficult for those with greater cultural capital. For example, the game *Spacechem* requires players to synthesise chemicals using particular combinations of atoms in a way that requires and develops understanding of chemical engineering.

Some non-commercial games are used to drive citizen science. Players gain the reward of contributing to scientific knowledge. For example, the players of *Stall Catchers* helped a small team of professional scientists complete the world's first crowd-sourced analysis of an Alzheimer's study in much less time than it would take without the help from volunteers.

Minecraft can be used in a similarly immersive way to 'core' games such as the role-playing and adventure games. As we have seen, it offers community both in its gameplay and in online help and mods. It generates a sense of a *Minecraft* community for players to join and show off their creations using screenshots. Its pleasures of design and strategy appeal to both genders and all ages. It does not require cultural capital, as the building blocks of the game are so simple, but the end results can be complex and aesthetically pleasing.

Minecraft has been used in non-commercial settings such as education. The *Minecraft Education Edition* can be of use in coding, but also in subjects as diverse as Chemistry and English Literature.

Social and economic contexts

Changing attitudes to sexualities may influence the willingness of players in role-playing games to adopt an avatar of a different gender to themselves

> **Revision activity**
>
> Conduct an informal survey among people you know who play the games, to find out similarities and differences in how they use video games. You might ask how much time they spend playing, where they play, individually or multiplayer, whether they prefer easy or difficult games, whether they play for entertainment or to learn skills, and whether they consider themselves part of a gaming community.

and, in some games, such as *Dragon Age*, choose the sexual orientation of their character.

Social anxieties about isolation and addiction may have limited the appeal of gaming to some audiences in the past, but the advent of mobile gaming seems to overcome this.

Economic growth in China, for example, has fuelled the rise in game-playing by making the hardware and software available to more citizens.

Mass and specialised audience needs

As in film, there are mainstream and independent sectors in the video game industry (see pages 100–21 on blockbuster and art house cinema). High-budget games have to offer mainstream gaming pleasures aimed at the mass audience. Thus, for example, *Super Mario Odyssey* has a low PEGI rating, a series of colourful, imaginatively designed worlds, cartoonish characters familiar from earlier instalments, some difficult challenges but easily comprehensible tasks, and elements that refer back to previous versions to reward long term players.

Independent games are lower budget and can afford to take more creative risks, so players of such games may require a higher standard of sophistication in the concept. The exploration of the experience of mental illness in the game *Hellblade Senua*, for example, won it a 2018 Bafta award in the category 'Games Beyond Entertainment', which celebrates new releases with a political or social message. *What Remains of Edith Finch* offers pleasures of narrative ambiguity and difficulty in the same way as art house film. Low-budget video games can more easily reach audiences due to the technology of digital downloading, which means that the game does not have to struggle to be circulated (as films do to find cinema screens). On the other hand, the lack of a large advertising and marketing budget means that such games will rely heavily on reviews and awards to gain word-of-mouth recommendations.

Minecraft is unusual in being both an independent video game – low budget in its design and open-minded in its collaboration with prosumers – and backed by a very large digital media corporation, Microsoft. It has become a mass-market product – selling more than 100 million copies – by becoming increasingly sophisticated while never losing its original appeal.

Now test yourself

TESTED ☐

1 For video games, you study media industries and economic and historical contexts only. True or false?
2 State three ways *Minecraft* reflects its independent roots.
3 State three ways a video game can earn revenue.
4 The VSC is the statutory body responsible for the age rating of video games in the UK using the PEGI system. Explain what this means.
5 Name the creator of the *Minecraft* game.
6 Which gamer motivations does *Minecraft* appeal to?
7 Name the country with the largest video game audience.
8 How does *Minecraft* offer interactivity?

Answers on p. 206

Radio

Radio: media industries

Radio production, distribution and circulation

Radio, like television, developed as a centralised medium because of how it is distributed. Radio transmission is limited in bandwidth, meaning only a few channels can transmit, so some central control is required. Radio therefore evolved as a one-way medium in which a few producers addressed a mass audience who listened on domestic radios.

The nature of radio production, distribution and circulation – few producers targeting large audiences – means that it is a mostly mainstream media form. Popular music radio in particular does not tend towards the experimental. There is some variation in the music played, but little in the formats. This tendency has been accentuated by the regulated nature of the media form, where legitimate radio stations need to be awarded a licence to transmit.

In Britain, radio remained a monopoly of the BBC until the first commercial radio stations were licensed by the broadcasting regulator in 1973. The BBC's monopoly allowed it to decide what the nation's taste in music should be, so access to pop music was very restricted in the early 1960s, until the competition from pop music **pirate radio stations** forced the BBC to develop a pop music station – Radio 1 – in 1967. This was modelled on the pirate radio stations, which were themselves modelled on American pop music radio.

Local radio started in the 1960s. Some large commercial stations such as Capital (music radio) and LBC (speech radio) have since expanded through DAB and internet radio to a more national scale. LBC, originally the London Broadcasting Company, now broadcasts nationally on DAB radio under the slogan 'Leading Britain's Conversation'.

Radio, especially popular music radio, is a relatively cheap medium to produce. Hence the appeal of pirate radio, which expanded again in the 1980s to serve certain mostly urban communities, often defined by race and ethnicity. It was renowned for its authenticity and roots, causing some to criticise the decision of some pirate stations, such as Kiss radio, to apply for a licence and become more mainstream.

The Radio 1 Breakfast Show is produced by the BBC from its own studios at Broadcasting House in London. The Breakfast Show is considered the **flagship programme** for Radio 1 and the appointment of a new presenter makes the mainstream news. The presenter was once chosen for their popularity in order to boost audiences, but the attempt in recent years to offer more niche programming aimed at a young audience led to Nick Grimshaw taking over as the fifteenth presenter in 2012. Nick was 11 years younger than the previous presenter and part of his remit was to 'scare away the over 30s'. The programme ran with the same presenter from Monday to Friday until June 2018, when the Friday programme was rebranded as Radio 1's Weekend Breakfast as part of a move to keep it relevant with a youth audience with hosts – Dev and Alice Levine – who were established Radio 1 weekend presenters. Nick Grimshaw stepped down as presenter in August 2018 and was replaced by Greg James.

Pirate radio stations: Unlicensed and therefore illegal radio stations sometimes operated from ships (hence the name).

Flagship programme: A television or radio programme that gains a lot of attention so helps define its channel as a brand.

Music on daytime Radio 1 is governed by a **playlist**. The playlist is partly guided by what's already popular with young people online; many older artists are not included as the network is trying to keep an under-30 audience. There is, however, an attempt to choose music that is not already popular, particularly by British artists, in order to make the output more distinctive.

Cultural, political and economic contexts

Radio was the first domestic electronic medium and so was subject to political control. However, the notion of a free media is central to democracy, and state media are associated with dictatorships, so it is politically important in countries such as the UK for any political control to be at arm's length. This was first achieved by allowing the BBC a monopoly and then, when commercial rivals started, establishing a separate authority (the forerunner of Ofcom) to regulate radio without direct state interference.

Popular music radio operates in a cultural context where pop music is seen as inferior to other art forms, due to its commercial success and accessibility. This is because cultural conservatives, who have an important influence in cultural politics, value the high culture found on Radio 3 precisely because it is 'difficult' and not commercially successful. This context is key in understanding political debates about the role of BBC Radio 1. Politicians, especially those on the right and those opposed to public institutions such as the BBC, sometimes argue that there is no reason why licence fee payers should pay for Radio 1 when it is delivering content that can be accessed easily from commercial radio stations.

BBC Radio 1 creates the economic context in which commercial radio has its audience and profits reduced by having to compete with a publicly funded institution. A government committed to the free market can apply pressure on the BBC by reducing its licence fee – an economic pressure on Radio 1 to provide distinctive content even if that means losing audiences.

The ownership and control of radio

Commercial radio was originally set up in the 1970s to be 'independent local radio' but ownership is becoming concentrated in fewer hands, which are not necessarily local to the areas they serve. Global Radio, for example, owns many of the largest commercial radio brands:

- Capital
- LBC
- Classic FM
- Heart
- Smooth.

However, Global Radio, as its name suggests, specialises in radio and is very small scale when compared to the media conglomerates who dominate in film, video games and television.

The BBC is a publicly funded corporation. It collects the licence fee, which is then allocated to the BBC by the Department of Culture, Media and Sport (DCMS), who use some of it to fund broadband roll-out and the Welsh channel S4C. The licence fee is designed so that the BBC does not have to chase ratings or serve the parts of the population most attractive to advertisers, but can supply **Public Service Broadcasting (PSB)** to the whole population of the UK.

Playlist: Where radio management choose a list of songs (e.g. around 40 records each week for Radio 1) for repeated daytime play. This is common in popular music radio, where presenters are given little choice in what music to play in order to increase accessibility.

Exam tip

You do not need to learn this list, just to understand that commercial radio has concentrated ownership.

Public Service Broadcasting (PSB): Broadcasting intended for public benefit – these benefits (especially those for the BBC) are the subject of vigorous political and cultural debate, and are overseen in Britain by the regulator Ofcom.

In 2016/17 Radio 1 had a budget of £34.7 million (over £6 million less than it had in 2013/14). Radio 1 costs 1.2p per user hour (about the same as Radio 4 and less than a quarter of Radio 3).

Cultural, political and economic contexts

The fact that the Radio 1 budget comes from the licence fee enables Radio 1 to chase a young **niche audience**, even though this audience is more likely to use online media rather than radio and so can't be relied on for audience figures. The fact that popular music programming is much cheaper than classical music programming means that Radio 1 can offer value for money even if its audiences shrink. Thus, this economic context allows the political drive for more PSB content as expressed in the Radio 1 remit (see below).

The BBC faces a cultural context in which compulsory charges such as the licence fee are starting to seem old-fashioned in a media world that emphasises consumer choice over public service but where public support for the BBC as an institution remains high.

Radio industries and audiences

See also 'How radio producers target, attract, reach, address and potentially construct audiences through content and marketing' below.

Most radio audiences are local or national. Broadcasters such as the BBC maintain national audiences with national radio stations providing high-quality content and local audiences through local radio offering specific local content, such as local news, sports coverage, traffic updates and information on local events. However, the BBC World Service addresses a global audience through its content – either by international content in the English language or by content in the national languages of the services for specific countries. In 2016/17, about 154 million people per week accessed BBC World Service radio.

The Radio 1 Breakfast Show audience and for Radio 1 generally is declining, as the controller attempts to attract the target demographic of 15–29 year olds and send older listeners to Radio 2.

Over the same period audiences have been increasing for the BBC's digital music station Radio 6 Music.

Cultural, political and economic contexts

The Radio 1 Breakfast Show faces increasing competition for its audience from commercial radio rivals and from online content, especially music-streaming sites such as Spotify and video-sharing sites such as YouTube. Increasing numbers of people are choosing to stream only in their homes and not pay the licence fee. However, the political context in which a 'too successful' Radio 1 is seen as a threat to commercial interests and an abdication of PSB requirements means that declining audiences for Radio 1 are not viewed as a major problem by the BBC.

The role of the BBC World Service reflects the political context in which 'soft power' is seen as important in today's world, so major economic powers such as the UK should project their image in the world.

The impact of technological change on radio

The range of radio stations available was massively expanded by digital radio such as DAB radio and internet radio stations. Plus, digitally

Niche audience: A specialised audience; the opposite of a mass audience.

Revision activity

Access the latest BBC annual report at www. bbc.co.uk/aboutthebbc/ insidethebbc/howwework/ reports/ara and look at the page on radio.

convergent media allow sound-only media like radio to offer images via social media such as Twitter, Instagram and Snapchat.

The BBC says that Radio 1 should encourage the take-up of DAB and other digital technologies, in particular by promoting 1Xtra and making high-quality content available on digital platforms. The broadcast output should be complemented by an online presence with interactive features, including some use of visual enhancements, which enable the audience to engage with the output and share their views with both the station and other listeners. Radio 1 should experiment with new technologies as they become available to ensure its young audiences have the maximum opportunity to access programmes as and when they want.

The Radio 1 Breakfast Show uses social media accounts to create an interactive relationship with its audience: the Radio 1 Twitter and Facebook accounts are highly active with 3 million followers in 2018, when the YouTube channel had more than 5 million subscribers. The BBC iPlayer Radio app allows streaming of the programme, podcasts, playlists and mixes on mobiles and tablets. The programme encourages texting and emailing, for example, Greg James marked the opening of his first show in 2018 by asking listeners to choose his first record by texting live on air (audiences were given 30 seconds to text in).

Revision activity

Access Radio 1 social media feeds (or Breakfast Show feeds if these are currently available) and review the followers/subscribers and content.

Cultural, political and economic contexts

For many years, Radio 1 was only available on medium wave frequencies, reflecting the low cultural evaluation given to pop music in this low-quality listening experience compared to FM frequencies.

The use of digital platforms by radio depends on the economic context of the rapidly decreasing cost of computing power and storage and the growth of the internet, the cultural context of audiences' expectations that any serious media outlet will be online, and the political context in which the BBC is charged in its Charter (created by the DCMS) with 'helping to deliver to the public the benefit of emerging communications technologies and services'.

The role of regulation in radio

Radio in the UK is regulated by Ofcom and, from April 2017, Ofcom became the BBC's first external regulator, replacing the previous system by which the BBC regulated itself. The BBC is expected to uphold higher standards than the commercial sector because of the way it is funded. The BBC's first director general, Lord Reith, introduced many of the concepts that would later define PSB in the UK when he adopted the mission to 'inform, educate and entertain'. The BBC has been judged on delivering 'Reithian values', such as raising the cultural standards of the nation by educating and informing, particularly via channels such as Radio 3, with its commitment to the 'high arts', and Radio 4, with its commitment to information and education.

Ofcom's duties by law, which apply to all UK radio broadcasters, are to ensure that:

- a wide range of high-quality radio programmes are provided, appealing to a range of tastes and interests
- radio services are provided by a range of different organisations
- people who listen to the radio are protected from harmful or offensive material
- people are protected from being treated unfairly in radio programmes, and from having their privacy invaded
- the radio spectrum is used in the most effective way.

Ofcom does not regulate radio adverts. Nor does it regulate internet-only radio stations – a classic example of the effect of digital technologies on regulation as Ofcom could not licence foreign-based internet stations nor enforce broadcasting rules.

Ofcom holds the BBC to account, ensuring it keeps to its Charter and Agreement (which were renewed in December 2017). The Royal Charter is the constitutional basis for the BBC. It sets out the public purposes of the BBC, guarantees its independence from the government and outlines the duties of the BBC Board. It sets out how the BBC should work and states its mission, which underpins all its regulation:

- to act in the public interest
- to serve all audiences
- to be impartial
- to make high-quality programmes
- to be distinctive
- to inform, educate and entertain.

Because they are PSB, Radio 1 programmes should be one or more of the following:

- high quality
- original
- challenging
- innovative and engaging
- nurturing of UK talent.

Radio 1's remit is to:

- expose listeners to new and sometimes challenging material they may not otherwise experience
- reflect a diverse range of new and UK music
- offer a daytime mix of music, information and entertainment, and use an extensive playlist to introduce unfamiliar and innovative songs alongside more established tracks
- offer specialist presenters in the evening, covering a broad range of musical genres
- cover a wide range of live events and encourage its listeners to take part in music events and activities
- include documentaries and social action campaigns in its schedule
- provide accurate, impartial and independent news.

The BBC Radio 1 Breakfast Show is perhaps the least PSB programming on the BBC. It largely consists of recorded music, much like any commercial popular music radio station. There are, however, some elements that reflect the Radio 1 PSB remit:

- the high proportion of UK music played

Revision activity

Search 'Ofcom Ruling' on the internet to investigate recent examples of Ofcom applying the regulations. For example, see Ofcom's ruling in 2018 against the BBC Radio 4 *Today* programme that allowed Nigel Lawson, a campaigner against the idea of climate change, to state without immediate challenge that there was no evidence for extreme weather events. Ofcom received complaints that the interview broke the UK broadcasting rule stating that 'news, in whatever form, must be reported with due accuracy and presented with due impartiality' and upheld this view.

- the high-quality presentation – the show is 'good of its kind', the traditional BBC standard for entertainment content
- the regular news bulletins – every half hour
- the address to a specifically young audience helps the BBC fulfil its PSB requirement to reflect and represent the whole UK population.

As the showcase programme in a popular music radio channel, *The BBC Radio 1 Breakfast Show* is best judged within the context of the range of BBC programming and channels. Rather than expecting it to exhibit Reithian values, its role is to attract young audiences who might later graduate to more 'high art' BBC content.

Cultural, political and economic contexts

Ofcom taking over regulation of the BBC was the result of some political controversy. Some right-wing commentators, especially in newspapers such as the *Daily Mail*, are highly critical of the BBC's 'liberal bias'. Many saw the BBC as an unaccountable, over-powerful public body, protected from free market competition. Even the BBC's supporters felt that the previous self-regulatory regime was ineffective, allowing, for example, BBC executives to earn very high salaries without proper oversight.

The cultural context in which popular music, especially recorded music, is considered low status, explains the other requirements placed on Radio 1 to try to achieve PSB status: innovative and challenging music, UK talent, live music, and speech programming. Radio 3's remit refers to 'great composers', there is no such reference to 'great popular musicians' in Radio 1's remit. This low cultural status influences political debates about privatisation of parts of the BBC; these invariably assume that the BBC would retain core PSB elements such as Radio 3 and sell off the more commercial Radio 1.

The economic context in which live music is much more expensive than playing recorded music influences its status as a PSB element. The licence fee provides sufficient income for the BBC to be able to afford live music, where most commercial stations cannot.

The effect of individual producers on radio

Presenters are the public face of programmes and in some cases – such as the legendary *John Peel Show* – can shape the content of the programme itself and cultivate a loyal following. Nick Grimshaw did bring a rather camp, northern persona to *The BBC Radio 1 Breakfast Show*, but the bulk of the show consists of playlisted music.

Radio: media audiences

REVISED

How the industry categorises radio audiences

Audiences are categorised and measured by **Radio Joint Audience Research (RAJAR)**. Data freely available on the RAJAR website uses the following categories:

- age
- class (A, B, C1, C2, D, E) – see page 44 for an explanation of these categories
- region.

> **Radio Joint Audience Research (RAJAR):** The official body in charge of measuring radio audiences in the UK, which is jointly owned by the BBC and the Radiocentre on behalf of the commercial sector.

Cultural, political and economic contexts

Commercial radio is interested in categorising audiences in order to sell them to advertisers. The BBC, on the other hand, only needs to categorise audiences in order to measure how far Radio 1, for example, is serving its core target audience of 15–29 year olds and how far all its stations are serving a diverse audience. This diversity includes serving all the nations and regions of the UK. It includes groups defined by race and ethnicity as well as age, gender and social class. The BBC's performance review from 2015 measured audiences in terms of:

- age
- class (A, B, C1, C2, D, E)
- gender
- race/ethnicity – White or **BAME**
- nation (Wales, England, Scotland, Northern Ireland).

> (BBC Trust Service Review Radio 1, 1Xtra, Radio 2, Radio3, 6 Music and Asian Network, (March 2015): downloads.bbc.co.uk/bbctrust/assets/files/pdf/our... radio/performance_analysis.pdf)

> **BAME**: Acronym for 'Black, Asian and minority ethnic'.

This showed that Radio 1, among 15–29 year olds:
- was losing its audience as fewer listened to the radio
- was gaining BAME listeners, but the station has a much higher reach among White listeners
- was slightly more middle class than the population as a whole
- was slightly more female than the population as a whole.

These figures were different for Radio 1Xtra, which has a much higher reach among the BAME 15–24-year-old target audience than the White audience, is more male, and still slightly more middle class. The Asian Network audience is 85 per cent Asian with an even spread across the age groups. Radio 2 is very successful in reaching most of its over-35 target audience across class, gender and the nations (though not among BAME groups). This all suggests that the mix of popular music radio stations does address diverse audiences, though older Black audiences may be less well served.

Targeting and addressing radio audiences

Radio audiences may be:
- local
- national
- international
- fans of music or speech radio
- defined by musical taste
- defined by demographics.

Local or regional radio stations will try to attract a broad demographic by offering a range of programming, serving different tastes in music, and offering local information and services such as local news, travel reports, school closures, sports coverage and so on. These have the advantage of addressing an audience with a strongly defined local identity.

Commercial national radio stations have to target demographics that are attractive to advertisers. Some chase the mainstream audience by offering classic music from a particular decade (e.g. Absolute 80s) or accessible music (e.g. Smooth Radio, Classic FM), others target specialist interest groups, such as Talksport with sports fans.

The BBC, as we have seen, offers a stable of radio stations that are designed to cover the range of tastes and cater for every audience, including:

Radio station	Targets
Radio 1	15– 29 year olds with popular music
Radio 1Xtra	15– 24 year old fans of Black music
Radio 2	A mass audience of over-35 year olds with a mix of speech and music
Radio 3	Fans of high culture with classical music, arts programmes and drama
Radio 4	An educated mass audience with news, current affairs, comedy, drama, magazine programmes and documentaries
Radio 4 Extra	A nostalgic Radio 4 audience with repeats of old programmes dating back as far as the 1940s
Radio 5 Live	News and sports fans
BBC 6 Music	Discerning popular music fans by including rarities and older music
BBC Asian Network	British Asians
BBC local radio	Urban, regional and rural audiences with its 40 stations
BBC World Service	Diverse global audiences with its number of stations in English and local languages

The BBC targets audiences primarily through content rather than marketing, although cross-promotion on other BBC radio stations is now routine.

Radio 1 increasingly relies on the online social and participatory media to reach its target young audience. Radio 1's controller Ben Cooper has argued that the station should not be judged solely on RAJAR figures:

> Radio 1 is evolving with its young audiences as we live through changing times for traditional radio, so it's particularly gratifying to see that in addition to around 10 million listeners, we have seen record figures for Radio 1 videos on Facebook with 80 million monthly views, and 1.4 billion total views on Radio 1's YouTube channel. You can't judge Radio 1 on RAJAR figures alone – just as you can't judge a newspaper solely on physical sales – you have to take into account our digital innovations as well.

Nick Levine, 'Nick Grimshaw's Radio 1 breakfast show ratings fall to new low', *NME*, 18 May 2017

Nick Grimshaw was brought in to the show in 2012 to feature his celebrity connections and to address a young audience, perhaps as a best friend. Greg James, in 2018, appears to be developing a greater focus on the listeners; so his version of the show has dropped the 'zoo' format (multiple presenters). The musical content of the show is mainstream contemporary pop music with some older music – the 'greatest hits' – that date back as far as the 1990s. The show is primarily music and any speech segments are short, as befits a morning show where audiences will not be expected to have long concentration spans. The tone is upbeat to 'get you up and out in the morning'.

The Radio 1 schedule is **stripped** so audiences are familiar with the format and listening can become a ritual pleasure. The traditional schedule runs identically from Monday to Thursday with different Friday and weekend programming. *The BBC Radio 1 Breakfast Show* has a regular running order for a similar reason, to encourage habitual or ritual morning listening.

> **Stripped schedule**: A television or radio schedule that repeats the same programme at the same time every day.

Cultural, political and economic contexts

Audience targeting by BBC radio is influenced by the political context of debates about PSB, as outlined on page 127. *The BBC Radio 1 Breakfast Show* needs to attract a large enough audience to justify its licence fee funding, a specialist enough audience to help meet diversity targets, and to meet PSB criteria, so serving all audiences through the provision of impartial, high-quality and distinctive output and services that inform, educate and entertain.

Technologies, audience consumption and response

Radio is most often used as a **secondary medium** because of its audio-only quality. This means it is listened to in the home, while driving (morning and evening drive-time periods are the peak audience times for radio) or while at work. RAJAR figures for 2017 suggest the following breakdown of the audience location for radio:

- home   60 per cent
- car   24 per cent
- work   16 per cent.

> **Secondary medium**: A media form normally consumed while doing something else.

Many audiences use radio for background noise, companionship and for structuring other activities around predictable repetition. The development of DAB technology has allowed many more national stations to compete for audiences. Digital listening is now about half of all radio listening, with most of that being DAB and a little online and on digital television. This has enabled more specialist channels to flourish, such as the BBC's Radio 1Xtra, Radio 4 Extra, Radio 5 Live and Radio 6 Music.

Young listeners are increasingly listening to radio as podcasts. This gives audiences the opportunity to play programmes at the time and place of their choosing and to fast-forward through items they don't like. Mixtapes are only useful if audiences access them online at a time of their choosing.

> **Revision activity**
>
> Check the Radio 1 schedule to see if it has changed since publication of this book.
>
> Access *The BBC Radio 1 Breakfast Show*'s online presence and note how it addresses its audience; play some interviews and note the presenter's style and audience address.
>
> Listen to *The BBC Radio 1 Breakfast Show* and note how the current presenter(s)' style(s) try to address and engage Radio 1 listeners.

Cultural, political and economic contexts

Audiences, especially younger audiences, have consumerist cultural expectations of choice, immediacy and media plenty, which radio needs to fulfil if it is to compete with the online media. On the other hand, the **curated** quality of radio may appeal to audiences suffering 'choice fatigue', especially in the mornings.

The replacement of FM radio by DAB technology is ultimately a political decision. The FM switch-off has been delayed already by the government as some areas of the country are still not served by DAB.

> **Curated media**: Media where a professional has made a judgement about what is good, so the audience can relax and don't have to make a choice.

Audience interaction and prosumers

Although radio is a classic 'old' medium in that centralised producers address a mass audience, its audio-only quality has enabled a long history of cheap audience interaction by means of phone-ins (which do not work so well on television). Most of the BBC radio stations use phone-ins to involve their audiences in production. Even that bastion of high culture, Radio 3, has audience members sending in texts, emails and tweets to its more populist programmes.

The BBC Radio 1 Breakfast Show uses audience interaction by posing questions, such as 'Things you pretend to like for the sake of your

> **Revision activity**
>
> Conduct an informal survey among people you know who listen to radio to find out how they do this: on FM radio, on digital DAB radio, on television or online. To what extent does this affect how and when they consume radio?

partner', playing live phone conversations on the phone, as well as texts, tweets and emails. Occasionally, audience members will choose tracks. Quizzes are an opportunity to chat to listeners.

The audience is encouraged to share on social media and this promotes the sense of an audience community – Greg James announced in 2018 that his version of the show would be a safe place for people to confess things and be weird.

The BBC Radio 1 Breakfast Show tends to present the music in a straightforward way, without making judgements on its quality and this, together with the show's probable use as a secondary medium, means that audiences are likely to do less interpretation than of many other media products, other than enjoying or not enjoying the music and the presenters.

Cultural, political and economic contexts

Audiences today have much higher cultural expectations of interactivity and participation, due largely to the development of the internet but also to the decline of the traditional deferential culture in which 'your betters' (e.g. the BBC) knew best. This has been caused by the rise of consumerism and thus audience expectations of consumer choice and service rather than passively accepting a restricted choice.

Audience interpretations and contexts

The different BBC radio stations each tend to develop a separate culture that they share with their audience. For example, a Radio 3 audience, used to the conventions of classical music culture, might find the pop on Radio 1 to be very loud, unchallenging and repetitive. A Radio 1 audience, on the other hand, might find Radio 3 to be unexciting and stuffy, with strange moments of silence. These differences reflect the different cultural expectations of high culture and popular culture.

Even within these categories there will be differences in interpretation. Lovers of more extreme popular musical genres such as death metal would deride the more mainstream pop of *The BBC Radio 1 Breakfast Show*.

The BBC Radio 1 Breakfast Show is designed to fit the cultural expectations of a young pop music-loving audience – it strives for a friendly, informal and inclusive mode of address that engages with the everyday activities of its audience, such as revising for exams or news items about the difficulties young parents face in buying a house.

The ways different audiences use radio

Different types of radio channels will be used in different ways by audiences. One major distinction is between local radio and national radio. Local radio will be used by audiences sharing the same or similar local identities irrespective of other **demographics** or **cultural capital**. National stations may appeal to a mass audience or to niche audiences. Let's take some BBC radio channels as examples.

Radio 1 is used by young audiences to support a youthful identity, for entertainment, and in order to keep up to date with developments

Revision activity

Pick one episode of *The Radio 1 Breakfast Show* and note:
- how different audiences might interpret it differently
- how audiences are invited to interact with the show.

Demographics: Measuring audiences in terms of social characteristics, such as age, gender, class, region, nation, race and ethnicity.

Cultural capital: Capital is wealth you can invest to make more money. Cultural capital refers to aspects of culture such as education that help a person progress in society. Media literacy (a knowledge and understanding of media forms) is part of cultural capital in modern society.

in contemporary popular music. It is used by middle-aged audiences, although not targeted at this group, also to keep up to date and to maintain some sense of youthfulness. It requires little cultural capital apart from an understanding of popular culture. Its upbeat tone makes it useful as a background companion for younger audiences. *The Radio 1 Breakfast Show*, for example, offers short pieces of music and speech segments so it does not require concentrated listening.

Radio 3 is used by older, more middle-class audiences to maintain a 'cultured' identity, for education and for entertainment. It requires a degree of cultural capital. Audiences need to understand the role of genres, composers and performers in different historical periods, should be able to concentrate through long pieces of music, and be familiar with high drama, poetry and literature. The more challenging music played in the evening is not intended as background listening.

Radio 5 Live is used by a more male audience to support an identity as a sports fan, for entertainment and information to keep up with the news and sport. It requires some cultural capital – an understanding of sport and its importance in British culture and internationally. It is designed for more attentive listening than background material, especially its live sports coverage.

Cultural, political and economic contexts

The BBC for many years resisted the separation of types of radio into distinct channels serving different audiences – this was because of the Reithian mission to 'improve' the culture of the nation by introducing lovers of popular culture gradually to high culture by maintaining a mix of programmes on radio channels. Such cultural elitism was largely blown away by the consumerism of the 1960s, expressed partly in youth culture and pop music. The importation of American pop music radio formats via the pirate stations led to a separate BBC pop music station – Radio 1 – as well as the segregation of high culture to Radio 3 and Radio 4.

The economic imperative of the BBC's funding by the licence fee means it needs to address large and diverse audiences to justify this funding. Hence it must find out how audiences use its services through audience research.

Mass and specialised audience needs

The needs of mass and specialist audiences are met in different ways by different radio channels.

The entertainment needs of a mass audience such as that of Radio 4 will be met by a mix of programming offering a variety of entertainment (quiz and panel shows, comedy drama, soap opera, chat shows, and so on). The entertainment needs of a niche audience such as that of Radio 3 may be met by more restricted programming addressing the specific needs of that audience – classical music lovers. In the same way, Radio 1 restricts its programming to mostly pop music programming.

The **surveillance needs** of a mass audience may be met again by a range of information-giving programming. Radio 4 offers news, current affairs, documentaries, and magazine programmes on film, the media, medicine, science, gardening and so on. The needs of a niche audience, as for the Radio 1 audience, may be met by some youth and sport-orientated news

> ### Revision activity
>
> Conduct an informal survey among people you know who listen to the radio to find out similarities and differences in listeners to different stations. You might ask how much time they spend listening, where they listen, what else they are doing at the time. Discover whether they listen for entertainment, for information or both, and whether they think of themselves as fans of that radio station.

coverage but primarily through giving a sense of keeping up to date with music and sampling 'greatest hits' from the past.

The **social needs** of mass audiences will be met by programming that addresses a wide range of audiences and uses an inclusive mode of address that alienates as few listeners as possible. Stations aimed at niche audiences can make their listeners feel part of a group by adopting the communicative style of that group. For instance, Radio 5 Live is more informal and opinionated in its news coverage than is Radio 4. *The Radio 1 Breakfast Show* adopted a 'mates round the table' collective presentation style until August 2018, part of an informal mode of address that makes the audience feel part of that group, sharing experiences and celebrating the everyday. This **parasocial interaction** – interacting with the media as if with friends – is an important pleasure of radio as a medium, especially for people trapped in their home or cars.

The **personal identity needs** of mass audiences may be more diffuse than those for niche audiences. The BBC found to its cost (or it may have been a cunning plan) that Radio 6 listeners are highly committed to the channel when it suggested taking it off air. Many older pop music fans of a more alternative kind felt that the channel belonged to them and that a part of their culture was in danger.

Cultural, political and economic contexts

The rise of marketing as a major force in media funding means that advertisers are looking for niche audiences at whom they can aim specialist brands – this fuels the market in niche audience media products. While this economic context does not directly affect the BBC, the general culture of consumerism of which it is a part certainly does. Hence the BBC now markets its channels to mass and niche audiences rather than, as it used to, expecting audiences to accept what they are given.

The cultural and political context of the BBC's position in PSB means that it has to be seen to be addressing the needs of a diverse range of audiences.

Reaching specialised radio audiences

We have seen above how the BBC uses different radio channels and online media to reach specialised local, national and international audiences.

Cultural, political and economic contexts

While global audiences might be most cheaply reached through the internet, the BBC still uses radio transmission as radio is a cheaper technology and therefore more accessible in poorer countries where access to the internet is more limited.

The global recognition of the BBC as a brand is an important cultural context facilitating its global reach. This recognition is aided by the fact that the World Service broadcasts in both the world's common language – English – and in local languages. This was considered so politically important that the service was for many years funded by the Foreign Office.

Surveillance needs: How audiences use the media to learn what is going on in the world by seeking information and analysis.

Social needs: How audiences use the media to help their social interactions, to feel they are members of society, or as a substitute for real social interaction.

Parasocial interaction: When audiences use media products to provide a sense of companionship and care about media characters in the way they would care about real people.

Personal identity needs: How audiences use the media to find role models, to build up their sense of who they are, to reinforce their beliefs and values, or by identifying with characters.

Now test yourself

1 State three elements of the BBC Radio 1 remit.
2 How large is the audience for *The Radio 1 Breakfast Show*?
3 How does *The Radio 1 Breakfast Show* meet PSB requirements?
4 Which five audience categories did the BBC Trust use to measure audiences in 2016?
5 Which BBC radio station is most targeted at a mass audience?
6 Which BBC radio station is most aimed at a niche audience with high levels of cultural capital?
7 How can audiences access Radio 1 apart from live radio?

Answers on pp. 206–7

Exam practice

Now practise answering exam practice Questions 1 and 2 on pages 98 and 99 and compare your answers to those online.

ONLINE

How to prepare for the exam

- Revise media industries for film as a media form, revise how economic and historical contexts influence the film industry, and practise using the two versions of *The Jungle Book* as illustration for these points (plus any other relevant film releases). You do not need to watch the films.
- Revise media industries and audiences for video games as a media form, revise how economic and social contexts influence media industries and audiences for video games, and practise using *Minecraft* as illustration for these points (plus any other relevant video games). You should briefly play the game or watch a walkthrough on a video-sharing site.
- Revise media industries and audiences for radio as a media form, revise how economic, political and cultural contexts influence media industries and audiences for radio, and practise using *The Radio 1 Breakfast Show* as illustration for these points (plus any other relevant radio stations or programmes). You should have listened to one complete episode of the show. You may want to keep listening to the show as revision.

► Paper 2 – Section B: Long form television drama

What you have to do

This section of the exam asks two questions on your study of long form television drama (LFTVD).

Which areas of the theoretical framework must I study?	
LFTVD	The whole theoretical framework: ● media language ● representations ● industries ● audiences Social, cultural, economic, political and historical contexts Academic ideas and arguments (theories)

The two questions in Section B will be as follows:

Q3	30 marks	This will be a complex question including a number of bullet points which guide you to complete all the relevant tasks. These will include: ● showing knowledge and understanding of the influence of media contexts on LFTVD ● analysing the set products you have studied, probably in terms of media language or representation (this might entail comparing the two) ● making judgements and drawing conclusions. This extended essay should take about 50 minutes to plan and write, and should be well structured with a clear conclusion.
Q4	10 marks	This question asks you to evaluate an academic theory in relation to LFTVD. You may or may not be given a choice of writers to evaluate. This question does not ask you to lay out the writer's ideas in detail, rather to explain how useful they are in understanding LFTVD. This short essay should take about 17 minutes to plan and write.

Question 3

What this question involves

The following information is based on the specimen assessment materials produced by OCR. These are likely to be the format of exam questions in the live exam papers, but OCR reserves the right to make changes to this format if this turns out to be necessary.

Question 3 will probably ask for all three of:
- your knowledge and understanding of the influence of media contexts on LFTVD
- analysis (probably of media language or representations)
- judgements and conclusions.

Timing

As Question 3 is worth 30 marks, you should spend about 50 minutes answering this question.

> **Revision activity**
>
> Past papers and practice papers are published on the OCR Interchange – ask your teacher to access these so you can check whether the format for Question 3 has changed over time.

What the examiner is looking for

REVISED

In Question 3 examiners are looking for:
- you to cover **more than one of** the four areas of the theoretical framework and contexts
- how comprehensive and accurate is your knowledge and understanding of the influence of media contexts
- how comprehensive, accurate and detailed is your application of knowledge of the area of the theoretical framework, contexts and theory to analyse the set product(s)
- how convincingly, accurately and perceptively you analyse the sources, with logical connections and lines of reasoning
- how accomplished and developed are your judgements and conclusions.

Exam practice

Question 3*

In this question you will be rewarded for drawing together elements from your full course of study, including different areas of the theoretical frameworks and media contexts.

Why do long form dramas from different countries offer different representations?

In your answer you must:
- consider the contexts in which long form dramas are produced and consumed
- explain how media contexts may have influenced the representations in the set episodes of the two LFTVDs you have studied
- make judgements and reach conclusions about the reasons for the differences in representation between the two episodes.   [30]

Sample answer available online

ONLINE

Extended response questions

REVISED

The asterisk (★) next to the exam practice Question 3 is to signpost that this is an extended response answer, meaning that you will be marked on the quality of your essay:
- how well you develop a line of reasoning
- how relevant your answer is throughout
- how well you provide evidence for the points you make.

Making judgements and reaching conclusions

If a question asks for the reasons for the differences, as in this question, then that must be the focus of your conclusion, which one bullet point will ask you to provide. In exam practice Question 3 you might argue one of the following:

● that the differences in representation **do** reflect media contexts
● that the differences in representation **do not** reflect media contexts but other factors such as media industries or audiences or generic conventions
● that the differences in representation reflect both media contexts and other factors.

Examiners will be told to credit any argument that is backed up by analysis of the extract, so there is no 'right answer' to these questions with which you have to agree. In fact, examiners are told to reward nuance in the conclusion, meaning that careful and thoughtful views will be rewarded more highly than simple assertions. This means:

● it would be good practice to offer some counter-argument within the essay and test ideas against the evidence before coming to a conclusion based on your analysis
● your conclusion can argue that both sides of an argument are correct to some extent.

You may find it useful to end this type of essay with a paragraph starting with the phrase 'In conclusion' – reminding you to reach a conclusion and signalling to the examiner that you are drawing one.

Example

In conclusion, the differences in representation between *Mr. Robot* and *The Killing* reflect generic conventions more than national contexts. It is perfectly possible to imagine a Danish corporate conspiracy thriller and an American social realist police drama using conventions similarly to represent a strong female detective protagonist and a troubled masculine protagonist. These are globalised televisual genres, even though each may be inflected differently according to the national context (e.g. the cynical New York culture expressed in *Mr. Robot*, the small-scale Danish community values in *The Killing*). The themes of both programmes – fear of digital control and fear of violent crime – are universal, though the former reflects the political and economic context of the uncontrolled expansion of the digital industries and the latter reflects specifically Danish concerns about local coalition politics that reflect a national context. The fact that both programmes have enjoyed success outside their national origins, despite *The Killing* being in Danish, suggests that both offer representations that are attractive to modern audiences – a strong feminist representation on the one hand, an anarchic 'outsider' representation on the other. Here again, the appeal to audiences relies on the contexts in which audiences find themselves – in a post-feminist and postmodern, hyperreal world in which both genders struggle to construct identities with fewer fixed points of reference. To this extent, media contexts and other factors such as genre and audience are inextricably linked.

Exam tip

Simply repeating or rephrasing the question in an opening paragraph often suggests a middling or low-quality answer. Examiners always mark each answer on its merits, but a good initial impression cannot do any harm. So if you know what conclusion you are going to reach, you can state this at the outset.

This would count as a conclusion. It is nuanced as it covers both sides of an argument. It appears to rely on the analysis already made earlier in the essay.

However, if you see immediately that the analysis would point to a definite conclusion to a particular question, it is perfectly fine to start the essay with a strong assertion of this conclusion. This is because a confident beginning to an essay often suggests to the examiner that this might be a high-quality essay.

'Full course of study' questions

REVISED

Question 3 will start with this sentence:

> In this question you will be rewarded for drawing together elements from your full course of study, including different areas of the theoretical frameworks and media contexts.

The statement means you must cover more than one of the four areas of the theoretical framework – media language, representations, industries and audiences – to achieve the top of the highest mark band.

The conclusion to Question 3 above does cover both audience and representations and contexts, and touches on Baudrillard's theory, so it would not have its marks limited for covering only one area.

Recommended revision for this question

REVISED

For media **language**, you should:
- analyse and explain the combination of elements to create meaning using **semiotics**
- analyse and explain the **generic conventions** of LFTVD, looking at variations, change over time, **genre hybridity** and challenging/subverting conventions
- analyse and explain the relationship between media language and technology
- analyse and explain examples of **intertextuality**
- analyse and explain the way media language incorporates viewpoints and **ideologies**
- practise applying the ideas of Barthes, Todorov, Levi-Strauss, Neale and Baudrillard in analysing LFTVD
- analyse and explain media language in LFTVD in terms of media contexts.

> **Semiotics**: The study of signs. (See Barthes in the Academic Theories section.)
>
> **Generic conventions**: The shared understandings of what elements fit in which genres.
>
> **Genre hybridity**: The stable mixing of different genres in one product. Many genres are commonly hybridised with romance, for example, to increase their audience appeal.
>
> **Intertextuality**: Media products (texts) that refer to other media products.

> **Ideologies**: Sets of beliefs, values and assumptions shared by a social group and embedded in social, cultural, political and economic institutions. Usually thought to reflect the interests of powerful groups. Consumerism, freedom, equality and individualism are often considered dominant ideologies in free market capitalist societies as they reflect the economic basis of these societies.

For media **representations**, you should:
- analyse and explain how selection and combination create representations of events, issues, individuals and social groups

- analyse and explain how LFTVD makes claims about **realism** and constructs versions of reality
- analyse and explain the impact of the media industry and social, cultural and historical contexts on how producers choose to represent events, issues, individuals and social groups
- analyse and explain positive and negative uses of **stereotyping**
- analyse and explain how social groups may be under-represented or misrepresented
- analyse and explain how representations, particularly those that systematically reinforce values, attitudes and beliefs about the world across many representations, invoke **discourses** and ideologies and **position audiences**
- suggest how audience response and interpretation reflects social, cultural and historical circumstances
- apply the ideas of Hall, Gauntlett, Butler, Van Zoonen, hooks and Gilroy in analysing LFTVD.

Realism: Realism is the set of conventions by which audiences accept a representation as 'real' or 'realistic'. If an Ancient Roman character in a period drama used a mobile phone this would break the rules of realism. If she or he spoke in English, a language not yet invented in Ancient Roman times, this would not break the rules. This suggests that, as with language or genre, the rules of realism are arbitrary, unwritten, and only noticed when broken. There are different sets of rules for different genres and for different media forms, and there are many different forms of realism. A very expressionist supernatural horror media product should still have emotional realism, for example, and should obey its own internal rules.

Stereotyping: A commonly repeated generalisation about a group, event or institution that carries judgements, either positive or negative, and assumes any example of this group, event or institution will fit the stereotype. This generalisation is inaccurate because it is an over-simplification, even if it is based in reality. It can refer to a representation that comprises a simple stereotyped characteristic rather than a complex and individualised set of characteristics.

Discourses: A system of shared knowledge embedded in social institutions, such as medicine, that exercise power over people.

Positioning audiences: How products try to put their audiences in particular positions. This might be emotional positioning (e.g. making them feel fear or sympathy), cognitive positioning (how they think about representations in the products), social positioning (e.g. as males or females) or cultural positioning (e.g. being positioned as British or American).

For media **industries** you should know:
- how television is shaped by how it is **produced, distributed and circulated**
- the ownership and control of television
- economic factors such as funding for television
- how television industries maintain audiences nationally and globally (this is covered under audiences)
- the impact of technological change, especially digital convergent media platforms, on television

Production, distribution and circulation: Production is the making of the product, distribution is getting the product to the retailer, circulation is how the product is consumed.

- the role of regulation in television and the impact of digital technologies on regulation
- the effect of individual producers on television
- the influence of social, cultural, economic, political and historical contexts on television industries
- the ideas of Curran and Seaton, Livingstone and Lunt, and Hesmondhalgh on industries.

For media **audiences** you should know:
- how audiences are categorised by industries
- how producers target, attract, reach, address and potentially construct audiences through content and marketing
- the interrelationship between media technologies and consumption and response
- how audiences interpret the media form, interact with the media form, and can be actively involved in production
- the way in which different interpretations reflect social, cultural and historical circumstances
- the different ways audiences defined by **demographics**, identity and **cultural capital** use the media form
- the different needs of mass and specialised audiences and their significance to the media form
- how specialised audiences can be reached through different technologies and platforms, nationally and globally
- the influence of social, cultural, economic, political and historical contexts on television audiences
- the ideas of Bandura, Gerbner, Hall, Jenkins and Shirky on audience.

Demographics: Measuring audiences in terms of social characteristics, such as age, gender, class, region, nation, race and ethnicity.

Cultural capital: Capital is wealth you can invest to make more money. Cultural capital refers to aspects of culture such as education that help a person progress in society. Media literacy (a knowledge and understanding of media forms) is part of cultural capital in modern society.

Set products

REVISED

You will have chosen:
- one English-language LFTVD
- one non-English-language LFTVD.

Exam tip

The recommended revision above has been taken from the subject content on pages 23–27 of the specification but condensed for clarity. Examiners may write their questions using the same wording as the subject content, so please read through the subject content to check you understand all the wording as well as revising the content below.

Exam tip

Concentrate on the content for your two set products. You can ignore the analysis of the set products that you have not chosen to study.

English-language LFTVDs

Mr. Robot, episode 1

This psychological thriller premiered in 2015 on the US cable network USA Television. It is available in the UK on Amazon Prime. Three seasons; ran from 2015 to 2017.

Key characters

Elliot – the protagonist and narrator (voiceover); his narrative is probably unreliable as he has delusions and lies constantly

Mr. Robot – the man who recruits Elliot to a group of hackers

Angela – Elliot's work colleague, old friend and love interest even though she has a boyfriend that Elliot hates

Gideon – Elliot's boss

Krista – Elliot's therapist

Colby – E Corp's Chief Technology Executive ('E might as well stand for evil')

Tyrell Wellick – Senior Vice President Technology for E Corps

Plot of episode 1

We learn of 'The Conspiracy – the guys that play God but without permission'.

Elliot, our narrator, works for Allsafe, a cyber security company run by Gideon, a kind of father figure for Elliot (who later tells him that he is gay), who is in a panic about cyber-attacks on the firm's clients. At night Elliot cries with loneliness, takes morphine, has sex with his dealer and undertakes hacking to expose a paedophile, find out about Angela's boyfriend's affairs and protect his therapist, Krista, from her married lover. He hates corporations, heroes, social media and consumerism. He has delusions about 'men in black'.

Allsafe's biggest client, E Corp, the largest conglomerate in the world, visits the office and Elliot meets Tyrell. They bond over Linux. E Corp suffers a denial of service cyber-attack which Elliot solves, but he finds a message in the attack code telling him to 'leave me here' in the root server, which he does, and pointing him to 'fsociety' and thus to Mr. Robot. He is like a very alternative father figure to the corporate Gideon and he introduces Elliot to a collective working on something called 'the project' in Coney Island. The members of this collective are hyper-vigilant around Elliot but seem to ignore Mr. Robot. One young woman – Darlene – wants to know when he's going to give them the code. Elliot wonders if Mr. Robot is simply a paranoid delusion and next time he looks the collective appears to have vanished. Mr. Robot tells Elliot that the project is to take down money, starting by erasing all the debt controlled by E Corps.

Elliot is told to plant incriminating evidence against Colby; at first he is unsure about doing this but then Colby mistreats Angela in a meeting, so Elliot changes his mind.

Elliot confronts Krista's lover and takes his dog. Angela asks Elliot to let her lose rather than sticking up for her. Elliot looks like he might realise that his desire to control others may have negative consequences, then finds out that Colby has been arrested. It's happening! Elliot is taken to meet 'The Conspiracy' – a group of men in suits. One of them is Tyrell Wellick.

House of Cards, episode 1

This political drama, a remake of a British TV series, premiered on Netflix in 2013. Seven seasons; from 2013 to 2017. Then Netflix announced that the eighth season would be the last.

Key characters

Frank – the protagonist and narrator (to camera), the House Majority Whip

Claire – Frank's wife, who runs the Clean Water Initiative

Zoe – a young journalist just starting her career

Russo – a congressman who Frank manipulates into helping him undermine Kern

Kern – Frank's rival who gets the Secretary of State post he coveted

Vasquez – the president's Chief of Staff, a powerful Latino woman

House of Cards, episode 1

Doug – Frank's sidekick

Walker – the President elect

Plot of episode 1

We first meet Frank strangling an injured dog while speaking a monologue about necessary brutality.

Vasquez tells Frank that he is not being nominated for Secretary of State; Kern is instead. Meanwhile Claire is expanding her staff, expecting a big cheque from a donor. Frank gets home crestfallen. Claire wants him to be angry at his treatment and insists 'My husband doesn't apologise. Even to me'. Frank declares 'I love her more than a shark loves blood'. Frank devises a plan to eliminate his opposition one by one, starting with Kern.

Zoe is trying to get ahead at work but is frustrated. She has a confident, assertive sexuality. She has a photo of Frank looking at her backside and offers discretion in return for information.

Claire is making redundancies at her office despite the pain this causes her staff. Frank sweetens her donors by getting them tickets for the Jefferson Ball.

Doug offers to help make the police commissioner mayor in return for letting Russo off a drunk-driving charge, so Frank can later demand his 'absolute unquestioning loyalty'.

Vasquez has asked Frank to water down an education bill so it can pass; he pretends to shred the draft bill, then passes it on to Zoe, whose boss declares that this will 'put Walker on his arse'. Walker is inaugurated and announces a new education bill while Frank gives a knowing look to the camera.

The next day Frank visits a cafe to eat ribs. He sees the front page lambasting the education bill and that there has been a dog hit and run arrest. He'll have a second helping. He's feeling hungry today.

Homeland, episode 1

This spy thriller, a remake of an Israeli programme, premiered in 2011 on the US cable channel Showtime. It was shown in the UK on Channel 4. Seven seasons; ran from 2011 to 2018, when it was announced that the eighth season will be the last.

Key characters

Carrie – our protagonist, a CIA operative

David – CIA Deputy Director and head of counter-terrorism

Saul – CIA Middle East Division Chief

Nick Brody – a rescued Al-Qaeda prisoner of war

Jessica Brody – Nick's wife

Mike – Nick's best friend who is in love with Jessica

Abu Nazir – a high-ranking member of Al-Qaeda who has 'turned' Brody

Plot of episode 1

The episode opens with Carrie in Baghdad on the phone to David, her boss, while trying to reach a man in prison who she will help in return for information about an attack by Abu Nazir.

10 months later

Carrie is still obsessed with Abu Nazir and taking medication for bipolar disorder. David announces that Brody has been rescued from Al-Qaeda captivity. Carrie tells Saul that she has information about an America POW who has been turned; he asks for hard evidence. Carrie has Brody's house bugged.

The army and CIA try to make Brody look like a hero as he returns. His wife has been sleeping with Mike, thinking that he was not returning, so the homecoming is very awkward. Jessica tries to look alluring but Brody is very jumpy. They have violent sex.

➜

Homeland, episode 1

The next morning Carrie asks Brody in his debrief if he ever met Abu Nazir; we see a flashback of Nazir giving him water, but Brody claims never to have met him. Carrie later discovers him lying to fuel her suspicions. David warns Saul that Carrie is causing trouble. Brody meets the wife of his fellow captive marine, Tom, to comfort her. Saul goes to Carrie's house to tell her he is reporting her. She fails to seduce him and he leaves. Carrie is manic. Meanwhile Mike is at a barbeque with Nick and Jessica, who tells Mike she can't leave Nick.

Carrie has a realisation – Brody is sending a message when on television with his finger movements. We see Brody running, then a montage of Brody killing Tom, Nazir comforting him, and the steps of the White House.

Stranger Things, episode 1

This generically ambiguous programme – a mix of science fiction, supernatural horror, investigative and coming-of-age drama – premiered on Netflix in 2016. Two seasons; ran from 2016 to 2017, a third is in production in 2018 and more will probably follow.

Key characters

Joyce – Will's mother

Jonathon – Will's brother

Hopper – the police chief, an alcoholic

Will – a boy captured by an unknown force (later in the series revealed to be a monster from the 'Upside Down', an alternate dimension discovered by Hawkins Laboratory scientists)

Eleven – a mysterious girl with telekinetic powers

Dustin – Will's friend

Lucas – Will's friend

Mike – Will's friend

Nancy – Mike's sister

Steve – Nancy's boyfriend

Dr Brenner – Head scientist at the laboratory

Plot of episode 1

At Hawkins National Laboratory, Department of Energy alarms are sounding as a scientist flees. He is devoured.

In a suburban home four friends are playing Dungeons and Dragons. They are told to finish just as Will throws a seven (which means he will be eaten but only aficionados of the game will know this). Cycling home, Will passes a protected area where he comes across an unseen growling thing. He rides home and is caught at the shed.

Chapter One

Home. Will is missing. Joyce and Jonathon were both at work last night. Will's three friends are bullied at school, one for his disability. Nancy meets Steve at school. Hopper is still drunk and is uninterested in Will's disappearance, advising Joyce to contact his dad, Lonnie.

Meanwhile, investigators arrive at the lab with guns; they see black roots and flesh-like substances on the walls. Brenner reassures them that 'The Girl' can't have got far.

Eleven, dressed in hospital garments, enters a diner where the owner feeds her – she makes a fan stop rattling by staring at it.

At school, the teacher has acquired a new radio, the friends are members of the AV club. Hopper interviews them and tells them to go straight home. There is a flashback of Joyce taking Will to see the film *Poltergeist*. She and Jonathon search for Will at his fort in the woods, Castle Byers. Hopper finds Will's BMX bike. The team at the lab listen in to phone conversations. Hopper searches Will's home and is going to investigate noises in the shed (the light fails again) when he is interrupted. Hopper calls a search.

Stranger Things, episode 1

Mike and his family argue over searching for Will; his father is insensitive while his mother tries to hold the family together. Mike is angry about a lack of interest in Will.

Searching in the woods, Hopper talks to the teacher about his lost daughter. Mike and Lucas arrange to meet and Steve arrives at Nancy's bedroom to revise and try to have sex.

The 'social services' arrive at the diner with Brenner, shooting the owner but Eleven escapes.

Joyce and Jonathon get a mysterious phone call from someone who might be Will.

Dustin, Mike and Lucas find Eleven in the woods.

Non-English-language LFTVDs

The Killing, episode 1

This hybrid of police and political drama premiered on Danish national television channel DR1 in 2007. It was available in the UK on BBC Four. It ran for three seasons from 2007 to 2012.

Key characters

Sarah Lund – our protagonist, a police inspector

Jan Meyer – Lund's replacement for when she moves to Sweden

Theis Birk Larsen – the father of the murdered girl, Nanna

Pernille Birk Larsen – Nanna's mother

Lisa – Nanna's friend

Vagn – Theis's employee

Troels – a local politician running for election

Mayor Bremer

Plot of episode 1

A young girl is chased through the woods in the dark.

Day 1

Lund is moving to Sweden with her children to be with her partner. Her colleagues organise a practical joke and a Swedish-themed party to mark her leaving. Jan Meyer arrives and together they investigate bloodstained clothes found in the country, including a video card belonging to Theis.

At work, Theis smooths over an argument with an Arab shopkeeper over Vagn's incompetence and racism, then returns home to fix a dishwasher flood and has sex with Pernille. He has a surprise plan for Nanna's apartment.

At City Hall, there's an election in prospect. Troels is at his wife's grave then in a meeting planning to undermine Mayor Bremer, who asks him to wait before running for office. Troels refuses.

Lund and Meyer ask Pernille what Theis was doing at the weekend. Nanna was supposed to be staying at Lisa's. Lund calls it in as a missing person.

At school, Lisa denies knowing anything about Nanna. The political duel between Troels and Bremer is to be held there, but is cancelled when Lund arrives to interview Nanna's classmates. Lisa runs out to ask her friends if Nanna is with her ex-boyfriend, Oliver.

At home, Pernille is in a panic. Theis takes Vagn to see the house he has bought to house the family; he gives Vagn some money to avoid him committing a criminal act. Pernille arrives and tells him that Nanna is missing, but he is sure he knows where she will be. He finds Lisa, who tells him about Oliver, so Theis sets off to get her, but she isn't there.

Meyer searches the woods with dogs and finds only a fox.

Lund drops her son off at her mum's. She only realises when her boyfriend rings that she is going to miss the plane.

➡

The Killing, episode 1

Troels is suspicious; how did the Mayor know his key facts? He discovers that someone is digging for dirt on him.

A car is found in a waterway. Theis comes across Lund and Meyer searching it and finding Nanna's body. Pernille overhears on the telephone. The car belongs to Troels' campaign.

Borgen, episode 1

This political drama premiered on Danish national television channel DR1 in 2010. It was available in the UK on BBC Four. It ran for three seasons from 2010 to 2013.

Key characters

Birgitte – our protagonist, the leader of the Moderates, a centrist political party

Phillip – Birgitte's husband

Kasper – Birgitte's communications chief

Hesselboe – Prime Minister and leader of the Liberal Party

Ole – Hesselboe's public relations advisor

Laugesen – Labour Party leader

Katrine – a television journalist

Hanne – Katrine's colleague

Torben – Hanne and Katrine's boss

Bent – the older man with the beard who mentors Birgitte to power

Plot of episode 1

Caption: 'A prince should have no other aim or thought but war and its organisation and discipline.' Machiavelli.

Pre-title sequence: We see Birgitte with Kasper preparing for a television appearance in make-up. It is three days until the election. We see Hesselboe advised by a British PR firm. Katrine interviews Birgitte; although she is in coalition with Laugesen's party (as the opposition), she breaks the coalition live on air because of his negative comments about asylum seekers.

Episode 1 Decency in the middle

Hesselboe is in London with his wife, who is drunk and out of control, and he has to use a ministry Eurocard to make a purchase to keep her quiet.

Birgitte is angry with Katrine, who has been in a relationship with Kasper. Kasper speaks to Ole to sound out a coalition, but can't sell the idea to Birgitte and Bent. She is going to take her children to a party. We later see her with her husband, who looks after the children.

At an apartment. Katrine is with Ole – he's going to leave his wife – they have sex, then he dies. In a panic, she rings Kasper who rushes over then cleans up to protect her job. In doing so, he discovers the receipts from Hesselboe's misuse of the credit card.

Kasper tells Birgitte he has information that could blackmail Hesselboe to get her into office and form a coalition or use it against him. Birgitte doesn't want to come to office in that way. Kasper thinks that means she never will.

Birgitte meets Laugesen. She is principled, he will do anything for power, including attacking asylum seekers to stop voters going to the far-right Freedom Party. He offers her extra ministries to stay in coalition, she refuses. At home, she prepares to resign after the election – to allow her husband to pursue his career as she's had her five years in the deal she had proposed to him.

Laugesen chats with Kasper, they are both equally ambitious and cynical about politics. Kasper tells Laugesen about the information.

Torben sacks Hanne over her alcoholism. He furious with Katrine for not answering phone calls, but has to offer her the final debate tonight.

→

Borgen, episode 1

Kasper tells Birgitte to wear a black dress and has written her a tactical speech for the debate. She can't fit into the dress and doesn't want to be tactical.

Kasper asks Laugesen not to use the information. In the two-minute final speeches Birgitte improvises, making an honest speech, in favour of a multi-ethnic society, against widening inequality, and about the need for a new politics. Bent, watching on television, is impressed. Kasper is distraught, then impressed.

Laugesen reveals the credit card receipts; Hesselboe storms out. Birgitte fires Kasper for giving away the information.

Morning. Birgitte cycles to work. Bent tells her the Labour Party are rebelling against Laugesen and events could come to a head very soon.

Election night. Phillip has bought Brigitte a new black dress. The Moderates have gained 15 seats and Hesselboe is in trouble. He and Laugesen have lost seats. All the press want to hear from Birgitte. Bent insists that this is a new beginning and that she must now lead her party to power.

Kasper is out in the cold. Katrine finally collapses from grief.

At daybreak, Birgitte gets home. They want her for Prime Minister.

Trapped, episode 1

This police drama premiered on Icelandic national television channel RUV in 2015. It was available in the UK on BBC Four. A second series is planned for 2018.

Key characters

Andri – our protagonist, the local police chief

Hinrika – Andri's female junior officer

Ásgeir – Andri's male junior officer

Agnes – Andri's ex-wife

Søren Carlsen – Danish ferry captain

Hjörtur – the young man whose girlfriend died in the fire

Plot of episode 1

Hjörtur and his girlfriend Dagný speed on a motorbike through snowy countryside towards an abandoned factory, where they come to drink, smoke and have sex. When Hjörtur goes downstairs, he discovers that a fire has broken out. He desperately tries but fails to rescue Dagný from the flames.

Seven years later

Andri gets the kids to school. Their mother is coming to town with her new boyfriend.

A mutilated torso is caught in fishing nets just off the local harbour, shortly before the arrival of the ferry from Denmark. Andri starts the investigation with Hinrika and Ásgeir. The discovery of the torso is initially linked to someone aboard the ferry. Andri therefore orders that no one may leave the vessel, pending the arrival of the investigation team from Reykjavik. The ferry captain doesn't want the ship searched.

There is a town meeting about Chinese investment in a new port.

Hjörtur returns to town.

The owner doesn't want the torso kept at his fish factory.

Hinrika questions the passengers on the ferry, despite the Reykjavik detectives' opposition to Andri's 'meddling'.

Andri's children are bullies. When Andri goes to the school the teacher knows about the torso. Agnes meets the children. Andri is still wearing his wedding ring.

A blizzard sets in, preventing detectives from Reykjavik from reaching Seyðisfjörður.

→

Trapped, episode 1

The passengers, frustrated by the delay in disembarkation, are eventually allowed off the ship after ferry captain Søren Carlsen shuts down the heating system – he is congratulated for causing chaos by an unknown character.

Ásgeir tracks down a Lithuanian criminal involved in human trafficking. Andri chases him as he drives off in a campervan with two imprisoned African girls, he crashes then escapes and the girls run off.

Deutschland 83, episode 1

This spy thriller was premiered on the US cable television channel Sundance TV, then the German commercial broadcaster RTL. It was available in the UK on Channel 4, branded under *Walter Presents*. A second series is planned for 2018.

Key characters

Martin – the protagonist, a young East German asked to spy on the West

Leonora – Martin's aunt, cultural attaché of the East German Permanent Mission in Bonn

Walter – works for the East German Foreign Intelligence Services

Annett – Martin's girlfriend

Tobias – a sleeper agent (a university professor) in Bonn and Martin's handler

Kramer – a fellow spy

General Edel – a West German General who liaises with the Americans

Plot of episode 1

Pre-title sequence: in the East German mission, Bonn, West Germany, Leonora watches Ronald Reagan make a bellicose speech.

Martin, a border guard, interrogates West German students, lectures them on socialism, lets them go, leaving behind their Shakespeare book, then laughs.

Leonora meets with Walter. The West is on the offensive. She has a plan to replace a 24-year-old aide de camp with Martin.

At a family party Martin gives his mother the Shakespeare book, we discover that Leonora is Martin's aunt and meet Annett.

The programme titles include Cold War footage and end with an atomic bomb.

Leonora brings Walter to visit. In return for taking this job she will get his mother on the kidney transplant list. Martin doesn't want to go. His coffee is drugged.

Martin wakes up in a strange city (in Bonn, the capital of West Germany). Leonora and Tobias brief him: he's to work for General Edel who is attached to Pershing missiles (deployed in West Germany by the Americans in 1983 and seen as escalating the arms race). Martin runs away. He is shocked by the plenty in the local supermarket. Tobias tells him he can't run; they are close to a third world war and his country needs him. They eat fast food.

Martin is trained, including understanding the differences between the two Germanies, and is given the cover name Moritz Stamm. He meets his fellow spy Kramer at the camp, General Edel, and Edel's son, who shocks Martin with his Green politics. Martin is also surprised by the cynicism and lack of enthusiasm in West Germany for the Cold War, the arms race and the Americans.

At home his mother has to brush off Annett about where Martin is.

US General Jackson arrives to discuss the Pershing 2 missiles with Edel. Martin photographs the contents of Jackson's briefcase, but fails to lock the secretary's drawer in time.

At a barbeque, Martin passes the photos to Tobias. Martin sneaks into the house to ring Annett but is overheard by a relative, so Tobias gives Martin a drug to put in her drink. That night he drives the woman home; she won't remember anything in the morning.

Next morning, Martin meets Leonora – he has photographed a list of East German targets. The Americans are planning an attack, next he must find out when. He wants to go home but Leonora insists that his mother's life depends on him staying.

Long form television drama

LFTVD: media language

Semiotics: combining media language elements

For an explanation of Barthes' semiotics, see page 7 under Paper 1, Questions 1 and 2. See the analyses below for an application of this theory.

Historical, cultural and economic contexts

Long form television drama offers media language characterised by high production values that in the 1970s would have been considered characteristic of cinema. Compare a popular 1970s American television programme such as *Starsky and Hutch* with recent LFTVD and the former appears cheap, relatively studio-bound, conventionally shot and edited, with crude apparently under-rehearsed performances. Recent LFTVD has developed as a quality product due to the economic context of increasing competition in the television market with the development of more channels, leading to the search for quality drama as flagship programming. This raised audience expectations of television drama, given the cultural context in which the programmes were made, and hence increased the pressure to provide high production values.

Current LFTVDs are expected to include stars or highly skilled actors, sophisticated production design, cinematic-style camerawork, lighting and editing, **through-composed music** and sophisticated sound effects. They offer complex **serial narratives** with **multiple narrative strands**, and detailed and possibly ambiguous characterisation.

Analyses

Let's analyse one key scene from each drama in terms of their use of media language to create meaning. Key scenes will be taken from the opening of each programme as this is a crucial period for establishing tone, character and location, the narrative setup, and generic possibilities. (The last two will be investigated later under Genre and Narrative Theory.) Issues of ideology will be dealt with later.

Through-composed music: The music has been commissioned specifically for the drama to fit its tone and particular scenes, and runs throughout the drama rather than using existing music.

Serial narrative: A narrative in which a story develops from episode to episode leading to a narrative resolution in the final episode (as opposed to series narratives, which have resolutions at the end of each episode, though some series narratives also offer some serial narrative arcs).

Multiple narrative strands: A narrative in which several parallel storylines progress (as in a soap opera) that may or may not affect one another. More complex serial narratives may tie together all these strands in the final resolution, but some may be left hanging.

English-language LFTVDs

> #### *Mr. Robot*, episode 1 – opening sequence
>
> The sequence starts with a voiceover while black-on-white titles play. The voiceover addresses the audience directly but connotes uncertainty by referring to itself as a conversation with someone only in the protagonist's head and technophile sophistication by starting with a phrase – 'Hello friend' – commonly use to describe a computer virus. The flat monotone connotes perhaps lack of interest and authenticity in its refusal to try to sell to the audience. The first slow tracking back shot – of the conspiracy – links silhouetted men in suits, who slowly come into focus, to an urban skyline to connote power and mystery. The closely mic'ed voice starts off against silence, then a build-up of orchestral music connoting mystery climaxes on a fade to black.
>
> Our first view of Elliot is in a shot that conveys alienation, matching his flat voice. Located in a subway train, the lighting is sickly, creating a yellow-brown colour palette. Elliot is clearly the subject, but is placed at the bottom of the frame on the extreme right-hand side so some of his close-up face is outside the frame. His large eyes (unlit by an eye light, giving them a slightly dead look) in a pale, thin face are looking around in a paranoid manner. The soundtrack highlights the screeching noises of the train. This all activates a Barthesian myth of 'urban alienation', a myth recognisable from countless media products.

→

Mr. Robot, episode 1 – opening sequence

The scene continues with a conventional shot reverse shot of Elliot and the men he thinks are following him. It then contrast cuts on Elliot's 'Instead I went to …' to a shot of him in a different location, a café. The abrupt edit draws attention to the expressionistic manner of the editing, which contrasts with the **social realism** of the mise-en-scène, but further connotes that the whole narrative is Elliot's version of events. Despite the abrupt change of location, the mise-en-scène is linked by similar lighting and colour palette.

The café scene is mostly conventionally shot and edited, with shot reverse shot on Ron and Elliott that becomes more close up as the tension builds. The soundtrack starts with banal 'dinner jazz' music among the background sounds, but non-diegetic music starts as Elliot tells Ron that he has hacked him, connoting tension as it is based on bass guitar beats like a heartbeat. Shots of Elliot sometimes have him strangely placed in the centre of the frame – a weak position that reflects his ambiguous and held-back performance. This scene leads up to the title frame in a very old-fashioned, doubled, blocky red font.

This media language meets the contextual requirement for high production values as its highly stylised nature suggests an 'authored' product – reflecting the personal vision of its writer-producer. It breaks with the conventionality of traditional television drama to fit the alienation of its unreliable narrator. The narrative is ambiguous and complex.

Social realism: The set of conventions by which audiences accept a representation as reflecting real social conditions, especially the plight of the poor and powerless. The term may imply the depiction of a social group or social truth that is under-represented in other media products.

House of Cards, episode 1 – opening sequence

The sequence starts with the sound of a car crash and a yelping dog over a black screen. This fades, motivated by the sound of a door opening, to an almost unlit exterior night shot as Frank opens his door in long shot, walks to the camera in mid-close-up, turns and walks down the sidewalk. This stylish shot connotes sophistication, as does Frank's white shirt and braces and his colleague's dress shirt and bow tie. Both actors perform as men of power. Neither have eye lights, giving them dead-looking eyes in the low lighting. As they approach the dog, they look down in a low angle point-of-view shot from the dog's perspective, conveying that the programme will address the audience in an ambiguous manner. The next shot sees Frank walk towards the out-of-frame dog into a mid-shot, then address the audience directly looking into camera, connoting that he is now letting us into his world. His killing of the dog is connoted by sound effects and performance alone while he delivers a monologue about pain. The juxtaposition of his calmness and the brutality of the act connotes his ruthlessness, his willingness to do whatever is required. The whole scene is shot in very long takes, particularly the shot of the killing and monologue, an editing style that focuses attention on the performance. The music – piano and orchestra – has both sinister and sophisticated connotations, which tie in with the upmarket mise-en-scène and atmosphere of cold brutality.

The next scene sees Frank washing, including a mirror point of view shot that enables Frank to give the audience a knowing look. He glides into shot behind Claire, both in formal dress, in an underlit house interior with a white/grey colour palette that connotes coolness and that they are lurking in their lair.

The final scene is again characterised by very slow editing pace, performance to camera (explaining the political context and characters), and camera movement around a large crowd scene in a ballroom motivated by Frank's performance with cutaways to key characters. This connotes Frank's expertise and control. The mise-en-scène suggests an attempt to look festive that is undercut by the tawdriness of the decorations, the Auld Lang Syne diegetic music, and the performances of insincerity (e.g. by Vasquez smiling briefly for the camera). This all activates the Barthesian myth of the insincere World of Politics.

This media language meets the contextual requirement for high production values due to its star casting and its highly stylised nature suggesting an 'authored' product – in this case the influence of star film director David Fincher as well as the writer Beau Willimon. The very knowing media language fits the programme's ironic tone and a narrative in which the protagonist constantly breaks the fourth wall by speaking or acting directly to the audience to let them in on the dramatic irony.

Homeland, episode 1 – opening sequence

The sequence begins with an establishing shot of the Baghdad skyline followed by some documentary-style shots of people in the streets. All the shots in Baghdad are hand-held, connoting documentary realism, as does the use of natural lighting and thriller-style urgency. The soundtrack is dominated by the sounds of the streets with a call to prayer in the background, activating a Barthesian myth of the Middle East. Then Carrie's voice, closely mic'ed, dominates the soundtrack and we cut to a view out of her car window then close-ups of Carrie with loud diegetic sounds of driving. This contrast cuts to gallows in a prison, back to Carrie and then a series of edits between the parallel action of Carrie driving and walking through Baghdad and David at the other end of the phone conversation. The rapid editing and change of locations connote energy and urgency, but the shots of David at a formal gathering are shot with much more controlled camerawork, conventional lighting, quieter background sound and more formal mise-en-scène such as David's dinner jacket. These shots of David connote power and authority in contrast to Carrie's increasingly desperate pleas.

At the prison, the contrast between inside and outside is emphasised by the changes in background sounds from loud traffic noises (though there is no traffic) and a call to prayer to quieter sounds of footsteps, a wireless buzz, the sounds of the guards arriving and the use of visual framing devices such as the window in the cell door and the corridor walls to connote being shut in. As the guards drag Carrie away, the violence is conveyed by fast-paced editing and chaotic hand-held camera movement. The scene ends with a reverberant sound like a door slamming.

This media language meets the contextual requirement for high production values due to its star casting and use of exotic locations (for American television). The documentary realist features of the opening fit the real historical context of fears of terrorism explored by this spy thriller. The narrative is made more complex by the mental health issues suffered by our protagonist – is the information whispered to her real?

Stranger Things, episode 1 – opening sequence

The opening sequence starts with a scene at the laboratory, seen first in a tilting exterior establishing shot with caption, then as a series of interiors. A slow track into a door with a quiet soundtrack creates a jump scare as the door slams open, a man runs through, and alarms sound. The mise-en-scène is expressionistic – oppressive corridors and flashing lights, camerawork using fluid movement to emphasise the speed of the scientist running. The moment he sees his attacker is connoted by animal noises on the soundtrack and a striking overhead shot connoting the attacker's point of view before the attack. The immense strength of the attack and the fact the attacker is unseen connotes the Barthesian myth of The Monster.

A contrast cut to a close-up of a lawn sprinkler connotes a return to a familiar reality, the Barthesian myth of small-town America. The rest of the sequence is shot at night with low-key lighting in naturalistic suburban mise-en-scène. This conveys both a sense of security and a possibility of threat. The four friends playing a game are cast for their physical dissimilarity, which is emphasised by their different costume. This connotes a gang of individuals. Their game is dramatised with loud sound effects, use of close-ups, and fast-paced edits to connote excitement.

A high-angle and low-angle shot reverse shot sequence of Mike and his mother, conveying their relative power, ends the game. Synthesised music starts to build, connoting the 1980s as do the props such as a 1980s-style record player and a cathode ray tube television with an indoor aerial.

As the children leave the large car port of Mike's house the light begins to flicker, perhaps referencing the flashing lights of the laboratory. The music swells to connote the power and pleasure of cycling home together, reinforced by the tracking low-angle camerawork, the backlighting as they race, and the way their movement motivates the framing.

A crane shot shows Will on his own and then the sign for the restricted area, juxtaposing the two to connote danger as the soundtrack changes to quiet diegetic sounds. A sound effect draws attention to Will's light failing. The monster is back-lit and shown very briefly to merely suggest his shape, his monstrosity connoted by a sudden wild sound and the chaos of Will's crash by fast cuts to unclear movement. Fluid camerawork follows Will home through beautifully side-lit gardens. At home, tracking shots follow Will's running, echoing those in the laboratory and the soundtrack of suspenseful orchestral music, the dog barking, and the monstrous noises on the telephone, which all signal danger. The shadowy monster's power is shown by its ability to unlock the door chain. There is a beautifully cinematic tracking shot of Will running through the garden into the light from the shed. The initial low-angle shot of its interior emphasises the light bulb for the first time. The camera tracks slowly towards the door, echoing the shot in the laboratory, as Will loads his gun.

➡

> ### *Stranger Things*, episode 1 – opening sequence
>
> As he waits, there is a movement behind him, he turns to look, and we cut to a craning high-angle point-of-view shot of Will's terrified face with growling on the soundtrack, a close-up of the light bulb, which burns bright, accompanied by the sound of screaming synthesisers, then dims to the sound of the wind. Cut to the shed from the same low angle as before, but Will is missing. Fade to black.
>
> This media language meets the contextual requirement for high production values as it consciously emulates the lush cinematography and use of enigma characteristic of Spielberg films such as *ET*. These cinematic qualities fit the highly intertextual nature of the series. The narrative is complex and ambiguous.

Non-English-language LFTVDs

> ### *The Killing*, episode 1 – closing sequence (47.34 to end)
>
> This sequence was chosen to illustrate the coming together of the programme's three narrative strands as the opening sequence is not typical of the programme as a whole.
>
> The sequence starts with a slow tracking shot across the canal bridge, ending with a focus pull to the chains that will raise the car from the water. Slow ominous orchestral music signals the catastrophe ahead, matched by slow editing and lengthy shots of Lund's profile, connoting the seriousness of the situation. A beautifully cinematic long shot against a sunset background shows back-lit water gushing from the car hoisted above the water.
>
> Theis is seen in close-up driving his van; he is indistinct, reflecting his lack of certainty over where his daughter is. The cut to Pernille shows her very still, in contrast to his movement. As Theis arrives and gets out of the car the camerawork changes to hand held and he is lit by harsh light, connoting ugliness. Pernille, in parallel action, is shot pacing around the house, the everyday props linking back to their domesticity. Lund and Meyer find Nanna's body in close-ups under the same harsh light. Lund steps out to see Theis in a controlled static shot that contrasts with his agitated hand-held shots. As Pernille hears Theis's anguished sounds the camera tracks back as she collapses with grief, as if recoiling in shock
>
> A flash is used as a stylised transition from the photo of Nanna back to the crime scene. Meyer's announcement that the car is registered to Troels motivates a body wipe transition to the very different mise-en-scène of Hartmann's campaign, where out-of-focus extras move in front of a bright wall poster of the politician. A focus pull from Troels looking full of suspicion to his campaign organiser (and lover) connotes his distrust now he knows there is a spy in his office. This begins a montage ending set to rhythmic but questioning music, of Troels, the body, Theis looking stunned, Pernille overcome with grief, dusting for fingerprints and ending in a freeze frame of Lund in close-up looking determined.
>
> This media language meets the contextual requirement for high production values due to its use of location shooting and some more expensive, cinematic-style shots among the more conventional and cheaper camerawork and mise-en-scène. This episode suggests a rather lower budget than for some of the other LFTVDs, but its lack of showiness fits the programme's social realism. The narrative is multi-stranded with complex interrelationships between the strands.

> ### *Borgen*, episode 1 – opening sequence
>
> The sequence starts with the through-composed musical soundtrack over the Machiavelli quote, with a fade up to a close-up of a make-up brush, connoting artifice and preparation. This cuts to a close-up of Birgitte as she is made up, with the sound of an interview on television introducing her competitors. We see Hanne in a degraded picture connoting a television screen, then a big close-up of Birgitte's eye and a two shot of her and the make-up artist. The two connote calmness and professionalism, reflected in the cool, white, uncluttered mise-en-scène. This cuts to Kasper silhouetted in a grey, shiny corridor – these connotations of cool efficiency and power are reinforced by his decisive phone manner, his business suit, and the way he prowls around. The camera slowly tracks around the television studio – emphasising the constructed artifice of the television studio as it peers from behind cameras.
>
> The next scene contrasts in its mise-en-scène and soundtrack: a busy London street, with traffic noise and more sinister music. The camerawork retains the slow tracking style established before, but in a much more open-framed manner – extras pass in front of the camera – reinforcing the connotations of urbanism.

Borgen, episode 1 – opening sequence

The cut to Hesselboe in the PR office is motivated by speech in English from the PR consultant. The mise-en-scène is grey, with huge windows overlooking St Pauls, activating the Barthesian myth of 'Big Business'. The camerawork, though mostly handheld, is static, including one low-angle shot that emphasises the size of the table, connoting the trappings of power.

This contrast cuts to very fluid handheld shots in natural light of Laugesen descending exterior steps for an interview. His exaggeratedly dynamic movements and hair suggest immediately a narcissistic character.

Another contrast cut back to the studio where the final scene in the sequence is shot in three-way parallel action: Torben and the crew in the control room, Birgitte and Katrine in the studio, and Kasper watching horrified from the wings. All three are shot in a similar style, with slow camera movement, open framing, often including foreground objects out of focus, all suggesting a drama unfolding in a confined space. The mise-en-scène for each of the three is subtly different: the control room using low-key very white lighting reinforcing the technophile connotations of the set; the studio using conventional, warmer studio lighting; Kasper in a low-key light that combines with his very brown environment to make him look hidden away. The soundtrack reinforces these differences: the control room has busy, overlapping dialogue, both Torben and Kasper are closely mic'ed to connote their private conversations, while Birgitte is mic'ed more distantly so she has to publicly proclaim. The parallel action dramatises the pressure on Birgitte to stay with Laugesen. Her moment of decision is signalled by performance of increasing discomfort and signified by a sudden dropping of the suspenseful music, which returns after her decision and sweeps towards the title sequence.

This media language meets the contextual requirement for high production values due to the variety of sets and locations and the reasonably stylised media language that suggests authorship. The programme's relative lack of showiness fits its social realism. The narrative is complex, with a large ensemble of important characters.

Trapped, episode 1 – post titles sequence (05.10–08.32)

This sequence was chosen to illustrate the programme's two narrative strands as the opening sequence is not typical of the programme as a whole.

The location of the series and its weather serve almost as characters. The sequence starts with two long shots: of the harbour overshadowed by the mountains; of the snowy town at the foot of the mountains, which connote the power of nature and the isolation of the town. An extreme contrast cut to a photograph on the wall and domestic family sounds brings us indoors. The decor is plain and old fashioned, the lighting low key and naturalistic for a grandparents' house. We are in the world of social realism. This is reinforced by **naturalism** in the casting – Andri is not a conventionally attractive man, though he has a bear-like solidity.

Simple piano music starts to signal the transition to the next scene, outside in the snow. A cutaway to a large mountain with avalanche defences foreshadows the weather's role in the plot. A beautifully cinematic telephoto long shot of the ferry, out of focus on the horizon as if emerging from another world, establishes the location for the contrast cut to the kitchen – a close-up of knives, which may again foreshadow events. The soundtrack on the ferry consists of ambient sounds, dominated by the low rumble of the ship's engines. One key shot shows the huge mountains of the harbour framed by the ship's windows. Contrasting shots of the fishing boat – from a wobbling hand-held camera and much smaller-scale sounds of water – connote its small size. A shot of the ferry dominating the frame emphasises the difference, then a reverse shot shows its bow wave disturbing the fishing boat, perhaps symbolising the **narrative disruption** the ferry will represent.

This media language meets the contextual requirement for high production values as the extensive use of location shooting and the use of a ferry, plus the cinematic quality in some camerawork, represents high expense for an Icelandic drama. The complex narrative interweaves Andri's family relationships with his police work.

Naturalism: The opposite of expressionism. Media language that is self-effacing to suggest a transparent window on the world. Often linked to **social realism**.

Narrative disruption: The event(s) that disrupt an initial equilibrium and drive a narrative towards a resolution. For example, a murder can disrupt the peace of a community and cause investigation and solution.

Deutschland 83, episode 1 – opening sequence

The sequence starts with a delicately lit exterior shot of Leonora's office block, connoting both institutional power and her need to work late into the night. Ronald Reagan makes a speech on the soundtrack, motivating a cut to the office where Leonora is watching television. She is smoking indoors. The decor matches the 1980s setting, the television is a cathode ray tube television. An unusual high-angle shot that emphasises the ceiling shows her walk to the telephone. This may connote surveillance, or may simply show off the 1980s production design. Slightly ominous music clashes with the beeps of the telephone. Leonora is stylishly dressed and well lit, connoting her important role.

Cut to a utilitarian corridor where, with rapid editing and a continuation of the music with more force, West German students are led to an office. The door slamming motivates the music to reduce to a thrumming under the conversation. The room is very plain and lit by unflattering but naturalistic fluorescent lamps. Martin's authority is connoted by his dominant body language, his uniform, the low-angle shots as if from the student's point of view, and the script, then is undermined by his giggles at the end. This scene contrasts the fearfulness of the authoritarian East German state with its citizens' everyday efforts to get by (Martin keeps one book to give his mother).

The next scene is located at Walter's office. The trappings of power are connoted by the overhead shot of Leonora's car arriving, the blank exterior and the large windows, but undermined by Walter's wince as he drinks the poor coffee. Again, the decor is very 1980s. The scene is edited slowly, naturally lit, with a fairly empty diegetic soundtrack, connoting a quiet chat between two powerful equals. Diegetic music kicks in only when Leonora hands over the file on Martin. This motivates a contrast cut to the next scene.

A handheld camera follows Martin into his mother's garden. His uniform stands out among the casually dressed party-goers. Leonora is revealed as his aunt. The noise and informality of the young people's party and use of diegetic pop music contrasts with all that has gone before. Both Martin and Annett have been cast with conventionally attractive young actors. Martin puts his hat on Annett and kisses her, connoting the throwing off of a formality and authority he does not really fit. A pop concert plays on the television.

An intimate scene between the two sisters, reinforced by use of two shots, connotes close family ties, but Leonora's look out of the hatch towards Martin suggests calculation rather than affection. The diegetic pop music on the soundtrack crashes into the title sequence.

This media language meets the contextual requirement for high production values due to its period mise-en-scène requiring meticulous production design, the use of German film actors and some cinematic shots. The narrative is not particularly complex in structure but is morally ambiguous.

Genre and LFTVD

Neale's theory

Neale argued that genre is a process by which generic codes and conventions are shared by producers and audiences through repetition in media products. The importance of this idea of a 'shared code' is that genres are not fixed, but constantly evolve with each new addition to the generic corpus.

There have been criticisms of this idea. Film noir, for example, while held to be a genre, is a label invented some time after most of the films now seen as 'film noir' were made (the 1940s and early 1950s), meaning that this label could not have been shared with audiences at the time. In a similar fashion, some LFTVDs such as *The Killing* or *Trapped* have come to be labelled 'Nordic noir' as they are seen to share similar dark themes, but this label is again retrospective.

Generic corpus: The body of media products in a genre. Each subtly adds to, and thus changes, the genre.

Revision activity

Pick two other key scenes from each of your LFTVDs and carry out a similar analysis of media language use.

Shared code: The idea the genres are defined by codes and conventions that come into existence in the interrelationship between media products, their producers and their audiences. A producer looks at existing products that have been successful with audiences and produces new products using the same conventions to meet the audiences' expectations, but with subtle variations to maintain interest.

However, Neale's concept of fluid genres explains the ease with which media products can play with genre codes and conventions, hybridise with other genres or have generic ambiguity. We can see the significance of these for LFTVDs in the analyses below.

Television and genre

Neale's theory was developed to explain genre in film but can apply equally to television. However, the differences between film and television have important consequences for genre.

Film, particularly when screened in cinema, is especially good at creating self-contained fictional worlds due to its mostly one-off narratives and conditions of viewing. Television, on the other hand, suffers interrupted and often less attentive viewing. This means that highly expressive genres such as horror or science fiction work better in film than on television. Antagonists in long-running television programmes become tamed by familiarity, unlike in the closed narratives of film. Romance may be more satisfying as a film genre than a television genre as couples cannot repeatedly fall in love; hence the use of unresolved sexual tension over several series of television dramas such as *The X-Files*.

However, television's repetition makes it very suitable for social realist genres with ensemble casts, who can become a sort of substitute family, as in police or medical dramas. This means that many forms of television drama tend towards soap opera with ensemble casts, multiple storylines, shifting perspectives and a strong sense of social realist location. The serial narratives of LFTVDs allow for these soap elements plus a drive towards narrative resolution.

The influence of historical, economic and cultural contexts

Long form television drama developed as a quality product due to the economic context of increasing competition with the advent of more television channels, leading to the search for quality drama as flagship programming. The need for distinctive programming means that generic hybridity is common. Programmes innovate through generic blending with the more adventurous attempting generic ambiguity or even deliberate confusion, as with the 'grandparent' of current LFTVD *Twin Peaks*. This appeared on first sight to be a detective series, but branched out in dizzying directions until it lost a sense of a firm generic foothold. Each generic innovation in the form has raised audience expectations of television drama, further raising the pressure culturally to innovate.

For **Public Service Broadcasting (PSB)** the cultural status of genres is an important context, which is undergoing a slow historical change. Generic mass media products are seen as having a lower cultural status than the more generically ambiguous high art. British television in the 1970s, for example, would fulfil its PSB obligations by screening single dramas such as *Play For Today*. The success of American quality drama such as *The Sopranos* (a complex, critically acclaimed gangster series) raised the cultural status of generic television drama. This, allied to the economic contexts of enormously increased competition for PSB broadcasters and their need to target programmes at the international as well as the national market, means that generic dramas can now be considered PSB programming, so long as they also contain culturally or politically significant messages.

> **Public Service Broadcasting (PSB)**: Broadcasting intended for public benefit – these benefits (especially those for the BBC) are the subject of vigorous political and cultural debate, and are overseen in Britain by the regulator Ofcom.

Generic analyses of set products

English-language LFTVDs

Mr. Robot, episode 1

This is a generically ambiguous programme, particularly as the narrator is so unreliable:
- it may be a conspiracy thriller (like the 1974 film *The Parallax View* in which a conspiracy does rule the world)
- it may be a psychological thriller (like the 2010 film *Shutter Island* or the 1999 film *Fight Club* in which the narrative occurs mostly in the character's mind)
- it may have romance elements given Elliot's relationship with Angela
- it may be a hacker drama (like the 1995 film *Hackers* in which hackers are the heroes)
- it may be a satirical comedy about corporate power.

This ambiguity allows *Mr. Robot* to go in a number of unpredictable directions as the season continues.

House of Cards, episode 1

This is a generic hybrid, combining political drama with an examination of a power marriage. However, rather than a *West Wing* drama dealing with serious political issues, the politics consists of scheming, lies and deceit. Rather than a romance, the Underwoods' marriage is one of equally corrupt, ambitious and powerful individuals. In this way, the conventions of both genres are subverted. Frank is cast as a pantomime character, a man of exaggerated venality, rather like a gangster.

Homeland, episode 1

This is a relatively simple spy thriller, with Carrie as the conventional maverick operative. So perhaps what is most generically unusual about the programme is that it has a female protagonist without a secondary romantic plot line. Moreover, the introduction of mental health issues into a genre already about conspiracy and obsession adds greater complexity and jeopardy.

Stranger Things, episode 1

This programme is generically complex as the first episode offers a number of directions the narrative could take. It includes:
- science fiction elements with the disruption emanating from a science laboratory
- horror elements with the monster (horror often being hybridised with sci-fi)
- conspiracy thriller elements with the sinister agents
- family drama in the relationship between Joyce, Jonathon and Will
- romance elements with Nancy and Steve
- coming-of-age drama with the boy gang
- police drama with Hopper's investigations and his troubled past.

Plus, throughout, there is a strong sense of cinematic homage lying just beyond the narrative.

Non-English-language LFTVDs

The Killing, episode 1

This programme interweaves three generically different narrative strands:
1. the police procedural drama investigating the murder
2. the family melodrama of Theis and Pernille (and, to some extent, of Lund's family)
3. the political drama of the mayoral election and the difficulties caused to Troels by the criminal investigation.

In addition – and this cannot be seen from the opening episode – the overall structure of the drama creates a murder mystery 'whodunnit' as different suspects emerge each episode. A PSB plotline of the impact of racism in society ties in to this as the killing is motivated by racism.

Borgen, episode 1

This programme is primarily a political drama, with Birgitte as a *West Wing*-style idealised politician, which interweaves other generic elements such as:
- romance (such as Katrine's doomed attempt in episode 1)
- workplace drama (within the political campaign and the media)
- family drama (Birgitte's relationship with her husband and kids).

Non-English-language LFTVDs

Trapped, episode 1

This programme is primarily a police procedural drama investigating the murder, with Andri as the conventional cop with misdemeanours in his past and a broken marriage, but also includes:
- a family drama (Andri's broken family and relationship with his in-laws)
- a small-town community drama of domination by Reykjavik and tensions below the surface.

In addition – and not apparent from the opening episode – the drama's overall structure creates a murder mystery 'whodunnit' as different suspects emerge each episode, with the suspects trapped in a snow-bound town rather than a country house or a train (as in Agatha Christie). The drama introduces PSB elements by reflecting Icelandic culture and covering issues of sexual exploitation and trafficking.

Deutschland 83, episode 1

This programme is primarily a spy thriller, but also includes generic elements of:
- romance (between Annett and Martin, plus other possibilities)
- political satire – aimed at both the East and West Germans and particularly the Americans
- family drama (concerning Martin's family).

Media language and technology

Economic contexts

An economic context is the reduction in cost of technology such as:
- CGI allowing visual effects even within television budgets
- drones allowing aerial photography at much lower budget levels
- high-definition digital cameras that can reproduce film-quality visuals, removing the need for the distinct studio video and exterior filmic camerawork typical of much earlier television. This enables much more extensive use of location and reduces the cost of editing. Modern video cameras can also shoot in much lower light levels, allowing low-key lighting at night.

Developments in streaming rely on economic contexts like the declining cost of computing power, political contexts such as the political drive to create high-speed broadband connections, and the cultural context of changing attitudes to what constitutes television. Streaming as a technology allows:
- programmes to be made without obvious segmentation in order to fit advertising breaks
- less adherence to rigid programme lengths
- less need for traditional narrative elements of weekly dramas such as 'previously on' sections and cliff-hanger endings as programmes can be watched as a complete series.

Streaming also means that programmes may be watched on phones and tablets as well as PCs and television, so the media language may need to adapt also to work on smaller screen sizes.

The role of intertextuality

Cultural contexts

The **postmodernism** of the 1990s in film, advertising and television has established **intertextuality** as culturally expected in much television drama. The extra complexity that intertextuality brings to a narrative can help meet the cultural expectation of quality in LFTVD. On the other hand, the need to both reflect the national context and appeal to international audiences may limit the opportunities for intertextuality in non-English

> **Revision activity**
>
> For each of your two chosen LFTVD episodes, note the key scenes that illustrate the use, hybridity or subversion of generic conventions in the drama.

> **Intertextuality**: Media products (texts) that refer to other media products.

language LFTVD. Local audiences might notice the references, but they may be missed by the international audience. It is no coincidence that the two most intertextual programmes among the set products – *Stranger Things* and *Deutschland 83* – reference internationally recognisable media products: Hollywood films in the former and television news about the Cold War and internationally successful pop music in the latter.

Postmodernism: A very general set of ideas about culture after modernism.

If traditional art forms use traditional conventions (e.g. traditional architecture) and modernism broke with these by breaking conventions to create something pure and new (e.g. modernist glass and steel towers), postmodernism uses conventions in a playful and ironic way to create something new out of intertextuality (e.g. mixing up different styles). Media products tend to postmodernism by their very nature because most use existing genre conventions to create something different.

The fact that postmodernism is difficult to pin down and define is itself quite postmodernist, as it reacted against the dogmatic ideals, truths and revolutionary breakthroughs that characterise modernism by adopting a certain fuzziness.

Set product examples

English-language LFTVDs

Mr. Robot, episode 1

Elliot thinks he sees 'men in black', possibly a reference to the conspiracy science-fiction film of that name.

Mr. Robot tells Elliot of his plans while the two are on a Ferris wheel. This is probably a reference to the 1949 classic *The Third Man*, where the morally compromised Harry Lime (Orson Welles) meets the protagonist on a Ferris wheel and delivers a very famous speech about good things coming out of destruction. Mr. Robot tells Elliot of his plan to bring down capitalism.

The use of the song 'If you go away' is untypical of the tone of the soundtrack and references the Belgian songwriter Jacques Brel, whose work signifies bohemianism and lacerating emotional honesty, reflecting Elliot's outsider status and intense loneliness.

There are countless cyber references, including the first words spoken, 'Hello friend', the name of a famous computer virus.

House of Cards, episode 1

For fans of the original series, the programme references the British version (1990–1995) in its tone and narrative, but also in its most famous line: 'You might very well think that but, of course, I couldn't possibly comment.'

Homeland, episode 1

Homeland doesn't appear to use intertextuality explicitly, though it probably references the original Israeli version. This may be because it is a thriller that tries to construct a coherent fictional world in which the threat is seen as real.

Stranger Things, episode 1

Stranger Things is explicitly a recreation of 1970s–1980s cinema, especially Spielberg, in overall style and tone. Like Spielberg's *ET*, the episode features a suburban location next to a wood, boys on bikes, missing fathers and ambiguous government agents in hazmat suits. Like Spielberg's *Jaws*, the peril is suggested rather than explicitly shown. Like Spielberg's *Close Encounters of the Third Kind*, an adult becomes obsessed. The boy gang is reminiscent of Reiner's *Stand by Me*. The girl with the ability to move objects is reminiscent of De Palma's *Carrie*. The soundtrack sounds like John Carpenter's scores and sound effects for horror films such as *The Thing*, whose poster is on the wall in the basement in Mike's house. There is an explicit reference to Hooper's *Poltergeist*, whose plot suggests the theme of being sucked into another world. The *Stranger Things* title has a retro look like that for *The Dead Zone*.

The 1960s song 'White rabbit' plays as Eleven escapes at the diner.

Figure 2.6 *Homeland* – the 'perfect' couple on Nick's release

Exam tip

It is clear that some set products use intertextual references more than others. Examiners cannot set exam questions that advantage some candidates over others, so questions on LFTVDs cannot assume that the products studied will include intertextual references.

Non-English-language LFTVDs
The Killing, episode 1
This programme's commitment to social realism means that it minimises explicit use of intertextuality.
Borgen, episode 1
This programme references Danish politics in some detail, with all the political parties in the programme having real-life counterparts. Beyond this, the programme's commitment to social realism means that it minimises explicit use of intertextuality.
Trapped, episode 1
This programme's commitment to social realism means that it minimises explicit use of intertextuality.
Deutschland 83, episode 1
This programme relies on intertextuality as part of its scene-setting; for example, the opening shot of Ronald Reagan's Cold War speech on television. Shots from East and West German television are used, in the titles for example, to establish the Cold War tension that forms the real historical context for these events. There are many other references, to different East and West German brands, for example, that may not resonate with international audiences but still signify cultural difference. Internationally successful pop music is used to evoke the period. The young people at the East German party are dancing to a German version of the international hit '99 Red Balloons'; in West Germany we hear western pop music such as New Order and Annie Lennox.

Viewpoints and ideologies in media language

The prime contexts influencing media language in television drama may be such ideologies as:

- **individualism**, e.g. focusing a drama on an individual protagonist
- **consumerism**, e.g. judging characters on their possessions or the desirability of their lifestyles
- **patriarchal** power and the challenge to this by feminism, e.g. using or refusing to use women's bodies as objects, or narratives that present a male, female or gender-neutral perspective
- racism and **ethnocentrism** and the challenge to those from multiculturalism and internationalism, e.g. narratives that present a monocultural, multicultural or minority perspective.

Revision activity

For each of your two chosen LFTVD episodes, follow up the references noted above by briefly accessing the referenced products.

Individualism: The ideology that assumes people are essentially individuals. Taking exams is an example of competitive individualism. The opposite is collectivism – that people are essentially collective, i.e. members of a group.

Consumerism: The ideology that we should judge ourselves and others on our material possessions, that our lifestyles (e.g. our clothes, houses, cars, media use) should define our individual identities. The opposite is ideas of duty or religious renunciation.

Patriarchy: The system and ideology of male power described by feminism. Literally it means 'rule of the father'. Patriarchal ideology includes the male gaze, stereotypes of male power (including violence) and activity, and female submissiveness and passivity, the ideology of romance and the family, and the separation of a masculine public realm from a feminine domestic realm.

Ethnocentrism: Belief that your own culture is natural and normal, and that other cultures are inferior and strange.

English-language LFTVDs

Mr. Robot, episode 1

The media language incorporates individualism through an individual narrator and protagonist, though this is undercut by making the character harder to identify with due to his flat delivery and unheroic appearance.

The programme appears to be anti-consumerist in its embrace of outsiders, such as Mr. Robot in his shabby clothes. In contrast, the smart suits of the E Corps executives appear to signify their low moral status. However, Gideon is shown surrounded by consumer goods such as a private jet and a managed 'out' lifestyle, yet is still cast and performed as sympathetic.

The narrative constructs a White American male perspective – Elliot's point of view. However, Elliot's outsider status, expressed in the programme's pessimistic and disorientating media language, problematises this White male American perspective.

House of Cards, episode 1

The media language incorporates individualism through an individual narrator and protagonist.

The programme incorporates consumerism in its mise-en-scène of balls and formal dress but also problematises this world by connoting its shallowness and naked ambition.

The narrative constructs a primarily White American male perspective – Frank's point of view. However, there is a narrative strand in which Claire is connoted as powerful without her husband. Frank's comments on Vasquez connoting her tokenism, drawing attention to the White perspective and thus de-naturalising it.

The cynical viewpoint of the programme is expressed in its slick and knowing media language.

Homeland, episode 1

The media language incorporates individualism through an individual maverick protagonist.

It also both incorporates and undermines consumerism. Carrie's character is expressed through her house and furnishings and her obsessiveness through her performance and some chaos in her house and lifestyle. This perhaps perversely reinforces consumerism in presenting her as unusual. Brody's family, by contrast, are presented as an apparently perfect all-American suburban family, but this image of consumerist perfection is undermined by their storylines of deception.

The narrative constructs a primarily female perspective – Carrie's point of view – within a world dominated by men, but also shows several scenes that objectivise women's bodies. The American perspective is constructed as multicultural. The thriller media language incorporates an American national security viewpoint, as threats to this security form the narrative disruption.

→

English-language LFTVDs

Stranger Things, episode 1

The multi-perspective narrative of this programme suggests a less individualistic ideology, though the perspectives of the lone individuals, especially Joyce and Hopper, and small groups such as the boys' gang drive the narrative. The perspective of the corporate force is not presented.

Consumerism is incorporated in the references to popular culture and consumer goods.

The social realism of the programme incorporates a pro-family ideology, as does the narrative disruption being the loss of a family member. The action elements in the episode incorporate an anti-authoritarian ideology, as the ruthless violence of the state is defeated by a small girl.

The narrative delivers a gender-neutral small-town American perspective. It is a matter of debate whether the casting of a Black actor as part of the gang suggests tokenism or multiculturalism.

Non-English-language LFTVDs

The Killing, episode 1

The media language incorporates individualism through an individual protagonist, but weakens this through two other intertwining storylines showing different perspectives.

Consumerism is incorporated through storylines showing Theis's efforts to create a better lifestyle and in the way the narrative disruption of the murder destroys this happy **narrative equilibrium** and Lund's search for a better life in Sweden.

The social realism of the programme incorporates a pro-family ideology, as does the narrative disruption being the loss of a family member.

The narrative constructs a primarily female perspective – Lund's point of view – within a world dominated by men, but also features one scene that presents Lund's body as an object of desire. In the secondary storylines we see a male perspective on politics and a gender-neutral perspective on the Birk Larsen family.

The programme suggests a primarily White perspective, but one that acknowledges racism and presents it as a social (and narrative) problem.

Borgen, episode 1

The media language incorporates individualism through an individual protagonist, but a protagonist who is in charge of a collective effort – forming a government.

The programme does not incorporate consumerism insofar as Birgitte is defined by her values and beliefs and willingness to stand up for these, in opposition to Laugesen's retail politics. There is some emphasis on the material trappings of power, but Birgitte is willing to sacrifice these. There is much emphasis on physical appearance – portrayed as a necessary evil.

The narrative constructs a primarily female perspective – Birgitte's point of view – within a world mostly dominated by men. The display of women's bodies is deconstructed in a feminist fashion in storylines about Birgitte's body shape.

The programme's suggests a primarily White perspective, but one that acknowledges racism and scapegoating of immigrants and presents it as a social (and narrative) problem.

The suspenseful elements of the narrative such as in moments of ethical decision-making present a viewpoint that political engagement and honesty are to be valued.

Narrative equilibrium: The state of stasis before the narrative disruption occurs. This is often inadequate in some way, so that the resolution leads to an improved equilibrium. The transformation from the initial to the final equilibrium suggests the key values or ideology of the narrative.

➜

Non-English-language LFTVDs
Trapped, episode 1
The media language incorporates individualism through an individual protagonist, but a protagonist who is embedded in a tight-knit community.
The programme's relationship to consumerism is ambiguous. Andri is building a new house to create a better life for this family and the community is trying to become rich by allowing the Chinese to build a new port, but money is obviously short in the post-financial crash period and the media language used to depict these enterprises suggests an element of desperation.
The narrative constructs a primarily male perspective – Andri's point of view – but his gender-neutral team each carry storylines and Andri is represented as a single parent. It is a White, Icelandic perspective, but one that acknowledges racism and sexual exploitation of women of colour as a social problem.
Deutschland 83, episode 1
The media language incorporates individualism through an individual protagonist, but a protagonist who is trapped by social forces beyond his control.
Consumerism is almost a character in this narrative. Explicit stories about the lack of consumer goods in East Germany are contrasted with material plenty in the West.
The narrative constructs a primarily male perspective – Martin's point of view – but the narrative is driven by a female power representative, Leonora. The perspective is German, but one that does not take sides between the East and the West – the key narrative disruption is American sabre-rattling and escalation of the Cold War arms race, a disruption that suggests a pacifist viewpoint. This programme has a primarily White perspective, but with multicultural casting.

Media language theories

Barthes has been covered on page 7 and pages 146–151, while Neale has been covered on pages 151-2; so this section will focus on the theories of Todorov, Levi-Strauss and Baudrillard in relation to the set products.

Todorov

Todorov's narratology can be used to analyse the narratives of the LFTVDs, but also has limitations.

The dramas can be analysed in terms of how they suggest or depict an initial equilibrium – a settled state that doesn't need to change – and how they disrupt this equilibrium with an event that creates a drive towards a narrative resolution.

Initial equilibrium and disruption
Mr. Robot

There are multiple disruptions, such as the conspiracy and the intrusion of the 'fsociety', which mean it is unclear from the opening episode where the series will go.

There is little sense of an initial equilibrium in the first episode as Elliot is so unhappy; perhaps untrammelled corporate power will prove to be the initial equilibrium.

> **Revision activity**
>
> Go back over your media language analyses of key scenes from your chosen LFTVD episodes and add references to how ideologies are incorporated in the media language.

> **Exam tip**
>
> This section overlaps with representation. Your exam question will be synoptic – allowing you to include all areas of the theoretical framework and contexts – so there is no need to establish clear differences between media language and representation as you can mix both together.

House of Cards

The narrative disruption is the thwarting of Frank's ambition by the decision to promote Kern instead of him. This suggests a narrative drive to see him achieve power.

The equilibrium is implied in the first episode: he has risen to limited power by playing by the rules.

Homeland

Abu Nazir's plot against America with Brody's release forming the narrative disruption. The narrative drive will be for Carrie to thwart this plot.

The initial equilibrium is implied rather than shown: his family life before his capture and American apparent safety before 9/11.

Stranger Things

The narrative disruption is the monstrous event at the start of the episode and Will's abduction at the end. The narrative drive will be the search for Will and resolution of the enigma that is the monster and its link to Eleven and her mysterious powers.

The initial equilibrium depicted in the episode is the settled and safe suburban lifestyle enjoyed by the gang of boys, if with inadequate fathers.

The Killing

The narrative disruption is the killing; the narrative drive will be to investigate the murder, to see its effects on the family and to see its effects on local politics.

The initial equilibrium is explored in the first episode: the Birk Larsen family's happiness, Lund's relationship with her family and a Swedish boyfriend, and Troel's rise to power in local politics.

Borgen

The narrative disruptions are Birgitte Nyborg's conviction politics, which breaks the coalition that constrains Birgitte, and Hesselboe's blunder, which undermines his Prime Ministership. The narrative drive suggested is Birgitte's rise to power and what she will do with it.

The initial equilibrium is implied in the first episode: the cynical but stable state of Danish politics.

Trapped

The narrative disruption is the murder suggested by the finding of the torso. Secondary disruptions include the intrusion of the ferry into the small town and the arrival of several outsiders – the people smuggler and the character from the initial sequence of Dagný perishing in a fire, Andri's ex-wife's new boyfriend. The main narrative drive will be investigating the murder.

The initial equilibrium of small-town life with minimal crime is depicted in the opening episode in the low-key police station.

Deutschland 83

The narrative disruption is US President Reagan's escalation of Cold War conflict in Europe, suggesting a narrative drive towards preventing nuclear annihilation.

The initial equilibrium presented in episode 1 is Martin's job as a border guard, his relationship with Annett and his mother.

Non-linear elements

Todorov's theory is designed to explain a **linear narrative** with a distinct ending, a narrative resolution. Long form television dramas are serial narratives, meaning that they do drive towards a resolution, unlike continuous serial narratives such as soap operas, where the narrative consists of constant disruptions and only brief moments of resolution. A LFTVD must offer a resolution for audience satisfaction, but the prime pleasure is in the delay of that resolution, a delay that creates anticipation by combining movement towards a resolution with other narrative strands with a life of their own. These might establish tone, develop characters, establish secondary and intertwining storylines, or spiral out from the main storyline in unpredictable directions. For example:

> **Linear narrative**: A narrative with a beginning, middle and end in which earlier events cause later events. This causal chain is key – the narrative can use flashbacks and flash forwards to change the order in which events are narrated.

Mr. Robot

The sequence in which Elliot exposes the child pornographer is an apparently self-contained narrative element that serves to establish Elliot as an individual campaigner for social good.

House of Cards

The initial story of the dying dog establishes Frank's character and enables a neat topping and tailing of the episode.

The secondary storyline about the ruthless way in which Claire runs the charity establishes her as having the same will to power as Frank.

Homeland

David's revelation that Carrie cost him his marriage suggests a relationship history.

The red herring of Brody secretly meeting Walker's wife delays Carrie's discovery of the truth.

Stranger Things

The Dungeons and Dragons sequence establishes the period setting, the close bond between the boys and Will's protective character.

The scenes with Nancy and Steve create a parallel romantic storyline and also establish Nancy's character as hard working and good at science.

The Killing

The sequence searching the cellar ending in a reveal that it is a practical joke establishes the popularity of Lund's character and the solidarity of the police as a team.

The parallel storyline of Troel's election campaign segments the murder narrative, only touching it at two points, introducing generic variation and a change in tone.

Borgen

The sequences showing Birgitte's relationship with her husband and children establish the close and equal relationship between the parents, her partner's honest but loving support and the children's pride in her work.

Kasper's relationship with Katrine allows his character to demonstrate a more caring and thoughtful side.

Trapped

Andri's difficulties in coming to terms with his break-up with Agnes add an emotional storyline to his detective work.

The storyline about the new Chinese port suggests that it may play an important role in the drama, as it involves all the local power-brokers.

Deutschland 83

The early interrogation of the West German students sequence establishes Martin as capable, well educated in socialist principles and happy to bend the rules to obtain a book for his mother.

Many sequences emphasise the differences between East and West, e.g. Martin asking where they hold the parades in the park in Bonn.

Enigma rather than resolution

The serial narrative of LFTVDs means that narrative closure is not required at the end of episodes. Most end with at least one enigma rather than a resolution:

- **Mr. Robot:** Who and what are the conspiracy and does the fsociety exist?
- **House of Cards:** How will the education bill revelations bring down Frank's enemies?
- **Homeland:** What is Brody's plan?
- **Stranger Things:** Where is Will?
- **The Killing:** Is Troels involved in the murder, how will the Birk Larsens cope, will Lund get to Sweden?
- **Borgen:** Will Birgitte become Prime Minister?
- **Trapped:** Has the Lithuanian escaped and is he the killer?
- **Deutschland 83:** What else will Martin have to do; how will he get home?

Levi-Strauss

Levi-Strauss's idea of the **binary opposition** – that the system of myths and fables was ruled by a structure of opposing terms such as hot–cold, male–female, culture–nature, raw–cooked – can be applied to these LFTVDs and can illuminate their ideological underpinning. The narrative suggests approval of the right-hand column terms in the following examples:

> **Revision activity**
>
> Find two more narrative strands that appear to be unrelated to the narrative drive towards resolution in each episode of the LFTVDs you have studied.

> **Revision activity**
>
> Note down any other questions or enigmas that need solving at the end of each episode of the LFTVDs you have studied.

> **Binary opposition**: This consists of two concepts that mean the opposite of each other, e.g. hot:cold. Levi-Strauss analysed communication in terms of these oppositions.

Mr. Robot		
Insiders	:	Outsiders
Corporations	:	Hackers
Inequality	:	Equality

House of Cards		
Washington	:	The Street*
Power/Money	:	Service
Cynical ambition	:	Authenticity

Homeland		
Outsiders	:	Insiders
Al Qaeda	:	America
Cruelty	:	Bureaucracy

Stranger Things		
Monstrous	:	Ordinary
Threat	:	Love/Companionship
Violence	:	Nurturing

The Killing		
Selfishness	:	Duty**
Violence	:	Nurturing
Racism	:	Inclusivity

Borgen		
Traditional politics	:	New politics – Birgitte
Cynicism	:	Principles
PR	:	Authenticity

Trapped		
Outsiders	:	Insiders***
Individuals	:	Family
Crime	:	Community

Deutschland 83		
State	:	Family
Manipulation	:	Love
Danger	:	Safety

*It is notable that the narrative for *House of Cards* mostly supports the opposite of Frank's world – life outside the power structures of Washington – which is shown only briefly at the end of the episode when he sits down to eat ribs.

**It is clear that Lund and Pernille clearly stand in the right-hand column, but it is not yet clear where Troels or Theis stand.

***The first episode deliberately sets up this inside/outside opposition, but as the series develops this simple reassuring set of oppositions is disrupted.

Baudrillard

Baudrillard argued that postmodern society is organised around 'simulation' – the play of images and signs. Differences of gender, class, politics and culture are dissolving in a world of simulation in which individuals construct their identities. The new world of 'hyperreality' consists of simulations that no longer have to refer to anything real, but to one another.

Any media product adds to hyperreality, so to this extent it is not really significant what the product contains. However, some of the set products appear to refer to this postmodern condition, so may be seen as commenting on or agreeing with Baudrillard's theory.

Mr. Robot

Elliot lives in a world of self-referential signs – computer code – that creates reality. Money, as Mr. Robot explains, is simply a series of electronic transactions. Further, the programme undermines its own realism by its mode of address to a 'fictitious' audience that Elliot thinks is only in his head, and this suggests that the whole narrative is a simulation within a simulation. It raises the question: does this reinforce hyperreality or weaken it by drawing attention to it?

House of Cards

Frank lives in a world of power plays that appear to have little relationship with the 'real' world (within the fiction) apart from how elements of it play out in media simulations. In this sense, the programme seems to present a hyperreality. This raises the question: does this reinforce hyperreality or weaken it by drawing attention to it?

Homeland

Attempts to ground itself in a real event – 9/11 – and its aftermath and creates fictional representations of a real threat to America. However, as Baudrillard can argue, all we know of 9/11 and the 'war on terror' is their media representations. To be intelligible, the programme relies on its audience understanding these simulations, and further adding to these simulations.

Stranger Things

Acknowledges and celebrates its intertextual references and, in doing so, its hyperreal nature. It refers to films that were representations both of their times but also of previous films. For example, the reference to John Carpenter's film *The Thing*, which was itself a remake of a 1950s film.

The Killing

Attempts to ground itself in real events – local government elections and the rise in racism in Danish society. Baudrillard might argue that the programme is part of hyperreality, but then this could be applied to any programme, as the theory is unfalsifiable.

Borgen

Attempts to ground itself in real events – national government elections and the role of the media in politics. Baudrillard can still argue that the programme is part of hyperreality – for international audiences this programme might represent all they know about Danish politics, for example.

Trapped

The programme attempts to ground itself in a real place – a small town often cut off by the weather and served by a ferry. Baudrillard can still argue that the programme is part of hyperreality – for international audiences this programme might represent all they know about Icelandic small towns, for example.

Deutschland 83

Attempts to ground itself very firmly in real events – the Cold War division of Germany, the rule by Communists in the East and Reagan's escalation of the arms race. This will be a period that many Germans remember from personal experience and the programme addresses that lived experience (by contrasting East and West German culture and consumer brands, for example). In this way, the programme appears to least fit Baudrillard's theory.

> **Revision activity**
>
> Write out revision cards for how each of the theorists – Barthes, Levi-Strauss, Neale, Baudrillard and Todorov – can be used to analyse your chosen LFTVDs.

> **Exam tip**
>
> These theory revision cards will be useful for Question 4 when you need to evaluate a theory.

Now test yourself

TESTED

1 Explain the economic context that has encouraged the production of high-quality LFTVD.
2 Explain the production values expected of LFTVDs.
3 How has the development of technology influenced LFTVDs?
4 Why don't the serial narratives of LFTVDs fully fit Todorov's theory?
5 Name the Levi-Strauss technique for analysing stories.
6 What did Baudrillard call the reality constructed by texts referring to other texts?

Answers on p. 207

LFTVD: media representations

REVISED

Representation: selection and combination

Media contexts

Social contexts include:
- the impact on television programmes of changes in gender roles, in gender, racial and ethnic inequalities, and in social attitudes to sexualities
- the influence of social anxieties on television programmes, for example the threat to the 'American dream' shown by representations of domestic terrorism and surveillance.

Cultural contexts include:
- the influence of national cultures on television programmes, for example the cultural importance of television dramas in reflecting, re-interpreting and re-enforcing national cultural identities (and, on occasion, challenging and subverting these representations to raise debates on representations and identity)
- the influence of **cultural globalisation** and **cultural hybridisation** on television programmes, for example the influence of postmodernism and the role of globalised generic conventions in the representation of events, issues and character types, and the cultural expectations of globalised audiences for representations of the local to have global resonances.

Historical contexts include:
- the influence of key historical events on television programmes, for example 9/11 and the 'war on terror' and how this affected the American psyche, or how the reunification of Germany influenced the region; how such events have been reflected and re-interpreted through television dramas
- significant historical changes in the other contexts – social, cultural and political change.

Political contexts include:
- the influence of politics on expectations of television drama, e.g. the pressure on national public service broadcasters
- the influence of attitudes to politics on television programmes including how television programmes can, and are expected to, reflect, reinterpret, amplify and satirise national political institutions and the mechanics of their working
- the need for the audience to have political knowledge itself to understand some representations in political dramas.

Economic contexts include:
- the influence of budgets and economic competition on the need for authored products requiring complex representations and for any localised representations to have universal appeal to attract global audiences.

The following table analyses representations in each of the set products, taking each of the above contexts in turn.

> **Cultural globalisation**: How modern media create a global culture based on shared use of media products such as globally successful film, television and popular music.

> **Cultural hybridisation**: How global cultural products may mix elements from different national cultures (e.g. the use of Chinese Kung Fu in Hollywood films).

> **Expressionism**: The opposite of naturalism. Media language that draws attention to itself, that expresses emotional states, e.g. harsh lighting might express alienation.

English-language LFTVDs

Mr. Robot, episode 1

How selection and combination create representations that reflect their social context:
- Elliot's workplace is represented as diverse, reflecting the context of contemporary New York's self-presentation as a 'melting pot' in which all the peoples of the world co-mingle. A liberal America, symbolised by New York, is suggested by Gideon's gayness being an incidental detail for his character. Unusually, an Asian has been selected as the paedophile character – this might suggest that the programme is so confident in its multicultural credentials that it is happy for minority characters to have major character flaws without being accused of racist representations.
- By contrast, the corporation executives and 'The Conspiracy' members are all White males, suggesting a deliberate strategy to negatively represent and critique the rich and powerful as White and patriarchal. The positively represented collective working on 'the project' on Coney Island is socially diverse in terms of race and gender.
- Episode reflects social anxieties about the power of giant corporations and modern society's reliance on digital technology, and perhaps anxieties about the mental health implications of young people spending long periods of time online.

→

English-language LFTVDs

How selection and combination create representations that reflect their cultural context:
- The episode shows the influence of postmodernism in American culture in that it represents a world of 'simulation', a world of computer code, of representations of self to others, a world with blurred boundaries between delusions and the real (reflecting theory such as Baudrillard).
- This postmodernism is apparent in Hollywood films (such as *Fight Club*) that have been cited as influencing the series.
- Urban alienation, exploitation and corporate domination represented as an oppositional view of the world firmly established in cultural movements such as romanticism and **expressionism**.
- Representation of an all-powerful conspiracy reflects a common theme in fiction and a widespread culturally shared belief.
- Representations of domination opposed by a hacking group fighting back against oppression may be signs of Elliot's alienation from the world or may be symptoms of his mental illness, or both.
- The representational complexity of the programme reflects the context of the high expectations of LFTVD.

How selection and combination create representations that reflect their political context:
- The opposition to the global corporate order in this programme reflects the influence of anti-globalisation protests in America and other countries.
- This drama is set in New York partly due to the political context of the divide in American society, with the east and west coasts representing liberal America and the heartlands representing conservative America.

How selection and combination create representations that reflect their historical context:
- The linking of issues of power and control to the digital industries reflects the growing dominance of these industries in contemporary society and the historic shift in the opportunities for power and control that this presents.

How selection and combination create representations that reflect their economic context:
- The complexity of the characterisation and representations reflects the economic pressure to create quality flagship programming.

House of Cards, episode 1

How selection and combination create representations that reflect their social context:
- The episode reflects socially contested gender and racial/ethnic relations: it suggests a degree of gender equality, e.g. Frank and Claire are both powerful individuals and are represented as having similar agency; Zoe is represented as assertive, ambitious and confident in her own sexuality. However, the narrative primarily follows the male protagonist and represents Washington politics as male-dominated and mostly White, with explicit tokenism in the hiring of a Latina Chief of Staff (reflecting bell hooks' theory).
- The episode shows the influence of social anxieties about politics falling into the hands of the power-obsessed.

How selection and combination create representations that reflect their cultural context:
- The episode reflects the American cultural preference for the rooted, honest, trustworthy hero in its representation of the opposite – the critical representation of the untrustworthy world of Washington politics.
- Series may be seen as an example of a globalised narrative as the original was set in Westminster politics and other versions could be set in many other countries; Frank and Claire are archetypal (i.e. universal) amoral power-seekers – Claire being likened to Lady Macbeth by critics.
- Representational sophistication of the programme reflects the context of the high expectations of LFTVD.

How selection and combination create representations that reflect their political context:
- The episode reflects cynicism and antipathy towards federal politics in the USA by representing politics as a naked struggle for power as an end in itself – politicians with beliefs, such as Donald, are represented as victims of the power-hungry.
- Representations are knowingly exaggerated for satirical effect, e.g. we first see Frank expressing his ruthlessness by strangling a dog, this exaggeration suggests an ironic distance in that we are not supposed to take them seriously (the author of the original novel was a politician satirising his trade from the inside).
- The series requires some understanding of Washington politics (but international audiences are used to being positioned as requiring knowledge of American society).

English-language LFTVDs

How selection and combination create representations that reflect their historical context:
- The episode reflects what might turn out to be the historical context of pre-Trump American politics.

How selection and combination create representations that reflect their economic context:
- The complexity of the characterisation and representations reflects the economic pressure to create quality flagship programming.

Homeland, episode 1

How selection and combination create representations that reflect their social context:
- The episode reflects socially contested gender and racial/ethnic relations: it represents a world in which apparent conformity to social norms masks underlying tensions and conflicts; in particular, we see Jessica rehearsing being 'the good wife' and the CIA desperately trying to persuade Brody to perform as the masculine 'hero'.
- The CIA management are male, reinforcing patriarchal power, but the narrative follows the agency of a female protagonist playing the role of the 'the maverick' who is proved right.
- Racial and ethnic representations are ambiguous: a Black man is poised to become Director of the CIA, the ultimate 'insider', but the 'enemy without' is an Arab.
- The episode shows the influence of social anxieties about the contemporary terrorist threat and about the state's response to that threat.

How selection and combination create representations that reflect their cultural context:
- The episode shows the influence of American culture's reaction to terrorism and international conflict – overt patriotism, militarism and the search for heroes.
- However, being based on an Israeli series, the series may reflect more universal cultural responses to and debates about the best way to respond to threats.
- The episode shows and critiques the influence of celebrity culture in the way Brody becomes an instant hero.
- The representational complexity of the programme, particularly the morally ambiguous heroine, reflects the context of the high expectations of LFTVD.

How selection and combination create representations that reflect their political context:
- Programme reflects cynicism towards federal politics in the USA by representing the White House as desperate for a 'win' in a foreign war.
- Series requires some understanding of the CIA and Washington politics (but international audiences are used to being positioned as requiring knowledge of American society).

How selection and combination create representations that reflect their historical context:
- The episode explores the historical trauma of 9/11 in the USA: the protagonist is haunted by her failure to prevent the terrorist attack, the returning 'hero' perhaps represents an American culture struggling to come to terms with faith-based terrorism.
- The shadow of previous difficult wars – in Vietnam and Iraq – is evident in the politicians' need to win the PR war as well as the actual war.

How selection and combination create representations that reflect their economic context:
- The complexity of the characterisation and representations reflects the economic pressure to create quality flagship programming.

Stranger Things, episode 1

How selection and combination create representations that reflect their social context:
- The episode intertextually reflects 1980s family and gender relations and is set within a Speilbergian, mostly White world of suburban family life, representing mothers as figures struggling to hold the family together, fathers as absent or insensitive and distracted, and young boys as establishing a fierce loyalty and masculine camaraderie in the face of a hostile world. Mike's teenage sister, Nancy, is represented in contradictory ways.
- The episode shows the influence of social anxieties about the consequences of scientific experimentation.

How selection and combination create representations that reflect their cultural context:
- The episode shows the influence of the cultural icon of the American small-town community. This representation has global recognition given the global success of the Hollywood blockbusters of the 1980s and their embodiment of this symbol of the American good life.
- The representation of Eleven as having supernatural powers reflects a cultural tradition of dangerous children in science-fiction literature such as *The Midwich Cuckoos*.

→

English-language LFTVDs

- The theme of science going wrong and producing monsters reflects a long tradition in literature, including classics such as *Frankenstein*.
- The representational complexity of the programme reflects the context of the high expectations of LFTVD.

How selection and combination create representations that reflect their political context:

- The episode reflects anxiety about the power of the central state in relation to the local community: the episode represents a shadowy world of possibly sinister enforcement agents, suggesting an all-powerful secret state, whereas the local police, by contrast, are represented in a humanised way: good-natured but complacent until forced into action. However, the representations are perhaps deliberately stereotyped for intertextual effect – to recreate the world of 1980s films – which may suggest a more **polysemic** reading.

How selection and combination create representations that reflect their historical context:

- Historic 1980s technology is represented in this episode, including walkie-talkies, high-performance radios and BMX bikes, all suggesting a more adventurous pre-internet age.

How selection and combination create representations that reflect their economic context:

- The complexity of the characterisation and representations reflects the economic pressure to create quality flagship programming.

Polysemic: Offering many meanings, so open to different readings.

Figure 2.7 *Stranger Things* – the strangeness of the character Eleven

Non-English-language LFTVDs

The Killing, episode 1

How selection and combination create representations that reflect their social context:

- The episode reflects socially contested gender relations: the police management and sparring politicians are male, reinforcing patriarchal power, but the narrative follows the agency of a female protagonist, whose professionalism and efficacy are foregrounded by her male colleague's contrasting boyishness and willingness to give up.
- Socially contested racial/ethnic relations are reflected: Denmark is represented as an avowedly multicultural society, with Vagn's racism represented as a character flaw in opposition to Theis's generosity.
- The episode shows the influence of social anxieties about the protection of children.

How selection and combination create representations that reflect their cultural context:

- The episode contains specifically Danish representations – the representation of rivalry with Sweden and the nature of Danish local politics, for example – but the crime narrative is of global cultural resonance, which may be why the programme was an international success.
- The episode shows and critiques the influence of celebrity culture in the way Troels is packaged by his campaign, for example the huge poster of a close-up of his face.
- The representational complexity and sophistication of the programme reflect the context of the high expectations of LFTVD.

→

Non-English-language LFTVDs

How selection and combination create representations that reflect their political context:
- The episode reflects a cynical view of spin-driven politics: the episode represents two separate worlds within the same society – that of family life and that of politics, the former with values of caring, solidarity and authenticity, the latter with values of competition, underhand point scoring and conspiracy.
- The episode reflects the context of immigration becoming an issue in Danish politics.
- The series requires some understanding of Danish local politics.

How selection and combination create representations that reflect their historical context:
- The representations of Theis and Pernille struggling to get ahead reflect the impact of the 2008 global economic crash.

How selection and combination create representations that reflect their economic context:
- The representation of Denmark via a conventional genre reflects the pressure to find international sales for a television product from a small nation.

Borgen, episode 1

How selection and combination create representations that reflect their social context:
- Episode reflects contested gender relations showing the impact of feminism on patriarchal society: politics and the media are mostly male dominated, but women are represented as skilled professionals and potential Prime Ministers, and Birgitte, in particular, is represented as decisive. Lesbians feature without comment. Many of the representations foreground the work of constructing femininity, especially for Birgitte and Katrine. However, Hesselboe's wife fits the patriarchal stereotype of the 'hysterical' woman.
- Masculinity is represented both positively from a feminist perspective, e.g. the ultra-supportive Phillip who has agreed to put his career on hold for Birgitte, and negatively, e.g. the sexually harassing, preening Laugesen, and sometimes both positively and negatively simultaneously, e.g. Kasper is caring and supportive but obsessed with winning power.
- Denmark is represented as an avowedly multicultural society; Laugesen's attack on asylum-seekers is represented as a deal-breaker by the heroine.

How selection and combination create representations that reflect their cultural context:
- The episode reflects Danish culture in its depiction of consensual decision-making and coalition politics, and its celebration of tolerance and inclusivity towards minority groups.
- Much of the politics is not only a representation of a national culture but of a globalised ideology of western liberalism.
- The representational complexity and sophistication of the programme reflects the context of the high expectations of LFTVD.
- The episode comments on the influence of celebrity culture in the way Birgitte gains instant celebrity by making one speech.

How selection and combination create representations that reflect their political context:
- The episode conveys a cynical view of spin-driven politics yet provides an optimistic vision of democratic politics: the political world is cynical, Machiavellian and driven by spin, but the voters respond to the honesty of a conviction politician.
- The episode reflects the context of immigration becoming an issue in Danish politics.
- The series requires some understanding of Danish national politics but does not assume this knowledge on the part of audiences – exposition enables politically literate audiences to understand the narrative.

How selection and combination create representations that reflect their historical context:
- Birgitte becomes Denmark's first female Prime Minister, reflecting the historical context of the rising power of women in Danish politics, which led shortly afterwards to a real female Danish Prime Minister.

How selection and combination create representations that reflect their economic context:
- The representation of purely Danish politics without recourse to popular genres reflects the economic success of previous Danish LFTVDs based in part on Danish issues.

Trapped, episode 1

How selection and combination create representations that reflect their social context:
- The episode reflects a mostly traditional society where patriarchy is only partially contested: the community is ruled by men – the mayor, the MP, the local businessmen, the police chief and the Reykjavik detectives are all men – suggesting a persistence of traditional gender roles, but the female police officer is professional and has agency within the narrative.

Non-English-language LFTVDs

- The community is monocultural, reflecting rural Icelandic society, but the programme represents racism and exploitation by a people smuggler, reflecting wider issues of race and immigration.
- The episode shows the influence of social anxieties about the exploitation of Iceland by economically powerful outsiders.

How selection and combination create representations that reflect their cultural context:
- The episode shows the influence of Icelandic culture in its representation of a very close-knit small community at the margins of civilisation, at the mercy of the elements, and held together by family and mutual aid.
- The choice of this location might reflect the influence of a return to traditional lifestyles and values by Icelanders after the 2008 crash caused economic ruin.
- The murder mystery narrative is reflected here as in other cultural products.
- The representational complexity of the programme demonstrates the context of the high expectations of LFTVD.

How selection and combination create representations that reflect their political context:
- The deference to Reykjavik shown by the local police reflects the capital's dominance within the country as a whole.

How selection and combination create representations that reflect their historical context:
- The representations of Andri struggling to complete his house reflect the impact of the 2008 global economic crash, which was particularly severe in Iceland.

How selection and combination create representations that reflect their economic context:
- The representation of Iceland via a conventional genre reflects the pressure to find international sales for a television product from a small nation.

Deutschland 83, episode 1

How selection and combination create representations that reflect their social context:
- The episode reflects the social contradictions in divided 1980s Germany: East Germany is represented as a rigidly controlled state that promotes women's equality, with Leonora as the powerful woman who sets up the spy operation, whereas in West Germany, which is less controlled, the military is represented as rigidly patriarchal.
- Both Germanys are represented as White and the representation of the racial integration of the American military appears to add to their 'otherness'.
- The episode shows the influence of social anxieties about facing up to Germany's divided past.

How selection and combination create representations that reflect their cultural context:
- The episode reflects specifically German concerns about cultural amnesia and remembering. The need to remember – recent media products have explored the East German experience in a way that represents how the ambiguities of that experience were buried in the triumph of the West at reunification.
- The spy narrative is of global cultural resonance, despite its local origin, and helps explain the international success of the series.
- The representational complexity of the programme reflects the context of the high expectations of LFTVD.

How selection and combination create representations that reflect their political context:
- The representation of concern in both Germanys about American sabre rattling may reflect either contemporary German political confidence, as the lead in European politics, or a liberal critique of American Republican politics by the programme's American writer, or both.

How selection and combination create representations that reflect their historical context:
- The episode explores the German division as it was in 1983: the East poor, controlled and firmly ideological; the West rich, free but self-doubting.
- The complex and ambiguous representations in *Deutschland 83* reflect the difficulties faced by Germany in coming to terms with its past, the political and military tensions of the early 1980s in divided Germany. The collapse of communism in 1989 meant that much of the East German experience was swept under the carpet.

How selection and combination create representations that reflect their economic context:
- The complexity of the characterisation and representations reflects the economic pressure to create quality flagship programming.

LFTVDs: realism and constructing reality

Media contexts

Television as a media form has a tendency to social realism, as befits a domestic medium that relies on repetition (see page 150). However, looking back, classic LFTVD in the USA includes very different modes: cable channel HBO made its name with highly social realist drama such as *The Wire* (2002), which stood out against mainstream television; at the other extreme, the acclaimed *Twin Peaks* (1990) on network television redefined the possibilities of LFTVD by its surreal style that brought together folksy detectives and supernatural happenings in an uncertain and disorientating mix.

The set product LFTVDs show very different levels and types of realism, as is typical of this form, but all retain some element of realism in the sense of creating a coherent fictional world that can be understood by audiences as relating in some way to the 'real' world. Some go further and offer social realism: a sense of addressing real-world social issues and the everyday concerns of 'ordinary' people.

Mr. Robot

Deliberately undermines its own realism by its **mode of address** to a 'fictitious' audience with Elliot thinking he is telling us events that exist only in his head. It comments on the real world by creating a self-consciously fantastic fictional world that contains social attitudes (e.g. Elliot's antipathy to social media and the hero status of Steve Jobs) that might apply in the real world.

House of Cards

Though set in the real world of Washington politics, the programme eschews social realism in favour of caricature. Characters have recognisable traits, such as Frank's ambition, but these are ironically represented and exaggerated to create a sense of theatricality rather than realism.

Homeland

Grounds itself in a real event – 9/11 and its aftermath – and tries to create fictional representations of a real threat to America. It suggests realism by representing recognisable events and social types that remain plausible within thriller conventions. Abu Nazir's plot, for example, is rather 'far-fetched', but this fact is used cleverly to enable others to cast doubt on Carrie's sanity. Far-fetched plots are conventional in the thriller genre and so suspension of disbelief for these is accepted by audiences. The casting of a film actor as Carrie might have disrupted the sense of realism, but this is countered by her un-starry performance as a tortured, flawed character.

Stranger Things

Acknowledges and celebrates its intertextual references and, in doing so, its lack of realism. However, it relies on a strong sense of time and place, so the mise-en-scène must work hard to maintain the realism of this time and place, and the script maintains consistent characters, no matter how extreme the events that occur.

> **Revision activity**
>
> Select three key scenes from each of your two chosen LFTVDs and analyse how they construct representations.

> **Mode of address**: How a media product addresses its audience. This might be warm and inclusive, or formal and objective, for example, as in tabloid and broadsheet newspapers.

The Killing

Attempts to ground itself in recognisable events – local government elections and the rise in racism in Danish society. It further suggests realism by representing events, locations and social types that remain plausible within the conventions of police, family and political drama. For international audiences this is helped by the casting of what were then unknown actors who brought no external persona to the product. The programme delivers a narrative that, though slightly stylised in its three intertwining plots, is driven by the characters' different reactions to unfolding events.

Borgen

Attempts to root itself in real events – national government elections and the role of the media in politics. It suggests realism by representing recognisable events, locations and social types that remain plausible within the conventions of political drama. The programme delivers a narrative that, though melodramatic in its coincidences and unexpected events (such as Ole's relationship with Katrine and sudden death), is driven by the characters' different reactions to unfolding events.

Trapped

Attempts to ground itself in a real place – a small town often cut off by the weather and served by a ferry. It creates a social realist version of a highly stylised genre – the country house murder mystery. The programme delivers a strong and consistent sense of place, plausible characters and a narrative that, though slightly melodramatic in its unexpected events (such as the discovery of the torso and the presence of a people smuggler), is driven by the characters' different reactions to unfolding events.

Deutschland 83

Attempts to ground itself very firmly in real events – the Cold War division of Germany, the rule by Communists in the East and Reagan's escalation of the arms race. Within this social realist context of recognisable events it creates situations and characters that remain plausible within the conventions of spy drama. These allow a certain level of implausibility in the service of suspense and intrigue (such as the unquestioned replacement of Moritz Stamm). The programme delivers a consistent sense of time and place via its highly controlled mise-en-scène, plausible characters and a narrative that, though melodramatic in its coincidences (such as Leonora being Martin's aunt), is driven by the characters' different reactions to unfolding events.

Stereotyping in LFTVDs

Media contexts

Stereotyping is commonly used in television narratives to enable easy audience comprehension. However, LFTVD has developed in the context of cultural expectations of narrative complexity and ambiguity, as befits a quality product. Moreover, the long form serial drama allows for considerable character development over the course of a season as characters react to events; plus, the more multi-perspective narratives often found in LFTVDs enable the drama to show characters in a number of different lights. Both of these mean that characters in LFTVDs

> **Revision activity**
>
> List the similarities and differences in how your two chosen LFTVDs construct a reality and make claims about realism.

> **Stereotyping**: A commonly repeated generalisation about a group, event or institution that carries judgements, either positive or negative, and assumes any example of this group, event or institution will fit the stereotype. This generalisation is inaccurate because it is an over-simplification, even if it is based in reality. It can refer to a representation that comprises a simple stereotyped characteristic rather than a complex and individualised set of characteristics.

are expected to be rounded individuals with a number of perhaps contradictory character traits, rather than simple stereotypes, even if they may start off with stereotypical traits.

Public service broadcasting programmes may be expected to use stereotypes in a positive way to reflect the national culture and to engage in social issues. They may also be expected to challenge and deconstruct stereotypes, either within the political context of state regulation or within the cultural context of expectations that PSB programmes will present an anti-sexist, anti-racist and anti-homophobic agenda.

Mr. Robot

The programme uses stereotypes such as:
- Elliot fits the stereotype of the socially awkward, possibly autistic, IT genius.
- His therapist is stereotypically female.
- The setting fits the stereotype of the grey, alienating city.
- The corporate executives fit the stereotype of being male, controlling, selfish and untrustworthy.
- Mr. Robot is acting out the stereotype of a homeless man harassing passers-by.
- Angela is a stereotypically warm and caring woman.
- Michael Hanson, the therapist's lover, is a stereotypical middle-aged male philanderer.

These stereotypes are complicated by:
- the fact they may all be figments of Elliot's imagination
- the anti-stereotypical representation of Gideon as a boss and father figure who incidentally is gay
- the anti-stereotypical representation of some hackers – the first Elliot meets is an older Black man
- Elliot's character develops beyond the stereotype; he can also be caring (e.g. to Gideon) and socially responsible (in exposing paedophiles)
- Angela's character develops beyond the stereotype; she is assertive in asking Elliot to let her fail rather than rescuing her.

House of Cards

The programme uses stereotypes such as:
- The politicians are stereotypically power-hungry and mostly male.
- The world of Washington politics (and charity fundraising) is stereotypically corrupt and driven by money.
- Stereotypically, Frank is the politician, Claire runs a charity.
- Zoe is the stereotypical ambitious young journalist who is out to make a name for herself.
- Russo is a stereotypical middle-aged male philanderer.

These stereotypes are complicated by:
- the theatricality of the representations – they *know* that they are stereotypes
- the anti-stereotypical representation of Vasquez, a Latino woman, as holding many of the reins of power
- the anti-stereotypical representation of Zoe as sexually confident and assertive
- Frank is outwardly powerful, but is seen to depend on Claire to maintain the mask, thus deconstructing the stereotype.

Homeland

The programme uses stereotypes such as:

- Terrorists are stereotypically represented as Arabs, or controlled by Arabs.
- The state is stereotypically run by older men.
- Brody and Mike as soldiers display a stereotypically taciturn masculinity and macho male bonding.
- Jessica is the stereotypical 'trophy wife' – thin, large eyes and conventionally attractive.
- Dana is a stereotypical moody teenager.
- Saul is a stereotypical wise older man and mentor figure.

These stereotypes are complicated by:

- the deconstruction of the stereotype as the programme shows the **gender performativity** behind Carrie and Jessica's bodies as objects (e.g. preparing themselves to be alluring to men)
- this is further deconstructed when the programme disrupts the voyeuristic audience position offered by having the audience watch Carrie watching sex as part of her surveillance, again disrupting the stereotype of women's bodies as objects
- the disruption of the stereotypical patriarchal order by the truth being discovered by what some male characters consider to be a stereotypical 'hysterical woman'
- the representation of Brody's stereotypical masculinity as a mask; his performance is made under pressure to conform to the model of a masculine hero and contrasts with his vulnerability in the final flashback and the tenderness offered by Abu Nazir.

> **Gender performativity**: The idea that gender roles are constituted in their performance ('we are what we do') and thus, for example, that there is no essential masculinity or femininity. The opposite theory is that which sees gender as grounded in biology.

Stranger Things

The programme uses stereotypes such as:

- The scientist is stereotypically studious-looking and dressed in a white coat.
- Mike's family is a stereotypical affluent, White, suburban, two-parent family.
- Nancy fits stereotypes of the teenage girl in her gossiping and concern for boys.
- Hopper is a generically stereotypical police officer haunted by his past.
- The agents are stereotypically faceless, powerful and ruthless.
- The mothers have the stereotypical role of holding the family together.

These stereotypes are complicated by:

- the fact that the representations are perhaps deliberately stereotyped for intertextual effect
- the unusual representation of a scientist as fearful and vulnerable
- the representation of Joyce's family as economically struggling
- Nancy's anti-stereotypical excellence at science
- the anti-patriarchal representation of fathers as insensitive and useless.

The Killing

The programme uses stereotypes such as:

- the stereotypical young female victim
- the stereotypically male political and police leaders
- stereotypes of Swedish blond Vikings and rotten herring
- it is stereotypically Pernille who waits at home while Theis goes out to search for Nanna

- Bremer is a stereotypical wily old politician, Troels the stereotypical young upstart
- Vagn is a stereotypical unintelligent racist.

These stereotypes are complicated by:
- The patriarchal order is disrupted by the narrative following a female character whose expertise and feminine empathy drive the investigation.
- Lund's agency is foregrounded by Meyer's boyishness and tendency to give up.
- Theis and Pernille's relationship is represented as one of equals – both run the business.

Borgen

The programme uses stereotypes such as:
- Politics and the media are stereotypically mostly male-dominated.
- Hesselboe's wife is a stereotypical hysterical woman.
- Laugesen is a stereotypically ambitious and cynical career politician.
- Kasper is a stereotypically ambitious and cynical spin doctor.
- Hanne is a stereotypical journalist with an alcohol addiction.
- Bent is a stereotypical wise older man and mentor figure.

These stereotypes are complicated by:
- Masculinity is represented as multifarious: the ultra-supportive Phillip has agreed to put his career on hold for Birgitte, the sexually harassing, preening Laugesen represents masculine narcissism, and Kasper is simultaneously caring and competitive.
- The representations foreground the work of femininity, especially for Birgitte and Katrine, thus disrupting female stereotypes by demonstrating the performative nature of femininity.

Trapped

The programme uses stereotypes such as:
- A community is stereotypically ruled by men – the mayor, the MP, the local businessmen, the police chief.
- Andri is a generically stereotypical police officer with a broken marriage and haunted by his past.
- Andri fits the stereotype of taciturn masculinity.
- Hjörtur and his girlfriend Dagný are stereotypical pleasure-seeking teenagers and Dagný's body is objectivised in the opening scene.
- Eirikur and Thorhildur are stereotypically traditional older people.
- The big city police are stereotypically arrogant and controlling.
- The mayor is stereotypically obsessed with protecting the town's image.

These stereotypes are complicated by:
- Andri's investigation of the case depends on his mixed gender team, in which Hinrika has equal agency in the narrative, disrupting patriarchal stereotypes.
- Male authority, especially that of the Reykjavik detectives, is represented as flawed – they are overconfident poseurs – and of no use against the power of nature.
- We gradually get to see behind Andri's masculine persona to the hurt underneath, when he snaps at the children, for example.

Deutschland 83

The programme uses stereotypes such as:

- Walter is a stereotypically ruthless male spymaster.
- The young people at the party are stereotypical pleasure-seeking teenagers.
- Martin is stereotypically flawed as a young man by lack of self-control and commitment to the cause, especially when it prevents him seeing his girlfriend.
- General Jackson is a stereotypically gung-ho American military man, unconcerned about local sensitivities.
- Yvonne is a stereotypically troubled and rebellious young teenager.

These stereotypes are complicated by:

- Martin starts as a stereotype but becomes a more complex character as we see beneath the mask of socialist righteousness in his family and then in his confrontation with the West.
- The representation of gender is complex: East Germany is represented as a rigidly controlled state that promotes women's equality, with Leonora as the powerful woman who sets up the spy operation, whereas in the less-controlled West Germany, the military is represented as rigidly patriarchal.

Under-represented or misrepresented groups

Media contexts

The increasingly globalised nature of television production (an economic and cultural context), especially with the rise of American-dominated video on-demand services, is increasing the over-representation of Americans in the world's media. Other countries, particularly poorer ones whose media products struggle to compete in the world market, are systematically under-represented. Nigeria's booming film production (normally distributed as video), for example, is significant enough to earn it the name 'Nollywood', but consists largely of low-budget productions representing Nigeria to Nigerians. British television, for example, has shown programmes from a variety of European countries but much less from other continents apart from North America and Australia.

The success of European LFTVDs has enabled the representation of the cultures of small countries – such as Iceland and Denmark – that are rarely, if ever, represented in globalised media. The fact that these are self-representations is vital in minimising misrepresentation. This has come about because audiences have become more accepting of the use of subtitles, which severely limited the reach of non-English language drama in the USA and Britain in the past. This cultural change is partly due to the success of non-English language LFTVD as video on-demand services and niche television channels are encouraged to distribute them.

There are some consistencies across the set products which suggest under-representation:

- There is under-representation of older people among the protagonists.
- There is under-representation of people of colour among the protagonists.
- There is under-representation of people with visible disabilities (though the protagonists in *Homeland* and *Mr. Robot* have mental health issues).
- There is under-representation of working-class people among the protagonists.

Revision activity

Make notes on how far and why your two chosen LFTVDs use stereotypes and/or anti-stereotypes. Are they similar or different in their use or avoidance of stereotyping?

- All the protagonists are heterosexual and apparently cisgendered (their gender identity fits their sex assigned at birth) and only a few examples of gay people are represented as minor characters.
- All the protagonists are from first-world countries.

Discourses, ideologies and audience positioning

Media contexts

Dominant ideologies fit the power structures and people's lived experience in the societies from which they arise, so are unlikely to be questioned. A pervasive ideology such as individualism is so rooted in Western societies that it is seldom questioned – people live their lives as individuals and expect everyone else to do the same. Dominant ideologies and discourses such as this will form the unexplored assumptions behind dramatic narratives.

Socially, culturally and politically contested ideologies and values are likely to be explored explicitly in quality drama as one of television's roles is to explore social issues that affect its audience. These might include:

- patriarchal versus feminist ideologies – traditional beliefs in male power challenged by demands for gender equality and liberation
- racist versus anti-racist ideologies – traditional beliefs in the superiority and inferiority of people defined by 'race' challenged by demands for equal rights from racially defined groups
- **heterosexist** versus **queer** ideologies – traditional beliefs in a 'natural' heterosexuality and homophobic reaction to deviations from this, challenged by demands for equal rights and recognition of the complexity of genders and sexualities.

> **Heterosexism/heterosexist ideology**: The idea that the norm is to be straightforwardly male or female and heterosexual. It follows that people who deviate from this norm, such as homosexuals, must be defined by this. The opposite of **Queer Theory**, which sees genders and sexualities as fluid.
>
> **Queer ideology**: Counters the idea of fixed and stable genders and sexualities (e.g. Butler's idea of gender being performative). Includes demands for LGBT rights and celebration of gender and sexual diversity.

These contested ideologies are evident in the set products:

English-language LFTVDs – contested ideologies
***Mr. Robot*, episode 1**
The White patriarchal order of powerful corporations may be brought down by an ethnically and gender-mixed collective of hackers. The male protagonist's inadequacies are foregrounded and countered by Angela, who almost manages to help Elliot see how his 'helping' is controlling. The audience are positioned as on the side of the mixed group who are challenging the old order.
The episode applies 'equal opportunities' in its distribution of character flaws among people of different races and ethnicities.
The episode tends to assume heterosexuality, but Elliot thanks Gideon when he comes out to him as he feels this is a moment of generosity. The audience are positioned as sympathetic to Gideon.
The programme represents anti-capitalist and anti-consumerist viewpoints in Elliot's diatribes against modern life.

→

> **Revision activity**
>
> Analyse the diversity of representation in your two chosen LFTVDs in terms of age, gender, sexuality, class, race and ethnicity, nation, disability and so on. Compare how far the two products attempt to depict under-represented groups and make notes on this.

English-language LFTVDs – contested ideologies

House of Cards, episode 1

The male protagonist is facing a powerful minority ethnic female foe – Vasquez – one of the few characters in the episode that he respects as much as his wife. The audience is positioned as relishing the fight that is to ensue.

While there is no evidence of anything except heterosexuality in the opening episode, the programme's melodramatic themes can suggest a queer reading. (Frank also has homoerotic moments in later episodes.) The audience is positioned as enjoying camp melodrama.

While the programme presents a critical view of politicians' flaws it does not criticise democracy itself.

Homeland, episode 1

The patriarchal order is represented in the episode then undermined – by Carrie's superior expertise and persistence, because male bonding is represented as being at the heart of the conspiracy and masks of heroic masculinity being the perfect disguise for a terrorist infiltrator. The 'male gaze' is disrupted by representation of women preparing their femininity. The audience is positioned as questioning gender roles.

The episode applies 'equal opportunities' in its distribution of character flaws among people of different races and ethnicities, with the CIA boss (David) whose ambition nearly undermines Carrie's investigation being a man of colour. The audience is positioned as non-racist.

While there is no evidence of anything except heterosexuality in the opening episode, Carrie's frank and pragmatic approach to sexual encounters disrupts conventional representations of female sexuality. The audience is positioned as open to disrupting traditional views of sexuality.

While the programme presents a critical view of politicians' and bureaucrats' flaws, it does not criticise democracy itself.

Stranger Things, episode 1

The patriarchal order is represented – by science, the family, the state and the local police in this episode – as deeply flawed and the audience is positioned as rooting for the underdogs: the single mother and the gang of children. This suggests a mix of pro-family and liberal feminist viewpoints.

Though the inclusion of one Black child in the gang may appear tokenistic, it may be deliberate as a period reference. The audience is positioned as non-racist.

There is no evidence of anything except heterosexuality in the opening episode, which may be deliberate as a period reference.

Figure 2.8 *The Killing* – lead character, Sarah Lund, taking agency in a male-dominated police/criminal world

Non-English language LFTVDs – contested ideologies

The Killing, episode 1

The patriarchal order is represented – by some objectivisation of Lund's body and by the leadership roles in politics, the police and business in this episode – but disrupted by Lund's superior expertise and persistence. The audience are positioned primarily to identify with Lund's desire to investigate, to grieve with both Theis and Pernille, and secondarily to care about Troels' leaky political team.

The audience is positioned as anti-racist as racism is represented and condemned in the episode.

The programme's concern for the human cost of crime suggests empathy with victims.

Borgen, episode 1

The patriarchal order is represented – by the leadership roles in politics and the media in this episode – but disrupted by Birgitte's superior expertise and refusal to compromise. The emphasis on constructing appearances undermines sexual objectification. The audience is positioned as wanting Birgitte to succeed (and to retain her extra-supportive husband) and as intrigued about how Kasper and Katrine's relationship will develop.

The audience is positioned as anti-racist as Laugesen's acceptance of implicit racism is condemned.

While the programme presents a critical view of politicians' flaws, it supports democracy itself, suggesting it can be used for good.

Trapped, episode 1

The patriarchal order is represented by the leadership roles in the police, politics and business in this episode, but as well as being intrigued by Hinrika, the audience is positioned to identify with Andri.

The audience is positioned as anti-racist, sympathising over the exploitation of the African girl who they see smuggled.

The programme appears to be presenting a pro-community viewpoint.

Deutschland 83, episode 1

There are contradictory representations of patriarchy in the West German military and gender equality in the East. The audience is positioned as identifying with the male protagonist Martin, because of his flawed character, but also as sympathising with Leonora in her pursuit of her patriotic duty, although perhaps shocked at her manipulative and calculating methods.

There are contradictory representations of race, showing the West German and American military as ethnically mixed and the East as monocultural. For German audiences this would reference historical experience – one difficulty after unification was integrating racist former East Germans into multicultural Germany. The audience is positioned as non-racist.

The programme seems to present the viewpoint that unification and ending the Cold War were historical blessings, but that the old East Germany was of real importance to those who lived in it.

Representation theories

Hall

Hall argues that representation is not about whether the media reflects or distorts reality, as this implies that there can be one 'true' meaning, but the many meanings a representation can generate. Meaning is constituted by representation, by what is present, what is absent and what is different. Thus, meaning can be contested. A representation implicates the audience in creating its meaning. Power – through ideology or by stereotyping – tries to fix the meaning of a representation in a 'preferred meaning'. To create deliberate anti-stereotypes is still to attempt to fix the meaning (albeit in a different way). A more effective strategy is to go inside the stereotype and open it up from within, to deconstruct the work of representation.

The sections above on selection and combination, stereotyping and ideologies all comprise applications of Hall's theory to the set products, and can be used to demonstrate the usefulness of this approach.

> **Revision activity**
>
> List the similarities and differences in how your two chosen LFTVDs reinforce values, invoke ideologies and position audiences. Start with the analysis of contested ideologies laid out here and add anything else that has come up in your analyses.

Gauntlett

Gauntlett argued that the media have an important but complex relationship with identities. In the modern world it is now an expectation that individuals make choices about their identity and lifestyle. Even in the traditional media, there are many diverse and contradictory media messages that individuals can use to think through their identities and ways of expressing themselves. For example, the success of 'popular feminism' and increasing representation of different sexualities has created a world where the meaning of gender, sexuality and identity is increasingly open.

The sections above on selection and combination, stereotyping and ideologies all comment on diverse and contradictory media messages within the set products, so this analysis may be used to demonstrate the usefulness of this approach.

Revision activity

List the diverse and contradictory media messages within your two chosen LFTVDs.

Van Zoonen

Van Zoonen argues that the way women's bodies are represented as objects in patriarchal culture is different to the representation of male bodies as spectacle. She agrees with Butler that gender is performative and contextual.

The sections above on selection and combination, stereotyping and ideologies all comment on patriarchal culture and the presentation of women's bodies, so this analysis may be used to demonstrate the usefulness of this approach.

hooks

hooks' concept of 'intersectionality' – that intersections of gender, race, class and sexuality create a 'white supremacist capitalist patriarchy' whose ideologies dominate media representations – is a high-level theory. While it cannot be tested against particular media products, it does draw attention to representations of those very intersections:

- In *Mr. Robot*, the powerful figures are White, male and middle class, which reflects the 'White supremacist capitalist patriarchy' but also criticises it.
- In *House of Cards* the powerful figures are White, male and middle class, reflecting the 'White supremacist capitalist patriarchy' but in a grotesque manner.
- In *Homeland* the powerful figures are male and middle class (David is Black and powerful, but he has the advantage of being male and middle class) – however these powerful figures are flawed.
- In *Stranger Things*, power does not necessarily reside with the 'White supremacist capitalist patriarchy' but with relative outsiders, implicitly criticising this power structure.
- In *The Killing*, a 'White supremacist capitalist patriarchy' is represented as in power, but a middle-class female has the agency.
- *Borgen* suggests that the 'White supremacist capitalist patriarchy' can be partially broken by a powerful woman.
- *Trapped* represents a 'White supremacist capitalist patriarchy', but the racist and capitalist aspects of this power structure are criticised.
- *Deutschland 83* represents two parallel power structures but criticises the socialist one in favour of the capitalist one, suggesting endorsement of the 'White supremacist capitalist patriarchy'.

Butler

Butler's theory of gender performativity is a very high-level theory that cannot be tested against particular media products, but it also draws attention to representations of those very performances. For example:

- Elliot's failure to perform masculinity effectively in *Mr. Robot*
- Carrie and Jessica's rehearsals to perform femininity and Brody's rehearsals to perform masculinity in *Homeland*
- Birgitte's rehearsals to perform femininity in *Borgen*.

Gilroy

Neither the USA, Denmark nor Iceland have an extensive colonial history like that of Britain, so may not suffer from 'post-colonial melancholia', but all were more or less tainted with racist ideologies used to justify slavery and colonialism in the modern era. The USA was founded upon racial and ethnic inequality as well as anti-colonialism. So any representation or lack of representation of race in their media products fits into this theory.

None of the products engages with what Gilroy calls the 'Black Atlantic'. This common culture gives the African diaspora an ethnic dimension (a sense of belonging based on inclusion) as well as a racial one (similar experience of exclusion). Many of the African-American characters are represented in bureaucratic roles such as the police chief in *House of Cards*, David the CIA director in *Homeland* or General Jackson in *Deutschland 83*, and Lucas in *Stranger Things* is represented as integrated into the culture of the predominantly White gang. They are all defined by the dominant White culture rather than members of a vibrant culture to be celebrated on its own terms.

> **Revision activity**
>
> Write out revision cards for how each of the theorists – Gilroy, hooks, Butler, Van Zoonen, Gauntlett, Hall – can be used to analyse your chosen LFTVDs.

> **Exam tip**
>
> These theory revision cards will be useful for Question 4 when you need to evaluate a theory.

> **Now test yourself** TESTED
>
> 1 Why might LFTVDs use stereotyping less than other programmes?
> 2 Which groups are under-represented among the protagonists in the LFTVDs?
> 3 Why does Hall argue against anti-stereotypes?
> 4 What does Gauntlett argue about media messages?
> 5 Give an example of a contested ideology in western societies.
> 6 What is Butler's key idea about gender?
>
> **Answers on p. 207**

LFTVD: media industries   REVISED

Television production, distribution and circulation

Social/cultural/economic/political/historical contexts

Changes in the political and economic contexts of television have altered the way it is produced, distributed and circulated. Traditionally broadcasters such as the BBC commissioned and produced their own programmes, then broadcast them on their own channels using their own transmitters. This control, plus a monopoly over production, allowed the BBC to impose **Reithian values**. Political pressure for competition in broadcasting led to ITV arriving in 1955 and ending the BBC monopoly. Political pressure to create greater diversity in television production and programmes led to Channel 4 being set up in 1982 as a commissioning-only organisation

> **Reithian values**: The values espoused by John Reith, the first Director General of the BBC, summarised as 'informing, educating and entertaining'.

with a remit to buy programmes from independent producers. Political pressure from a Conservative government then forced the BBC to commission programmes from independents. Many programmes are now produced by so-called independents for the mainstream channels. These are indistinguishable from other programming. Moreover, most independents are owned by multinational media conglomerates such as 21st Century Fox. This process reflects Curran and Seaton's argument that media industries follow the normal capitalist pattern of increasing concentration of ownership in fewer and fewer hands.

The political demand for high-quality and innovative television from PSB broadcasters, as expressed in Ofcom regulation, can be seen in the way both Channel 4 and BBC Four address niche audiences, and take risks, such as showing non-English language programming. This has subtly changed audience expectations – foreign language programmes are now culturally acceptable to larger British audiences. Evidence of this is that the 2018 series of *The Bridge*, a Danish/Swedish co-production was transmitted on BBC2.

> **Showrunner**: An individual (or a small team), usually a writer-producer, who places a personal stamp on a drama and gives it an 'authored' quality.

Television in the USA has always followed a free enterprise model with the government-funded PSB broadcaster being a small-scale provider of educational programmes rather than a competitor to the commercial networks. Under this model, television became dominated by a few networks, as in **Curran and Seaton**'s model. The rise of alternative providers such as the subscription satellite and cable service HBO in the 1990s shook up this stable model. Its programmes were not constantly disrupted by advertising breaks, unlike those on network television, and the social realism of its dramas represented a decisive break with the mainstream programming on the networks. This development provides a counter to Curran and Seaton's argument that concentration of ownership in the media leads to a narrowing of the range of opinions represented and a pursuit of profit at the expense of quality or creativity. It was the success of HBO that paved the way for subscription video on-demand services such as Netflix, and the international success of critically acclaimed series such as *The Wire* showed that there was a market for quality LFTVD.

Hesmondhalgh argued that risk is particularly high in the cultural industries because of the difficulty in predicting success, high production costs, low reproduction costs and the fact that media products are 'public goods' – they are not destroyed on consumption but can be further reproduced, hence the risk of piracy. This means that the cultural industries rely on 'big hits' to cover the costs of failure. Hence industries rely on repetition through use of stars, genres, franchises, repeatable narratives and so on to sell formats to audiences. While this is particularly true of the film industry, where the high level of risk leads to frantic attempts to avoid failure, it is less true of the broadcast television industry where scheduling alone can create an audience, especially where broadcasters are protected by public funding and public service broadcasting requirements. Simon Beaufoy, a successful screenwriter, has spoken about the difference between writing for film, where almost anyone can get you sacked, and writing for television, where the writer has much more creative control because of the lower risk (once a programme has been commissioned, it will be shown).

The new subscription video on-demand services such as Netflix and Amazon Prime need rapid expansion in order to achieve scale within the economic context of a crowded world marketplace. These services do fit

Hesmondhalgh's description of needing big hits as they require flagship programmes that they can heavily promote to achieve the levels of global word of mouth that one might expect of a Hollywood film. These products must be big budget, starry and culturally relevant to a global audience, but also, crucially, different enough from domestic television offerings in order to become 'must-see', culturally embedded products that everyone is talking about. These will attract new subscribers. Authorship becomes crucial – these products must be the creative vision of a '**showrunner**' to make them stand out from mass-produced network television. The showrunner would exercise quality control over the teams of creatives needed to work on long form serial drama (a practice already established in American network television).

The success of American quality drama inspired PSB broadcasters such as DR in Denmark to use similar showrunner production techniques for *The Killing*. This was a success on Sunday-evening Danish television, with what is in global terms a tiny audience, but the programme was conceived as a 'world class' product and was sold to 120 countries. The success of *The Killing* paved the way for other non-English-language LFTVDs to attempt to reach a more global audience.

The ownership and control of television

Social/cultural/economic/political/historical contexts

The founding of publicly owned broadcasters, such as DR in Denmark (*The Killing, Borgen*) and RUV in Iceland (*Trapped*), reflected the political pressure to control the new medium of television as it developed. Founded about the same time as the BBC in an era when the use of the media for propaganda purposes by authoritarian governments was growing, this historical context informed the need for state broadcasters that were not under direct state control. Like the BBC, DR is an independent institution funded by a licence fee. Like the BBC, RUV has a remit to inform, educate and entertain.

American media companies, by contrast, reflect the economic context of free market capitalism and the US political context of antipathy to any state interference in the free market that might be construed as socialism. American television companies are mostly publicly traded capitalist businesses. In the case of the set products:

Set product	Company	Publicly traded?	Background information
Mr. Robot	Comcast	Yes	Media conglomerate (owns the production company and the USA Network cable channel on which it aired)
House of Cards	Netflix	Yes	Netflix commissioned programming
Stranger Things	Netflix	Yes	Netflix commissioned programming
Homeland	21st Century Fox	Yes	Media conglomerate (owns the production company Fox 21 Television Studios) – currently subject to takeover bids; the programme is broadcast on Showtime, a cable channel owned by the CBS corporation

Deutschland 83 is a co-production between two commercial broadcasters: RTL, a German broadcaster, and Sundance TV, an American cable and satellite channel founded by Robert Redford and owned by the publicly traded commercial media organisation dedicated to speciality television and independent film. RTL is owned by Bertelsmann, a privately owned media conglomerate, which also owns UFA, the production company.

Control of television depends partly on ownership, but this is limited by the regulated nature of the medium (political context), the role of advertising in funding commercial media (economic context) or of PSB requirements for publicly funded media (political context), and the role of professional media practices and audience expectations in constituting acceptable media practices (cultural context).

Economic factors such as funding for television

Social/cultural/economic/political/historical contexts

Television has evolved three main types of funding:
1 public funding – e.g. DR, RUV
2 commercial funding by advertisers – e.g. RTL, Sundance
3 funding by subscription – e.g. Netflix.

These have come about, as outlined above, by a combination of:
- for public funding, public provision to provide social benefits (political context)
- for commercial broadcast television and subscription television, **free market capitalism** (economic context) and audience consumerist demands for increasing choice and availability (cultural context).

The economic and cultural contexts between Europe and the USA clearly differ, with the influence of social democracy in Europe leading to more state provision, while the private enterprise political and economic model in the USA leads to nearly fully commercial provision.

One effect of the subscription model is that providers such as Netflix attempt to increase the number of subscribers in order to establish a dominant position in the market, even at the expense of profitability. Netflix has spent so much on quality programming and films that it is not profitable and now has large debts to service. However it does have a large subscription base; by April 2018, Netflix had 125 million subscribers worldwide.

Free market capitalism: An economic system where the free market delivers most goods and services as commodities (things the consumer pays for). The opposite is socialism, where the state runs the economy. Social democratic states have a mix of free market and state provision.

The impact of technological change on television

Social/cultural/economic/political/historical contexts

The availability of streaming services depends on the economic context of the reduction in cost of computing power allowing the development of cheap smart televisions and the political drive towards increasing broadband speeds across nations as a necessary condition of modernity.

These services represent an economic challenge to network television: competition for audiences and for drama formats and creatives. This makes today an exciting time to be a production company, given the expanding opportunities for distribution.

These changes have led to the cultural context of audience expectations of choice, accessibility and immediacy, meaning that traditional broadcasters cannot rely on audiences waiting until next week for the next episode, but have to allow for **timeshift watching** and to offer on-demand 'binge watching' alongside traditional scheduling.

Timeshift watching: Recording scheduled television and watching at a different time.

Streaming technologies mean that the cultural role and context of television viewing is changing. Television watched on tablets or mobile phones is by nature a more individual activity and accelerates the move away from the cultural ideal of television-watching as a family activity, an ideal embedded in classic family-viewing shows of the 1970s. This weans the television industry away from mass audiences.

Advertising spend has changed. Technology such as recording devices that enable audiences to skip advertising have led to more emphasis being placed on sponsorship (as audiences will watch out for sponsorship credits while skipping through ad breaks) and brand promotion within programmes, such as **product placement**. The move away from overt advertising forced British regulators to abandon the previous ban on product placement in 2011, except on the BBC. Competition from the internet for advertising revenue has also hit traditional commercial television.

> **Product placement**: Placing brands in media products for payment. These might be props, brands featuring perhaps as background advertisements, branded vans or shops.

Regulation in television

Social/cultural/economic/political/historical contexts

Livingstone and Lunt studied how British television regulator Ofcom is serving an audience who may be seen as consumers and/or citizens, with consequences for regulation: consumers have wants, are individuals, seek private benefits from the media, use the language of choice and require regulation to protect against detriment, whereas citizens have needs, are social, seek public or social benefits from the media, use the language of rights and require regulation to promote the public interest. The citizen model reflects the traditional view of television as linked to public service principles, the consumer model reflects the cultural context of increasing consumerism. Traditional regulation is being put at risk by increasingly globalised media industries, the rise of the digital media, and media convergence.

One example of this difficulty for regulators is the 2017 Netflix drama *13 Reasons Why*, which raised the issue of regulating streamed television in the UK. The drama was controversial as it featured a teenage suicide and the 13 audio tapes left behind for different people to hear. British regulators would not normally allow the representation of dangerous acts, especially suicide, which might be imitated by a young target audience. However, unlike Amazon, Netflix was not located at that time in Britain, so could not be regulated by Ofcom.

In Britain, video on demand is age rated by the British Board of Film Classification (BBFC). The BBFC states on its website that:

> Providing BBFC age ratings for online content allows viewers to make the same informed viewing and purchasing choices for themselves and their families when using Digital Video Services, as they do when visiting the cinema or renting or buying DVDs and Blu-ray.

BBFC, 'BBFC Digital Age Ratings'

These ratings are voluntarily displayed on platforms such as Netflix and Amazon.

The effect of individual producers on television

Social/cultural/economic/political/historical contexts

We have seen already that quality LFTVD uses the 'showrunner' concept – that the series is under the control, of one person (see page 183).

Whereas in film the director is often seen as the 'author', the director's role is traditionally less venerated in television. Ken Loach, for example, now hailed as an 'auteur' in film directing, first came to fame as part of a television partnership with Tony Garnett, his producer. The essentially collaborative nature of television is often cited as the reason for this, but film is equally collaborative, so it is perhaps due to the lower cultural esteem in which television was traditionally held as a less artistic form than film.

The economic context in which the showrunner develops is the need for strong **brand awareness** in a very crowded television environment with little audience channel loyalty. In an era of increased availability, television programmes need their own image to attract audiences; the brand image of the channel no longer suffices when audiences can change channels so easily and frequently. Long form television dramas may be sold to audiences by their showrunners ('by the maker of …'), but their more important role is to create difference – some element of concept, tone, setting or casting that will establish brand awareness in the mind of the audience.

> **Brand awareness**: Public perception of a brand – knowing it exists, recognising it, showing interest in it, perhaps consuming it. Much advertising and marketing is aimed at increasing brand awareness.

Mr. Robot

Sam Esmail created the show and wrote most of the episodes, executive produced the show and directed many episodes. He has cited major influences like *American Psycho*, *Taxi Driver*, *A Clockwork Orange*, *The Matrix* and *Fight Club* as inspiring Elliot's disorder and the anti-consumerist, anti-establishment and anti-capitalist spirit of its characters.

House of Cards

The series was created by Beau Willimon, but the author of the original novel, Michael Dobbs, and the screenwriter for the British version, Andrew Davies, are both credited as executive producers, along with Willimon and David Fincher, who directed the first episode. The American series uses a similar tone and concept to the British series, despite the radical change in setting.

Homeland

The series was created by Howard Gordon and Alex Gansa, based on the Israeli series *Prisoners of War* created by Gideon Raff, who was also credited as an executive producer. Gordon and Hansa had previously created the very successful series *24*.

Stranger Things

The series was created, written and directed by the Duffer Brothers, who were young and relatively untried creators at the time Netflix commissioned the show. The show reflects the films of the 1980s – their young childhood.

The Killing

Søren Sveistrup was the series creator and head writer, though he worked closely with lead actress Sofie Gråbøl, who plays Sarah Lund, while writing (he approached her to play the part of Sarah Lund before work on the script began). Sveistrup did not reveal to the actors who the murderer was and only gave them the script one episode at a time.

Borgen

Adam Price (Danish, despite his name) developed and co-wrote the series but did not produce it, making this a more collaborative production.

Trapped

Baltasar Kormákur created the series, directing many episodes, but the showrunner was his co-developer Sigurjón Kjartansson, who is credited as executive producer. Baltasar founded RVK Studios, the production company for *Trapped*, and Sigurjón is its head of development.

Deutschland 83

The programme was created by the wife and husband team of Anna Winger and Joerg Winger; Anna, who scripted the programme, is an American novelist and Joerg, a German producer, is credited as producer. The series is reportedly inspired by Joerg's experience of military service.

Exam tip

You only need to know individual producers for the two set products you have studied.

Revision activity

Research the media industries and the production history of the two LFTVDs you have studied.

Now test yourself

TESTED

1 What are 'showrunners' and why do LFTVDs have them?
2 Which British broadcaster showed the non-English language LFTVD?
3 Why is traditional regulation of television at risk?
4 How is television funded?
5 Why is television less financially risky than film?
6 Why is branding increasingly important in television?

Answers on p. 207

LFTVD: media audiences

REVISED

How television audiences are categorised

Audience research in Britain is carried out by the Broadcasters Audience Research Board (BARB). It measures audiences for broadcast television in terms of the following categories:

- homes
- individuals
- adults
- men
- women
- children
- house persons
- social class.

BARB measures social class by the following 'social grades':

- AB – higher (A) or intermediate (B) managerial, administrative or professional
- C1 – supervisory or clerical and junior managerial, administrative or professional
- C2 – skilled manual workers
- D – semi-skilled and unskilled workers
- E – state pensioners, casual or lowest-grade workers.

Social/cultural/economic/political/historical contexts

Netflix does not release audience figures for individual programmes so it is not possible to know how it categorises its audiences. This may be because it does not need to sell its audiences to advertisers due to the economic and cultural contexts of increasing audience willingness to subscribe for advertising-free content.

Globalisation in the television industry (both an economic and cultural context) means that global services such as Netflix may not categorise audiences by social class, as this will vary in form so much across many different countries. However, subscribers are asked to select their favourite products from a list given to them at subscription, which enables Netflix to build up a psychographic profile of each subscriber (and their family members). Algorithms will then offer each subscriber a set of products on their home page that the service wants to promote to that type of subscriber.

Commercial television is interested in categorising audiences in order to sell them to advertisers. Publicly owned television such as DR and RUV may only need to categorise audiences in order to measure how far their stations are serving a diverse national audience.

Targeting and addressing television audiences

Social/cultural/economic/political/historical contexts

The economic and cultural importance of globalised television means that high-budget, high-quality television programmes must attract and address international as well as national audiences. This is true of global streaming services such as Netflix, for whom the US subscriber base is still a major part of their overall audience, as well as for commercial and publicly funded broadcasters. This is particularly true of smaller producers, such as Danish and Icelandic PSB television (DR, RUV), where co-production is necessary to provide the budgets required for high-end drama.

LFTVDs use similar production techniques to mainstream films to try to attract global audiences:
- use of the Hollywood star system – the American LFTVDs use recognised stars such as Christian Slater (*Mr. Robot*), Kevin Spacey (*House of Cards*), Claire Danes (*Homeland*), Winona Ryder (*Stranger Things*)
- high budgets and production values
- use of mainstream genres to increase accessibility
- use of generic hybridity to maximise audience attraction (e.g. family melodrama hybridised with a more action-oriented genre)
- development of franchises (all the LFTVDs have multiple seasons).

Unlike film franchises, LFTVD producers rely on television channels or streaming services to market the programmes, often using cross-promotion from similar programmes. The marketing will have a similar aim to that of film – to create a buzz around the programme, word of mouth that culminates in the opening of the series (for television channels) or the availability of the series (for streaming services). However, unlike film, television channels have a degree of audience loyalty linked to their ethos and brand image, so they know that the correct scheduling of a new programme will guarantee a certain size and type of audience.

If we look at the LFTVDs scheduled on British television:
- *Homeland* and *Deutschland 83* were scheduled on Channel 4, a channel that gets about a 5 per cent audience share. They were both scheduled at 9pm peak time after the watershed on Sunday night, up against more mainstream Sunday-night drama. *Homeland* gained about 3–4 million viewers, a very large audience for Channel 4. One and a half million viewers watched *Deutschland 83*, episode 1 live and 2.5 million once catch-up was included, making this the highest-rated foreign-language programme on British television

- *The Killing*, *Borgen* and *Trapped* were all scheduled on BBC Four, a niche channel targeting an educated audience which gets about a 1 per cent audience share. They were all scheduled in the channel's foreign-language drama slot – 9pm on Saturday night – with two episodes per week, a scheduling practice established by *The Killing* due to its very long series length. This slot offers an upmarket alternative to mainstream Saturday-night television on most other channels to those willing to read subtitles. *The Killing* averaged about half a million viewers, *Borgen* had over a million for its opening episode. *Trapped* was a **sleeper hit**, building up to well over 1 million viewers for the final episodes.

The marketing for the streamed LFTVDs reflects the authored elements of the programmes, as befits marketing for a subscription channel:

- The trailer for *House of Cards* emphasises its conspiratorial narrative, the casting of Kevin Spacey, and its melodramatic tone.
- The trailer for *Stranger Things* starts by emphasising the social realist small-town setting, contrasts Hopper's comic lines to Joyce with the horror of Will's disappearance, then creates a montage of characters and action set to quasi-religious choir and organ music, suggesting the range of generic pleasures on offer.

> **Sleeper hit**: A product that starts small but builds up a large audience through word of mouth.

The scheduling of *Mr. Robot* on USA Network was part of a rebranding campaign based on the slogan 'we the bold'. The channel was to be known for 'rich, captivating stories about unlikely heroes who defy the status quo, push boundaries and are willing to risk everything for what they believe in' (http://deadline.com/2016/04/usa-network-tagline-brand-we-the-bold-mr-robot-1201737705/).

The marketing reflects this strategy:

- The trailer for *Mr. Robot* retains its very downbeat and enigmatic tone, but adds some uplifting electronic music to counteract this, suggesting both its unusual media language and a more mainstream sense of excitement.

Public service providers such as DR and RUV have also to address their national audiences in order to fulfil their public service remit. They need to reflect their national culture, represent social, cultural and political issues, and demonstrate quality and innovation. The influence of these political contexts, however, ties in well with the requirement for international success of LFTVDs – to be high quality and innovative, and to exhibit an essential difference. In these cases, the representation of the national – Danish policing and social democracy or Icelandic policing and small-town isolation and community – creates difference in their exoticism for foreign audiences, offering them a form of cultural tourism. The very authenticity that is required for audience acceptance and popularity in the home nation also plays well with international audiences. All these public service programmes represent their society in microcosm: the narratives explore key social issues, such as political integrity, and anxieties, such as immigration, by means of the representation of particular individuals and communities. This strategy works on both the national and international stage in that audiences worldwide can see similar issues in their own societies to those represented in the programmes, but approach them afresh in a different context. Audiences are used to this in the cultural context of globalisation.

Deutschland 83 was produced by commercial broadcasters, but the fact that it was the first German-language programme to air on an American network shows that it shares similar advantages to the Danish and Icelandic dramas. East Germany would represent a particularly exotic location for American audiences brought up on the triumph of free market capitalism and notions of socialism as 'un-American'. Add to this the retro appeal of the programme and the German perspective on Americans – which might play well with liberal Americans – and the programme offers some sophisticated cultural tourism. That the programme represents the Cold War, which the USA won, might have helped as well.

Technologies, audience consumption and response
Social/cultural/economic/political/historical contexts

Media audience theory tends to take either an optimistic or a pessimistic view of the relationship between audiences and media products. Bandura and Gerbner are more pessimistic, seeing audience consumption and response as directly influenced by media products; Shirky and Jenkins are more optimistic, seeing audiences as active and emphasising what the audience do with the media rather than what the media does to them.

Bandura maintains that the media can directly influence people's values, judgement and conduct through media modelling. For example, media representations of aggressive or violent behaviour can lead to imitation. He argues that the evidence, especially where (as in television) the communication flow is one-way, best supports this idea of direct influence, rather than other models of media effects that have been put forward. These include:

- the two-step flow model (the media influence our opinion formers – people we look up to – who in turn influence us; this idea came from the study of elections)
- agenda-setting (the media doesn't tell us 'what to think' but 'what to think about', e.g. what counts as a social or political issue, what is trending)
- the media reflects the audience's existing attitudes and behaviour (i.e. the media 'giving the audience what it wants')
- that the media has no effects on its audience.

Gerbner argues, in an approach which disagrees with Bandura but still fits the pessimistic view, that exposure to television over long periods of time cultivates standardised roles and behaviours in the audience. Gerbner maintains that heavy users of television are more likely to:

- develop 'mean world syndrome' – a cynical, mistrusting attitude towards others – following prolonged exposure to high levels of television violence
- develop a common mainstream outlook on the world based on the images and labels on TV.

This is known as cultivation theory as it implies a long, slow process rather than a sudden influence.

The study of media effects by writers such as Bandura and Gerbner reflects the social, cultural and political contexts of anxieties about the effect of mass media consumption on mass audiences. These developed within the context of fewer television channels and larger audiences, before the audience fragmentation characteristic of current multichannel television and digital services. The optimistic approach tends to assume that these historical shifts in media availability serve to liberate audiences.

Jenkins, for example, argues that fans of media products, even one-way products such as television, act as 'textual poachers' – taking elements from media texts to create their own culture. For example, the 'cult' status of Faroese jumpers, worn in *The Killing*, generated their own fan website with advice on how to purchase or knit your own 'Sarah Lund' jumper.

Shirky goes further, discussing the end of old mass audiences and the development of the new media, with their amateur producers. This optimistic view does not fit the top-down, centralised nature of television production, especially high-budget, 'authored' forms such as LFTVD.

Different television technologies can affect audience media consumption. Streaming programmes allows for 'binge viewing', the equivalent of the DVD box set. The lack of interruptions from advertising on subscription services allows for more attentive viewing, encouraging more narrative complexity in the programmes, which further raises audience expectations of the attention required. The requirement for audience choice of a specific programme on streaming services, and thus the need for strong programme branding, means that their programmes require either a 'must see' quality or attract browsing viewers; this all adds to the sense of power and choice for the consumer.

Streaming may, in the long run, reduce the dominance of the discrete episode format in television, allowing audiences to skip sections or repeat sections, to create a flow of programming with minimal interruption. Netflix, for example, asks the viewer if they wish to watch the credits or skip straight to the next episode.

Broadcast television channels retain the traditional power of scheduling, although many offer plus one channels and catch-up opportunities to feed consumerist choice. Scheduling does allow for:

- appointment viewing – including the sense of anticipation in waiting for the next episode
- ritual viewing – the ability to organise the week around key programmes
- shared experience – the sense that others are watching the same programme at the same time and hence the opportunity for **second screening** and other forms of social interaction
- live television – such as the authentic suspense of watching a live sporting event or talent show.

Long form television dramas are well positioned to maximise these advantages of scheduling as they can develop a long narrative arc within an episodic framework. *The Killing*, for example, covered a different day of the police investigation with each episode while simultaneously cranking up the victim's family's grief. *Trapped* offered what felt like a different suspect every episode, with each new suspect undermining our sense of safety in the small community.

Second screening: Watching a media product and texting or posting about it simultaneously. Tends to encourage live television viewing, so is important for the future of linear (scheduled) television.

Figure 2.9 *Trapped* – the Icelandic backdrop

Audiences interaction and prosumers

Social/cultural/economic/political/historical contexts

Hall's 'encoding-decoding' model argues that media producers encode 'preferred meanings' into texts. These meanings will be those that fit the dominant ideologies – the set of basic assumptions, beliefs and values held in common and embedded in society, i.e. all the media contexts. Individualism is perhaps one such dominant ideology in western societies (see also page 156). Our society and culture treat us as individuals (for example, you sit an exam as an individual), our economy is based on competition between free individuals, we vote as individuals, our history is full of great individuals. However, unlike dominant ideologies, contested ideologies are easier to disagree with as other people may be doing the same in their social life, culture, work, or politics. For example, the impact of feminism has been that it is easier for women to name and disagree with sexism.

Media products may be encoded with particular ideologies but Hall argued they could be interpreted by their audiences in a number of different ways:

- the dominant-hegemonic reading: a 'preferred reading' that accepts the text's messages and the ideological assumptions behind the messages
- the negotiated reading: the reader accepts the text's ideological assumptions, but disagrees with aspects of the messages, so negotiates the meaning to fit with their 'lived experience'
- the oppositional reading: the reader rejects both the overt message and its underlying ideological assumptions.

Let's try applying this model to the English language LFTVDs:

- *Mr. Robot:* one ideology in the programme is individualism.
  - ○ The dominant-hegemonic reading: would identify with Elliot as a powerful individual.
  - ○ The negotiated reading: might agree with Elliot's sense of quest but disagree with his lying or think that the programme is unrealistic.
  - ○ The oppositional reading: might deride the plot (from a socialist point of view) as romantic individualistic nonsense – only collective political organisation can change the system.
- *House of Cards:* one ideology in the programme is competitive individualism.
  - ○ The dominant-hegemonic reading: would identify with Frank as a competitive individual trying to get ahead.

- ○ The negotiated reading: might think that Frank should play within the rules more or find the programme unrealistic.
- ○ The oppositional reading: might reject the programme (from a Marxist point of view) as American capitalist propaganda.
- **Homeland:** one ideology in the programme is patriotic duty.
  - ○ The dominant-hegemonic reading: would identify with Carrie as a committed individual concerned with saving lives.
  - ○ The negotiated reading: might agree with what Carrie is trying to achieve but disagree with her methods or find the programme unrealistic.
  - ○ The oppositional reading: might reject the programme as American propaganda.
- **Stranger Things:** one ideology in the programme is family values.
  - ○ The dominant-hegemonic reading: would identify with Joyce as a mother trying to hold her family together and with the programme's criticism of under-committed fathers.
  - ○ The negotiated reading: may not find the families very convincing or might have wanted a more positive view of family life.
  - ○ The oppositional reading: might reject the programme (from a feminist point of view) as relegating women to the family/domestic sphere and perpetuating patriarchy.

Audience interaction and active production are very limited with LFTVD as a media form. However, Jenkins' stress on fan appropriation and Shirky's on amateur producers do hold sway to some extent. Fans can post online fan fiction, fan theories, set up fan wikis and social media groups. All four English-language LFTVDs have extensive fan activity online. *Stranger Things* and *Mr. Robot* particularly attract fan theories. The non-English-language LFTVDs, on the other hand, are less well served.

The fan wikis – set up and collaboratively run by fans – are good examples of Jenkins' argument that in online 'participatory culture' audiences are active and creative participants rather than passive consumers, creating communities, producing new creative forms, collaborating to solve problems and shaping the flow of media. They also reflect Shirky's argument that amateur producers have different motivations to those of professionals – they value autonomy, competence, membership and generosity. User-generated content creates emotional connection between people who care about something. All this reflects the cultural context in which audiences are demanding interaction and providing it themselves online.

Audience interpretations and contexts

We have seen already how ideological stance can influence interpretations (see Hall above) and that ideologies reflect social, cultural and historical contexts. All the American English-language LFTVDs assume a positive view of America in order for their messages and viewpoints to be accepted. On the other hand, the European LFTVDs tend to reflect the more social democratic ideological context of Western Europe, which might appear strange or unacceptably radical to conservative America and even more so in authoritarian societies.

Social, cultural and historical contexts will affect the knowledge and experiences that audiences bring to products. American series will often make assumptions about audience knowledge of aspects of American

> **Revision activity**
>
> Discuss with other students what readings they make of the two set products you have studied. Make notes on the differences.

> **Revision activity**
>
> Look up fan activity online for your two set products and note down the differences and similarities between the fan activity for these products.

society. *House of Cards* and *Homeland* both require a basic understanding of the American political system, for example. *Mr. Robot* requires some understanding of computing for full appreciation of the references in the programme and assumes, for example, that audiences will know who Steve Jobs was. The warm intertextual referencing of the 1980s in *Stranger Things* will be interpreted differently depending on the audience's experiences of the 1980s.

Both *The Killing* and *Borgen* require some basic knowledge of Danish society, and *The Killing* opening episode makes more sense if the audience understands the cultural similarities and differences between Sweden and Denmark. *Borgen*, in particular requires some understanding of coalition politics, which is common in European countries apart from Britain. *Trapped* requires some understanding of Icelandic geography and culture. *Deutschland 83* relies in part on German (qualified) nostalgia for the old East Germany and recognition of key brands and locations.

Global mass and specialised audience needs

Social/cultural/economic/political/historical contexts

There are many different forms of television viewing, such as:
- comfort viewing – watching accessible and pleasurable television
- appointment viewing – watching gripping quality television with strong narratives or unusual representations that may have become a cultural event
- secondary viewing – leaving the television on while doing something else
- second screening – watching television and commenting live on social media, for example
- social viewing – collective viewing that bonds the viewers as a group (e.g. watching football in the pub)
- family viewing – intergenerational viewing
- individual viewing – perhaps in a private room, or on the move on a tablet or mobile phone.

LFTVD aspires to the status of 'must-see' television – appointment viewing – across an international market. This means that it transcends national identities to appeal to global audiences. In this, it is aided by cultural globalisation and hybridisation – the blending of cultural influences within a globalised culture, seen most powerfully in Hollywood appropriation of cultural elements from around the world, especially found in Disney products such as *Mulan*, *The Lion King* and *The Jungle Book*. This means that international audiences are culturally attuned to local narratives told within globally intelligible generic conventions.

In Britain, the scheduling of non-English-language LFTVDs suggests that audiences are defined by upmarket demographics. BBC Four, in particular, is a channel for educated audiences who demand intellectual stimulation and is watched by a primarily middle-class audience. Channel 4 also includes this demographic in its range of target audiences, especially on Sunday nights where, for example, *Homeland* was scheduled at 9pm followed by the *Walter Presents* strand of foreign-language programming at 10pm (showing a Flemish-language Belgian psychological thriller). Audiences will need an identity that encompasses a cosmopolitan openness to other cultures, and the cultural capital required to understand and appreciate cultural differences and to be comfortable with reading subtitles.

These audiences might use non-English-language LFTVDs in a variety of ways:

- as a way of informing themselves about other countries, languages, politics and history
- as a form of cultural tourism
- as a means of reinforcing a personal identity as a 'citizen of the world'
- in order to converse with their peer group and confirm their joint sophisticated identity
- to identify with rich and complex characters
- to escape into a complex and gripping narrative
- for a range of audience pleasures such as humour, pathos, suspense, action, narrative delay and resolution.

Revision activity

Check how this list applies to the non-English language LFTVD you have studied. Can you add to it?

Audiences for most English-language LFTVDs (except *Homeland*) in Britain are harder to investigate as there is very little information about Netflix or Amazon Prime subscribers. However, it is safe to assume that these audiences are less defined by identity and cultural capital than those who choose to watch foreign-language television. (Non-English-language viewers view dubbed versions in the local language on Netflix, for example, and world audiences are used to this for Hollywood films and American television imports already). A slightly younger audience profile for online media might be expected and a more upmarket audience profile due to the subscription element, but this cannot be confirmed.

Audiences are likely to use English-language LFTVDs in similar ways to the previous list:

- to identify with rich and complex characters
- to escape into a complex and gripping narrative
- for a range of audience pleasures such as humour, pathos, suspense, action, narrative delay and resolution
- in order to converse with their peer group about a television cultural event.

Revision activity

Check how this list applies to the English-language LFTVD you have studied. Can you add to it?

However, being positioned as an American is a very common experience for global audiences, so these programmes are less likely to offer exotic, cosmopolitan pleasures in the same way as the non-English-language LFTVDs.

Historically, the era of television scarcity encouraged channel loyalty and a sense that the audience's social and cultural identity would be linked to their loyalty to that channel. In the 1950s and 1960s in Britain, for example, it was common for households to consider themselves ITV viewers or BBC viewers. ITV was working class, regional, more adventurous and informal. The BBC was more middle class, more southern, more serious and more formal.

Several historical changes have disrupted this secure sense of channel loyalty and personal identity:

- the enormous growth of television channels and video on demand
- social changes complicating the old binary class structure so that classes are less distinct
- social and cultural changes in identity politics; feminism and multiculturalism mean that gender and ethnic/racial identity have become important complicating factors
- postmodern proliferation of identities in a consumerist media-dominated world.

The political context of pressure on publicly owned broadcasters to be especially distinctive in a multi-channel television age means that the needs of specialist, especially intellectually and culturally demanding, audiences must be met by these broadcasters. Channel 4 was successful with a French-language series, *The Returned*, in 2016 and had included an all-French-language advertising break to demonstrate the commercial as well as the PSB qualities of such drama. BBC Four is noted for its innovative approach within limited budgets, introducing both regular foreign-language programming and 'slow television' (long documentaries in which very little happens in a soothing manner). Both address specialist audience needs that are less likely to be served by other channels.

Now test yourself

1 Who measures British television audiences?
2 How do LFTVDs try to attract large audiences?
3 How do non-English language LFTVDs offer exoticism?
4 What are the advantages of scheduled viewing that LFTVDs can exploit?
5 Give an example of audience interactivity with LFTVDs.
6 How might British audiences use non-English language LFTVDs?

Answers on p. 207

Exam practice

Now practice answering exam practice Question 3 on page 134 and compare your answer to that online.

ONLINE

How to prepare for the exam

- Practise comparing and contrasting your two chosen LFTVDs across all four areas – media language, representation, audiences and industries – and all media contexts, paying particular attention to how you can relate each one of these to the others.
- Practise applying media theories to these products as part of your analysis of media language, representation, industries and audience.
- Watch other programmes in both series for background information on how the narrative develops, and look at reviews, critical writings and fan material on the series (though this is not compulsory).

Question 4

What this question involves

REVISED

This will be a question about evaluating one of the theories listed in the specification under the heading 'Academic ideas and arguments'. For the sake of brevity we will refer to these as 'theories'. In this question you will evaluate the usefulness of the theory in understanding LFTVD.

You may be given a choice of theories to evaluate or the question may only specify one theory.

Exam tip

This question is asking you to evaluate the theory, not to explain it. This means you only need to set out what the theory says in enough detail to evaluate its usefulness to the set product. You should not need to know any more about the theory than is stated in the specification.

Timing

REVISED ☐

Question 4 will be worth 10 marks, so you should spend about 17 minutes answering this question.

> **Revision activity**
>
> Past papers and practice papers are published on the OCR Interchange – ask your teacher to access these so you can check whether the format for Question 4 has changed over time.

What the examiner is looking for

REVISED ☐

In this exam practice Question 4, examiners are looking for:

- how comprehensive, detailed and accurate is your application of knowledge and understanding of media language to evaluate the theory
- how convincing, perceptive and accurate is your evaluation of the theory in understanding media language for LFTVD.

In short, you are being rewarded for using what you know to *evaluate* the theory (not for explaining the theory).

Exam practice

Question 4

Evaluate the relevance of Todorov's theory of narratology to long form television drama. [10]

Sample answer available online

ONLINE ☐

Recommended revision for this question

REVISED ☐

- The theories – these can be found in the Academic Theories section at: **www.hoddereducation.co.uk/myrevisionnotesdownloads.**
- In what ways each theory is useful in understanding LFTVDs.
- The limitations of each theory in understanding LFTVDs.

LFTVD: academic theories

REVISED ☐

Semiology – Barthes

How the theory is useful

- Can be applied to any sign, including language and image, to tease out connotations and ideology (see media language analysis under Question 3 on pages 146–51).
- Useful for 'micro' analysis of media language.

How the theory is limited

- Does not explain anything specific to LFTVD as it is a general theory of signification.
- Less useful for analysing 'macro' media language elements such as narrative and genre.

> **Exam tip**
>
> You should not try to guess which theory might come up but instead revise all the theories. Some theories apply better than others – as shown in the pages that follow. Those that work better may be more likely to appear in this question (and those that don't might be more likely to appear in Question 3).

- Does not reveal anything about the ownership and control of television and the process of mediation that leads to the narratives in television.
- Does not say about how audiences interpret LFTVDs and give meaning in different ways to the same signs.

Genre theory – Neale

How the theory is useful

- Was developed primarily to explain film genre, but can be applied to LFTVD as this is the most filmic form of television output, requiring an 'intertextual relay' of pre-publicity and reviews to generate the large audiences required.
- Draws attention to processes of difference-within-repetition (variation) and hybridity in LFTVD (see genre analysis under Question 3 on pages 151-4).
- The theory of genre as 'shared code' can be applied to the LFTVD itself as a form despite the fact that these dramas range across various different genres. For example, an early version of the form, *Twin Peaks*, established audience expectations of enigmatic narratives that have been developed through each addition to the generic corpus.

How the theory is limited

- Many LFTVDs have the resources to rely on elements such as high production values, the star system, tone and exoticism rather than genre to market themselves, emphasising individual difference rather than generic similarity.
- Some LFTVD generic descriptors, such as 'Nordic Noir' arose after the showing of some programmes, suggesting that this was not a 'shared code' with the audience at the time.

Structuralism – Levi-Strauss

How the theory is useful

- Can be applied to any cultural product, including LFTVDs (see analysis under Levi-Strauss for Question 3 on pages 162-3).
- Can be used to analyse LFTVD narratives, for example, by studying how they set up an 'inside' and 'outside' opposition, asking the audience to identify with the inside, and then in some cases (e.g. *Mr. Robot*, *Homeland*, *Deutschland 83*) playing around with this opposition to disorientate the audience.
- Can be used to analyse representations and their ideological effect, by establishing which side of an opposition the narrative values (see analysis under Levi-Strauss for Question 3).

How the theory is limited

- Does not explain anything specific to LFTVDs as it is an extremely high-level theory of culture.
- Does not tell us anything about the ownership and control of television and the process of mediation that leads to the narratives in LFTVDs.
- Does not tell us about how audiences interpret television and give meaning.

Narratology – Todorov

How the theory is useful

- Is sufficiently simple to be widely applicable, meaning that it is possible to identify the key elements – equilibrium (often implied) and disruption – in LFTVD (see analysis under Todorov for Question 3 on pages 159-62).
- Is very useful in teasing out the messages and values underlying a narrative, in pointing to the significance of the transformation between the initial equilibrium (displayed or implied) and the new equilibrium (see analysis under Todorov for Question 3).

How the theory is limited

- Was not designed to explain long form serial narratives but single narratives with resolutions, so does not explain complex narratives where climax and resolution are necessarily delayed and sometimes, in programmes that are designed to last many series, are never reached (see analysis under media language for Question 3 on pages 159-62).
- Does not help to understand television's tendency towards segmentation rather than linearity, e.g. the multiple segmented storylines of some long form dramas (see analysis under media language for Question 3).
- Does not help to analyse narrative strands that do not add to the narrative drive towards resolution but establish characterisation, spiral out from the main linear narrative or create cliffhangers (see analysis under media language for Question 3).

Postmodernism – Baudrillard

How the theory is useful

- Can be applied to any cultural product, including LFTVD (see analysis under Baudrillard for Question 3 on pages 163-4).
- May be celebrated in LFTVDs that refuse any simple identification of 'the real' in the fictional world (e.g. *Mr. Robot* – see analysis under media language for Question 3 on pages 154-6).

How the theory is limited

- Does not explain anything specific to LFTVDs as it is an extremely high-level theory of the postmodern world.
- Is unfalsifiable as it cannot be proved false or true.

Theories of representation – Hall

How the theory is useful

- Can be applied to any media product, including LFTVDs (see the selection and combination, stereotypes and ideology analysis under representation for Question 3 on pages 179 and 164-79).
- Draws attention to the role of power in representations – both the general distribution of power in society and the power of the television industry – but also the power of the audience to decode representations in different ways (see Hall on audiences on pages 192-4).

How the theory is limited

- Does not explain anything specific to LFTVDs as it is a general theory of representation.

Theories of identity – Gauntlett

How the theory is useful

- Can be applied to any media product, including LFTVDs.
- LFTVDs may tend to offer diverse and contradictory representations that audiences can use to think through their identity as they have the time and resources to develop complex representations (see analysis under representation for Question 3 on page 180).
- LFTVDs (especially the non-English-language examples) often attempt to reach and engage an international audience by offering a local representation with international resonance, thus increasing the diversity of representations of place and cultures (see analysis under audience for Question 3 on pages 164-79).
- LFTVDs may achieve cult status, adding to their value in helping create identities.

How the theory is limited

- Assumes that audiences are powerful, active agents and so may underestimate the power of media conglomerates and the forces of global capitalism to shape popular culture, tastes and identities.

Feminist theory – Van Zoonen

How the theory is useful

- Can be applied to any media product, including LFTVDs, especially representations of gender (see analysis under representation for Question 3 on pages 180 and 164-79).
- Can be used to apply the concept of patriarchy to the ownership and control of television, the recruitment and ethos of television professionals, and the representation of gender in LFTVDs, especially the representation of women's bodies.

How the theory is limited

- Does not explain anything specific to LFTVDs as it is a general theory of patriarchy.
- In prioritising gender inequalities, the theory may not aid analysis of other forms of inequality in representation in LFTVDs.
- In stressing the influence of social conflict on representations the theory may underestimate the influence of social consensus on representations.

Feminist theory – hooks

How the theory is useful

- Can be applied to any media product, including LFTVDs, especially representations of gender (see analysis under representation for Question 3 on page 180).
- Can be used to apply the concept of 'intersectionality' to misrepresentations and stereotypes based on one or more of gender, race, class and sexuality, and their interrelationship in any LFTVD representations (see analysis under hooks for Question 3).

How the theory is limited

- Does not explain anything specific to LFTVDs as it is a general theory of patriarchy.
- In prioritising gender linked to other inequalities, the theory may overlook similarities or equalities in representation in LFTVDs.
- In stressing the influence of social conflict on representations the theory may underestimate the influence of social consensus on representations.

Theories of gender performativity – Butler

How the theory is useful

- Can be applied to any media product, including LFTVDs, especially representations of gender (see analysis under representation for Question 3 on page 181).
- Can be applied particularly to LFTVDs where the performance of gender is foregrounded, e.g. through representations of women preparing to present their bodies for display, of people training or reinforcing characters in masculinity, or representations that expose or disrupt heteronormativity (see analysis under Butler for Question 3).

How the theory is limited

- Does not explain anything specific to LFTVDs as it is a high-level theory of gender.
- Is unfalsifiable as it cannot be proved false or true.

Theories around ethnicity and post-colonial theory – Gilroy

How the theory is useful

- Can be applied to any media product, including LFTVDs, especially representations of race, ethnicity and the post-colonial and post-slavery world (see the analysis under representation for Question 3 on page 181).
- Draws attention to the continuing role of racist ideology – of the superiority of White western culture – across a range of representations in LFTVDs (see the analysis under representation for Question 3).

How the theory is limited

- Does not explain anything specific to LFTVDs as it is a general theory.
- In prioritising race and the post-colonial experience the theory may not aid analysis of other forms of inequality in representation in LFTVDs.
- In stressing the influence of social conflict on representations the theory may underestimate the influence of social consensus on representations.

Power and media industries – Curran and Seaton

How the theory is useful

- Studying television as an industry draws attention to issues such as forms and effects of ownership and control, the working practices of creators, and issues of risk and profitability.
- Applies particularly to the international dominance of American television products and the American streaming services distributing many LFTVDs.

How the theory is limited

- In prioritising the effects of ownership and control on the content of LFTVDs this theory may not aid in understanding how ideologies, audience choice or media language conventions may determine media content.

Regulation – Livingstone and Lunt

How the theory is useful

- Applies in part to LFTVDs produced by European public service broadcasters, which may be regulated in the interests of citizens.
- Applies in part to LFTVDs produced by American cable and streaming services, which treat audiences as consumers and are only lightly regulated to avoid harm.
- Draws attention to the challenge of globalised television industries to traditional regulation.

How the theory is limited

- Only applies to the consumption of these LFTVDs in Britain or to British LFTVDs as the study of Ofcom was from a national perspective.

Cultural industries – Hesmondhalgh

How the theory is useful

- Draws attention to the forms and effects of ownership and control, such as the differences between the purely commercial American television products and the public service ethos of most European producers.
- Draws attention to the issues of risk and profitability in LFTVDs where high budgets are at stake and the ways producers will try to minimise these risks by using formatting – e.g. genres, the star system (and co-production deals for the smaller European broadcasters).

How the theory is limited

- In prioritising the effects of ownership and control on the content of LFTVDs this theory may not aid in understanding how ideologies, audience choice or media language conventions may determine media content.

Media effects – Bandura

How the theory is useful

- May apply to a wide range of media products, including LFTVDs.
- Draws attention to the need to investigate the direct effects on individuals who consume LFTVDs.
- Supports the arguments of those who think television should be regulated to avoid public harm.

How the theory is limited

- The complex and nuanced representations common to LFTVDs are less likely to cause a direct effect on audiences.
- Prioritising the effects of the media on the audience may mean that the effects of the audience on the media are underestimated (see Jenkins and Shirky).

Cultivation theory – Gerbner

How the theory is useful

- May apply to a wide range of media products, including LFTVDs.
- Draws attention to the need to investigate the longer-term effects on individuals who consume LFTVDs, especially heavy 'box set' users.
- Suggests, via its interest in the attitudinal effects of violent representations, that television programmes are possibly creating the belief in the audience that the world is characterised by negative/ dangerous events.
- Supports the arguments of those who think television should be regulated to avoid public harm.

How the theory is limited

- The complex and nuanced representations common to LFTVDs are less likely to cause an indirect effect on audiences.
- Prioritising the effects of the media on the audience may mean that the effects of the audience on the media are underestimated (see Jenkins and Shirky).

Reception theory – Hall

How the theory is useful

- May apply to a wide range of media products, including LFTVDs (see analysis under audience for Question 3 on page 36).
- Draws attention to different possible audience readings of a LFTVD's messages and values, while acknowledging the role of power in creating dominance within television messages and values.

How the theory is limited

- Assumes that there is one dominant meaning to which the audience responds – does not fit messages with a multitude of different possible readings (e.g. ironic messages such as those in *Mr. Robot*, *House of Cards*, *Homeland*, *Stranger Things*, *Deutschland 83*).

Fandom – Jenkins

How the theory is useful

- Applies particularly to the range and diversity of representations offered by LFTVDs to 'textual poachers' who wish to use these products to create their own culture, e.g. via fan sites.
- LFTVDs may achieve cult status, adding to their value for fans.

How the theory is limited

- This optimistic view of the power of LFTVD audiences may underestimate the power of the oligarchy of media conglomerates to shape and control television content (see Curran and Seaton).
- This view might underestimate the effects of LFTVDs on their audience (see Bandura and Gerbner).

'End of audience' theory – Shirky

How the theory is useful

- Draws attention to the way audiences for LFTVDs can provide value for one another by using websites to offer fan fiction, wikis, fan theories, merchandise (e.g. Sarah Lund sweaters) and so forth.

How the theory is limited

- Does not apply to broadcast television.
- Streaming services do not reflect the view of the online media proposed by Shirky insofar as they primarily operate like the 'old' media by offering centrally produced content.
- This optimistic view of the power of audiences may underestimate the power of the oligarchy of media conglomerates to shape and control television content (see Curran and Seaton).
- This view might underestimate the effects of LFTVDs on their audience (see Bandura and Gerbner).

Now test yourself

TESTED

1 What areas of the theoretical framework are ignored by Barthes' theory?
2 Why does the narrative form of LFTVDs mean that Todorov's theory does not fit them as well as it does single narratives?
3 How do the LFTVDs tend to fit Gauntlett's theory?
4 Can Butler's theory be proved wrong?
5 Name two optimistic theories of audience.
6 Name two theories that see conglomerates as dominating the media.

Answers on p. 208

Exam practice

Try answering exam practice Question 4 on page 197 and compare your answer to the sample answer online.

ONLINE

How to prepare for the exam

- You will need to learn the advantages and limitations of each theory in understanding the LFTVD in-depth study.
- While it is tempting to try to guess which theories may be paired with which in-depth studies, this doesn't really narrow down the choice very much, so it would be safer to assume that any combination could be asked for.
- Learning all this is a big task, so try to note all the repeated limitations and advantages as you may be able to fall back on these.
- Remember that the exam may give you a choice of theories to evaluate, so you can choose the one you feel most confident about.
- Practise applying the theories to your chosen LFTVDs so you have some detailed examples of how they have been useful in your analysis that you can use in your exam answers.
- Access the published OCR exam papers and practise answering the questions, checking your answers against the mark scheme.

Now test yourself answers

Paper 1 – Section A: News

Questions 1 and 2

1 Denotation is the literal meaning of a sign. A sign can have many connotations as these are the ideas, thoughts and feelings associated with a sign.

2 The gothic font connotes tradition, craft, solidity, reliability and so on.

3 Tabloid conventions: headlines (often banner) in bold, capitalised sans-serif fonts. Broadsheet conventions: headlines in serif fonts in sentence case.

4 They are both middle-market tabloids.

5 Broadsheets have more extensive use of colour, opinion, lifestyle and sports pieces on the home page, and some use of sans-serif fonts. Tabloids have fewer banner headlines, but a large number of headlines, most headlines are not capitalised, the home page layout is generally less photograph/image and headline dominated, hard news stories are covered on the home page.

6 Humour, parody, to honour the referred text, to create a flattering mode of address, to transfer the value of the referred media product, to create a sense of shared experience or code with the audience.

7 Sexism/patriarchal ideology, feminism, racism, multiculturalism, ethnocentrism, internationalism, materialism, consumerism, belief in welfare.

8 Because audiences can more easily choose how to interpret the messages in newspapers as they play a more active role in reading them compared to watching a film, for example.

9 The dominant reading, the negotiated reading, the oppositional reading.

10 Gilroy and/or hooks.

Question 3

1 The capitalist profit motive, or the flight of advertising revenue to online media.

2 Three news companies own more than 80 per cent of print circulation.

3 Newspapers may offer different political views to that of their owners because of a belief in press freedom, because it pleases the audience and makes money or because of the key role of the editor in setting the tone of the newspaper.

4 Three sources of funding for newspapers other than cover price or paywalls: events, sponsorship, advertising, membership, sales.

5 Two newspaper self-regulators: IPSO and Impress.

6 Three attributes of the *Daily Mail*'s audience: older, more female, middle market, C1C2s.

7 Three attributes of the *Guardian*'s audience: younger, more London-based, upmarket.

8 Any two newspapers from: *Jewish Chronicle*, the *Yorkshire Post*, the *Scotsman*, the *Voice*, the *Financial Times*, or similar.

Question 4

1 Binary opposition, useful for exploring 'us and them' oppositions in stories.

2 Baudrillard's theory: it is an example of hyperreality.

3 Social groups included are based on: race, class, gender, sexuality.

4 Bandura's theory.

5 Citizen journalism either in online newspapers or on social media.

Paper 1 – Section B: Media language and representations

Questions 5 and 6

Music videos: media language

1 To reflect the tone of the song, comment on the song, reflect the public image of the artist or the style of the producers.

2 Naturalistic media language: Corinne Bailey Rae, Massive Attack, or Emeli Sande.

3 Expressionist media language: Fatboy Slim, Radiohead, or David Guetta.

4 Performance and narrative videos.

5 The opportunities for music television offered by cable and satellite television, digital cameras and editing.

6 Celebrity culture and postmodernism.

Music videos: media representations

1 They use real locations; non-actors and an authentic performance style; continuity editing and naturalistic mise-en-scène; documentary conventions. They create a realist narrative and explore social issues.

...rms, they have to establish

...ty of the individual

...ges of identity for audience

..., fandom and musical taste,

...filiation.

...ising and marketing: media ...nguage

1 Slogans: Lucozade – 'In a different league/ Lucozade yes'; Shelter – 'We can help'.

2 OLD SPICE BAHAMAS SCENT COMES FROM AN ANTI-PERSPIRANT MINE IN THE BAHAMAS. THIS FACT HAS NOT BEEN FACT-CHECKED.

3 Key connotations: Lucozade – science, aspiration and passion; Shelter – humanity, care and realism; Old Spice – surrealist humour, pleasure.

4 Reason why/USP advertising, brand image advertising, lifestyle advertising.

5 Print technology enables advertisers to convey detailed information, create high-quality images, and use layout in striking ways.

Advertising and marketing: media representations

1 Old Spice.

2 Multiculturalism, postmodernism.

3 Positive, as ads aim to transfer positive values to the brand.

4 Women, older people, people with disabilities, single parents, LGBT people.

5 Consumerism.

Magazines: media language

1 Because it doesn't need to be recognised on newsagent shelves.

2 'A hand up, not a hand out'.

3 Magazines are displayed in shops by gender and frequency of publication (monthlies and weeklies).

4 Political contexts, e.g. debates about homelessness.

Magazines: media representations

1 'To dismantle poverty by creating opportunity'.

2 Operating by a code of journalistic ethics.

3 By allowing self-representations and celebrating the achievements of homeless people.

4 Women and people of colour.

5 Right-wing people, cultural conservatives.

Paper 2 – Section A: Media industries and audiences

Questions 1 and 2

Film

1 True.

2 About 4,000 in the USA and 600 in the UK (4,028 in the USA, 594 in the UK).

3 Any three of: big budgets, use of stars, saturation distribution, addresses a global mass audience, extensive promotion.

4 Free market capitalism.

5 China.

6 The trailers stressed the action elements rather than the musical comedy of the earlier version. The merchandising was more adult. The later film used adult-oriented social media.

7 Production: use of CGI, or high-quality digital sound, or high-quality 3D. Distribution: simultaneous saturation distribution, or use of social media to generate expectation. Exhibition: IMAX, or one-off exhibition, or high-quality digital surround sound.

8 'U' and 'PG' for the 1967 and 2016 versions, respectively.

Video games

1 False. You study audiences as well as industries, and social and economic contexts, not historical.

2 Its old-fashioned visuals, its modding community, its sandbox nature.

3 Any three from: subscription, paying for premium content, advertising, microtransactions, virtual currency, server leasing, merchandising outside the game, offer walls, offering a game in exchange for a link a to a site, donations.

4 The Video Standards Council has a legal duty to administer the PEGI age ratings (3, 7, 12, 16, and 18).

5 Marcus Persson.

6 Design, fantasy and community.

7 China.

8 By being a sandbox, world-building game, by encouraging modding, by encouraging a community of fans.

Radio

1 Any three of the following: engage young listeners, offer a range of music, offer live music, offer new music from the UK, include impartial news, documentaries and advice campaigns.

2 About 5 million.

3 High-quality presentation, a more diverse playlist than commercial stations, regular news bulletins, addressing a niche audience of 15-29 year olds.

4 Age, class, gender, race/ethnicity and nation

5 Radio 2.

6 Radio 3.

7 On social media such as Facebook and Twitter, by file-sharing sites such as YouTube, from the BBC iPlayer, or as podcasts.

Paper 2 – Section B: Long form television drama

Question 3

LFTD: media language

1 Increasing competition between television providers, including multinational streaming services, leading to the search for quality drama as flagship programming.

2 Starring highly skilled actors, sophisticated production design, cinematic style camerawork, lighting and editing, through-composed music and sophisticated sound effects, complex serial narratives with multiple narrative strands, and detailed characterisation.

3 Visual effects and aerial photography are affordable, digital cameras allow location shooting even in low-light levels, streaming programmes allows for less-interrupted narratives (e.g. no ad breaks, instant access to the next episode means less need for recaps).

4 The prime pleasure in a LFTVD is delaying resolution, developing narrative strands outside the main narrative that establish tone, developing characters, establishing secondary and intertwining storylines, or spiralling out from the main storyline in unpredictable directions.

5 Binary oppositions.

6 Hyperreality.

LFTD: media representations

1 The long narratives enable character development and multiple perspectives on events so characters are more likely to be represented as complex individuals with perhaps contradictory characteristics. PSB LFTVDs will work hard to avoid simple stereotyping.

2 Old people, people of colour, working-class people, LGBT people, people with visible disabilities, people from developing world countries.

3 Because anti-stereotypes try to 'fix' meaning in the same way as stereotypes, so are still the exercise of power.

4 That they are diverse and contradictory.

5 Examples of contested ideologies: patriarcha versus feminist, racist versus anti-racist, heterosexist versus queer.

6 Performativity – that gender is constructed in the act of performing gender roles.

LFTD: media industries

1 A showrunner is the person or people with creative control over a LFTVD, usually a writer-producer. They give the programme its 'authored' quality, helping it differentiate itself from other dramas in order to become a flagship programme.

2 BBC Four (*Killing/Borgen/Trapped*) or Channel 4 (*Deutschland 83*).

3 Because of global media producers using digital technologies such as international streaming services and online video-sharing sites; because online audiences are more resistant to traditional regulation.

4 By licence fee, by pay-per-view, by subscription, by advertising, by covert promotion.

5 Because television is very unlikely to fail to be distributed – i.e. if a channel commissions a programme, it will show it.

6 Because there are so many channels it is hard for anyone to stand out. Channel loyalty is declining so audiences need to quickly understand what the channel stands for. Because programmes are increasingly becoming brands.

LFTD: media audiences

1 BARB.

2 Stars, high budgets and production values, mainstream genres and hybridity, complex narratives and representations, franchises, cross-promotion on TV channels.

3 Through representation of national culture, issues and locations.

4 A sense of ritual, appointment viewing and a shared experience, making the programme easy to discuss with peers.

5 Active decoding of the product, online fan fiction, fan theories, fan wikis and social media groups.

6 As a way of informing themselves about other countries, and languages; as a form of cultural tourism; as a means of reinforcing a personal identity as a 'citizen of anywhere' or as culturally sophisticated; to identify with rich and complex characters; to escape into a complex and gripping narrative; for a range of audience pleasures such as humour, pathos, suspense, action, narrative delay and resolution.

ience or much of

less driven by movement

on of a disruption.

3 Due to their complexity they tend to offer diverse representations and engage fans.
4 No. It is unfalsifiable.
5 Shirky and Jenkins.
6 Curran and Seaton, Hesmondhalgh.